AGE OF PROPAGANDA

AGE OF PROPAGANDA

The Everyday Use and Abuse of Persuasion

Anthony R. Pratkanis and Elliot Aronson
University of California, Santa Cruz

W. H. FREEMAN AND COMPANY
NEW YORK

Portions of this book first appeared in *The Social Animal*.
Cartoons © 1991 by Sidney Harris

Library of Congress Cataloging-in-Publication Data

Pratkanis, Anthony R.
Age of propaganda : the everyday use and abuse of persuasion /
Anthony R. Pratkanis and Elliot Aronson
p.   cm.
Includes bibliographical references and index.
ISBN 0-7167-2210-0   ISBN 0-7167-2211-9 (pbk.)
1. Propaganda. 2. Persuasion (Psychology) 3. Public opinion. 4. Advertising. 5.
Television in propaganda. I. Aronson, Elliot. II. Title.
HM263.P715 1991
303.3'75—dc20   91-25616
                                                                CIP

Printed in the United States of America

1 2 3 4 5 6 7 8 9 0   VB   9 9 8 7 6 5 4 3 2 1

To the memory of my parents, Harry Aronson (1903-1950)
and Dorothy Aronson (1901-1989)
They had a wonderfully innocent, childlike trust that, in this country,
almost everything they read (especially if it was between
the covers of a book) was absolutely true.
E. A.

To my soon-to-be-born son
Chances are, he will grow up with a healthy skepticism but a regrettable
cynicism about the truth of everything he reads, hears, and sees.
A. R. P.

CONTENTS

COMMUNICATOR CREDIBILITY: REAL AND MANUFACTURED

THE MESSAGE AND HOW IT IS DELIVERED

EMOTIONAL APPEALS: TOUCH THE HEART, PERSUADE THE MIND

WHY WE WROTE
THIS BOOK

We are of different generations. One of us (EA) was born in 1932 and grew up during World War II. "At that time, I fervently believed just about everything I was exposed to in school and in the media. For example, I knew that all Germans were evil and that all Japanese were sneaky and treacherous, while all white Americans were clean-cut, honest, fair-minded and trusting. Perhaps you had to be eleven years old to take seriously the racial and national caricatures presented in the war movies of the early 1940s. But in those days, most grown-ups —including my parents (to whom this book is dedicated) certainly *wanted* to believe in the basic message of the war movies, and did, in fact, have a childlike trust in the media. They hung on every word President Roosevelt said in his famous fireside chats and never dreamed of questioning the nobility of the motives behind our national policy. They thought (and so did I) that the purpose of commercial advertising was to inform the consumer."

The world has taken a few turns since then. ARP grew up during the Vietnam war and was witness to the blatant lying by public officials of that era. "At the time, I sat riveted to my television screen, scared to death by the images of death and destruction beamed into my living room from Vietnam, all the while learning that politicians only lie when their lips move. I came of age during the Watergate era when a sitting president, Richard Nixon, was forced to resign when faced with the incontrovertible evidence (some of it supplied by his own tape recordings) of the lying, dirty tricks, and attempted cover-up that he and his cronies perpetrated on the American people. For me, commercials, whether for different brands of products or different brands of politicians, were entertainment designed to make someone rich or more powerful."

Unfortunately, no White House tape recorder was in use during the 1980s—so that President Reagan escaped the consequences of deceiving the American people (and the world) by subverting the constitution through the covert sale of arms to Iran and the diversion of the profits from that sale to support the Nicaraguan Contras. When confronted with evidence of these transactions, Reagan mumbled, "I think I don't remember."

It is a sad commentary on our times that, while the majority of the American people were furious at Nixon and his cronies, by the time of the Iran-Contra scandal, most Americans seemed to have developed a more cynical attitude about being deceived and did not seem displeased when Oliver North, John Poindexter, and President Reagan himself succeeded, for the most part, in "beating the rap." But such cynicism carries a price. A cynical electorate is a lackadaisical electorate—as evidenced by the fact that less than 50% of eligible Americans now bother to vote.

We wrote this book because we passionately believe that there are more than two choices: naive acceptance on the one hand and total cynicism on the other. It is important, especially in a democracy, during an age characterized by ever more sophisticated uses of propaganda techniques that Americans become informed about these devices, the psychological dynamics of what makes them effective, and how to counteract their effectiveness without withdrawing into abject cynicism. That's what this book is about. We are researchers who have been studying the nuts and bolts of persuasion techniques for a combined total of 45 years—and we believe we know something about what works and what doesn't work and why. Moreover, we believe we know something about how to guard against the abuse of these techniques by unscrupulous communicators—including (especially) those unscrupulous communicators who might be running for the highest political offices in the land.

In addition, our experience has led us to understand the difference between persuasion and propaganda. Thus, our book also contains advice for those of you who might want to be effective communicators in ways that are honest and above-board. We believe that, in an age of propaganda, the best thing for the survival of a democracy is the existence of communicators who know how to present their message clearly and fairly, coupled with an informed electorate who knows the difference between a fair presentation and a con job. It is toward achieving these ends that we wrote this book.

As with any effort of this size, there are a number of people that should be thanked. Vera Aronson, Mahzarin Banaji, Peter Farquhar, Craig Leve, Nathan Maccoby, Richard Petty and the Ohio State Research Group on Attitudes and Persuasion, Rosemarie Pratkanis, Michael Santos, and Carol Tavris provided helpful comments of an earlier draft. Marlene Turner provided continuous, invaluable feedback as the book was being written. (Dr. Turner also collaborated with her husband, ARP, on the second half of the dedication.) Our editor, Jonathan Cobb, reminded us what old-fashioned publishing must have been like—when editors truly loved books and ideas.

A. R. P. and E. A.
July 1991

AGE OF PROPAGANDA

OUR AGE OF PROPAGANDA

In the early 1990s, seventeen-year-old Demetrick James Walker was sentenced to life in prison for killing a sixteen-year-old. The reason for the slaying: Demetrick so wanted a pair of $125 Nike Air Jordans like the ones he had seen on TV that he put a .22-caliber pistol to the head of Johnny Bates, pulled the trigger, and walked off with a new pair of high-tops. During the trial, Houston prosecutor Mark Vinson placed some of the blame on the images created by advertising. Said Vinson, "It's bad when we create an image of luxury about athletic gear that it forces people to kill over it.[1]

The 1990 North Carolina U.S. Senate race was one of the most heated—and expensive—political contests in recent years. Going into the last weeks of the campaign, the black Democratic challenger, Harvey Gantt, held a slight lead in the polls over the white Republican incumbent, Jesse Helms. Eight days before the election, Helms broadcast an ad dubbed "White Hands." The spot showed a pair of white hands crumpling a letter of rejection. The voice-over: "You needed that job, but they had to give it to a minority because of racial quotas. Is that really fair?" Although Gantt was on record as opposed to quotas, the spot appears to have had its intended effect: Helms was reelected to the Senate, supported by a huge vote in white precincts.[2]

Some years ago, CBS aired the film *Cry Rape.* Essentially, the story made it clear that a rape victim who chooses to press charges against her attacker runs the risk of undergoing an ordeal that may be as harrowing as the rape itself. In this case the rapist, exuding boyish innocence, presented a convincing argument to the effect that he had been seduced by the woman. During the next few weeks, there was a sharp decrease in the number of rapes reported by victims to the police—apparently because victims, taking their cue from the television movie, feared the police would not believe them.

In October 1982, when seven people in the Chicago area died
after taking Tylenol headache capsules laced with cyanide,
the event was widely publicized by the national news media.
Indeed, for several days it was difficult to turn on the TV, or
radio, or pick up a newspaper, without encountering the
Tylenol poisonings. The effects of this prominent coverage
were immediate: Similar poisonings were reported in cities
across the country, involving the contamination of mouthwash, eyedrops, nasal spray, soda pop, even hot dogs.
Dramatically billed as "copycat poisonings," these poisonings, in turn, received widespread media attention. The
public reaction took on the properties of a spiral: Many
people panicked, seeking medical aid for burns and poisonings when they suffered from no more than common sore
throats and stomachaches. False alarms outnumbered actual
cases of product tampering by 7 to 1.

What do Demetrick James Walker, the voters of North Carolina, rape
victims, and, indeed, anyone who has ever watched television or read
a newpaper or magazine share in common? Every time we turn on the
radio or television, every time we open a book, magazine, or
newspaper, someone is trying to educate us, to convince us to buy a
product, to persuade us to vote for a candidate or to subscribe to some
version of what is right, true, or beautiful. This aim is most obvious in
advertising: Manufacturers of nearly identical products (aspirins, for
example, or toothpastes, or detergents, or political candidates) spend
vast amounts of money to persuade us to buy the product in their
package. Influence need not be so blatant—the impact of television
news shows and programs such as *Cry Rape*, for instance, extends far
beyond their most obvious effects as documentaries or dramatizations.
This influence can be very subtle indeed, even unintentional. As the
response to the movie about rape aptly illustrates, even when communicators are not directly attempting to sell us something, they can
succeed in influencing the way we look at the world and the way we
respond to important events in our lives. The purpose of this book is to
look at the nature of persuasion in our everyday life—to understand
how it influences our behavior, how we can protect ourselves from

unwanted propaganda, and how we can ultimately come to use persuasion wisely.

The primary vehicle for many persuasive appeals is the mass media. The statistics on the pervasiveness of the mass media are startling.[3] In the United States, there are 1,220 television stations, 9,871 radio stations, 482 newspapers, and 11,328 magazines. Americans have ample opportunity to consume mass media messages, and consume they do. Each year the typical American watches 1,550 hours of TV, listens to 1,160 hours of radio on one of 530 million radio sets, and spends 180 hours reading 94 pounds of newspapers and 110 hours reading magazines. Each year an American has the opportunity to read more than 30,000 new books in print. More than half of our waking hours are spent with the mass media.

If you watch thirty hours of TV per week (as does the typical American), you will view roughly 37,822 commercials per year. That works out to more than over 100 TV ads per day. You are likely to hear

"We limit him to an hour a day. He's up to March 29, 2014."

or see another 100 to 300 ads per day through the other mass media of radio, newspapers, and magazines.

And the advertising glut does not stop there. This year you will receive, on average, 216 pieces of direct mail advertising and about fifty phone calls from telemarketers, who contact 7 million persons a day. During the 1980s, American businesses spent $150 billion a year to hire more than 6.4 million sales agents. Approximately one in every twelve American families has a member working in sales. This force of millions attempts to persuade others to purchase everything from cars to shoes to small and large appliances, to contribute vast sums to needy charities, to enlist in the military, or to enroll in a specific college.

If you walk down just about any city street in America you will encounter countless billboards, posters, bumper stickers, and bus and cab displays, each with a separate advertising appeal. Your kitchen cupboard is probably full of product packages and labels, each containing at least one sales message. It seems that no place is free of advertising. Go to the racetrack and you will see 200-mile-an-hour race cars carry advertising worth $75 million per year. Go to a tennis tournament, a jazz festival, or a golf match and you will find corporate sponsors, such as the makers of Virginia Slims, Kool, and Doral cigarettes. Go to a movie and you will find that marketers have paid a handsome sum to have your favorite stars use their products in the film. Look at just about anyone in America and you will see human bodies turned into walking billboards with brand names appearing on T-shirts and ballcaps, not to mention the ubiquitous designer labels.

With 6% of the world's population, America consumes 57% of the world's advertising. Manufacturers spend more than $45 billion a year on advertising and more than $60 billion a year on product promotions (coupons, free samples, rebates, premiums, and the like). This corresponds to $200 per year per American spent on product advertising alone—a sum larger than the yearly income of a typical citizen of a third world nation.

But persuasion is not just the specialty of advertisers and marketers. The U.S. government spends more than $400 million per year to employ more than 8,000 workers to create propaganda favorable to the United States. The results: ninety films per year, twelve magazines in twenty-two languages, and 800 hours Voice of America programming in thirty-seven languages with an estimated audience of 75 million listeners—all describing the virtues of the American way.

Persuasion shows up in almost every walk of life. Nearly every major politician hires media consultants and political pundits to provide advice on how to persuade the public and how to get elected. Virtually every major business and special-interest group has hired a lobbyist to take its concerns to Congress or to state and local governments. In nearly every community, activists try to persuade their fellow citizens on important policy issues. The workplace, too, has always been fertile ground for office politics and persuasion. One study estimates that general managers spend upwards of 80% of their time in verbal communication—most of it with the intent of cajoling and persuading their fellow employees. With the advent of the photocopying machine, a whole new medium for office persuasion was invented—the photocopied memo. The Pentagon alone copies an average of 350,000 pages a day, the equivalent of 1,000 novels. Sunday may be a day of rest, but not from persuasion, as an army of preachers take to the pulpits to convince us of the moral course of action. They also take to the airwaves, with 14% of all radio stations extolling the virtues of Christianity.

And should you need assistance in preparing your persuasive message, millions stand ready in the wings to help (for a fee). Today there are more than 432,000 lawyers actively arguing and persuading in courts of law (a threefold increase in the last ten years). More than 300 companies (at billings of $130 million per year) provide "image consulting"—advice on how to make your personal image more appealing. Public relations firms can be hired to deal with any public opinion problem. There are more than 500 marketing research and opinion polling firms ready to find out what Americans think about any conceivable issue. These firms query more than 72 million Americans a year. The top ten marketing research firms alone have combined revenues of more than $1 billion.

Everyday we are bombarded with one persuasive communication after another. These appeals persuade not through the give-and-take of argument and debate but through the manipulation of symbols and of our most basic human emotions. For better or worse, ours is an age of propaganda.

Every society requires a mechanism for making decisions for resolving disputes and coordinating activities. Our society has opted for persuasion. In the Soviet Union, during the heyday of Communist Party rule, a bureaucratic Politburo attempted to regulate consumer tastes and choices. In our society, we ascribe that function to the persuasive skills of the advertiser. In traditional societies, marriages are arranged by parental authority according to rules and customs. In modern Western societies, love is left to the social-influence devices of the two potential lovebirds and their friends and families. During the Middle Ages in Europe, most disputes were settled by the decree of feudal lords or the papacy. Today, lawyers attempt to solve disputes by negotiating out-of-court settlements and, if that fails, argue the merits of the case before a complex system of judges. In many of the world's societies, rulers are selected by either the use of force or by family inheritance. The populace of the United States selects its rulers by a persuasion ritual known as the election campaign.

The roots of American persuasion practices go back to the founding of the nation.[4] The United States then, as today, was a diverse society populated by native Americans and people from England, Spain, Africa, Holland, and France, among other places. Each possessed his or her own beliefs and values. Although violence and threats of violence were frequently used to secure compliance, the bulk of the work of forging a new consensus from this diversity of opinion and perspective fell to persuasion. Early promoters induced settlers to the New World with promises of vast riches, cheap land, religious freedom, and a strange new world. Catholic priests and Protestant ministers preached to the converted and attempted to win over the unconverted, mostly native Americans, to the cause of Christ. The establishment of printing presses in America made it possible to distribute widely tracts, pamphlets, and newspapers designed to persuade fellow colonists.

Few places as vividly symbolize this early American fascination with persuasion as do Faneuil Hall and Quincy Market in Boston.[5] The hall, built in 1742 by Peter Faneuil, was originally intended to be a market "to Encourage and accommodate the Countrey People who bring Provisions into this Town." However, consumerism then as now was somewhat controversial, and to encourage the town of Boston to accept his gift, Faneuil added a meeting hall on the second floor, above the market stalls. Faneuil Hall has witnessed debate on nearly every major issue that has confronted the United States, including the decision for independence, slavery, temperance, and women's rights, as well as debate on every American war from 1812 to the Persian Gulf. The market, expanded 84 years later and renamed Quincy for the then mayor of Boston, is still in use today as one of America's oldest shopping malls. Not far away stand such monuments to persuasion as the Old State House and the Old North Church, the location of many of the first speeches and acts of the independence movement. Is it any wonder that the government these colonists helped to establish in the late eighteenth century had at its heart the art of persuasion?

However, it was not until the full force of the Industrial Revolution was felt in the nineteenth century that interest in, and organization of, persuasion emerged in earnest on a mass scale. The Industrial Revolution saw the invention of many new devices—steam engines, cotton gins, power looms, telegraphs, and assembly lines—resulting in the manufacture of more and more material goods for the mass market. Within a few generations, goods that could once be possessed only by the rich became the aspiration of almost everyone. An ever-increasing supply of products meant that items were purchased not solely because of need, but because of the dictates of fashion and style as well.

Consumers did not always buy the offered goods, however. There are a number of possible reasons for this. Potential customers might not know about the advantages of a certain product, or they might distrust the manufacturer, or they might consider the benefits of the product to be frivolous. They may not have had enough money to purchase immediately the offered goods. Out of necessity, manufacturers increasingly turned to sales and marketing to persuade people to purchase their products on a mass scale. With the rise of each of the mass media—printing presses in the seventeenth century, mass market magazines in the 1880s, radio in the 1930s, television in the 1950s, and direct-mail and telemarketing in the 1980s—manufacturers found an increasingly convenient way to do just that.

If we were to pick a specific date for the beginnings of our age of propaganda, however, we would select an obscure event that is not covered in most textbooks of American history. The modern age of propaganda began in Philadelphia in 1843 when a young man named Volney Palmer opened the first advertising agency. The shop was primitive by today's standards, serving only to broker advertising space between the newspaper publisher and advertiser.[6] Soon thereafter, full-service advertising agencies offering a wide range of client services such as media planning and the creation and preparation of ad copy appeared, along with a host of marketing research firms, publicity agencies, and opinion pollsters—all in the service of persuasion.

Academics were quick to get in on the act as well. By the early 1890s, new courses began appearing at universities with titles such as "Principles of Advertising," "Salesmanship," and "Wholesaling and Retailing." Academic textbooks with titles such as *Advertising and Its Mental Laws* and *Psychology in Advertising* were published and promised to teach the art of persuasion—at least as applied to advertising and sales.[7] Just after the turn of the century, the basic institutions of American propaganda were firmly established. The evolution of humankind from hunter-gatherers to shopper-disposers was complete.

It did not take long for the principles of advertising and marketing developed to sell consumer goods to be applied to the "sale" of political ideas and candidates. One of the first such applications came in the selling of World War I. In a book first published in 1920 and entitled *How We Advertised America*, George Creel, a publisher and head of the Committee on Public Information, proudly divulged how he and his committee used the principles of advertising to convince Americans to go to war against Germany.[8] Creel's success inspired others, most notably Adolf Hitler, to use and develop these techniques on a grand scale. The apparent success of such ventures has caused considerable concern—to say the least; modern critics have referred to persuasion as mind-control, brainwashing, and hidden seduction and have called attention to the damaging effects of propaganda.

The forms of persuasion that have come to dominate our twentieth century lifestyle are much different from those seen in any other age of persuasion—much different from those experienced by colonial

Americans. For this reason, we use the term *propaganda* to refer to the mass persuasion techniques that have come to characterize our post-industrial society. The word *propaganda* is of a relatively recent origin. The first documented use of the term occurred in 1622, when Pope Gregory XV established the Sacra Congregatio de Propaganda Fide. At the time, the Roman Catholic Church was engaged in mostly unsuccessful holy wars to reestablish the faith by force of arms. Pope Gregory realized that this was a losing effort and established the papal Propaganda as a means of coordinating efforts to bring men and women to the "voluntary" acceptance of church doctrines. The word *propaganda* thus took on a negative meaning in Protestant countries but a positive connotation (similar to *education* or *preaching*) in Catholic areas.

The term *propaganda* did not see widespread use until the beginning of the twentieth century, when it was used to describe the persuasion tactics employed during World War I and those later used by totalitarian regimes. *Propaganda* was originally defined as the dissemination of biased ideas and opinions, often through the use of lies and deception. However, as scholars began to study the topic in more detail, many came to realize that propaganda was not the sole property of "evil" and totalitarian regimes and that it often consists of more than just clever deceptions. The word *propaganda* has since evolved to mean mass "suggestion" or influence through the manipulation of symbols and the psychology of the individual. Propaganda is the communication of a point of view with the ultimate goal of having the recipient of the appeal come to "voluntarily" accept this position as if it were his or her own.

Not all persuasion is propaganda. The classical rhetoric theories of the early Greeks and Romans—which were avidly studied by those responsible for crafting the governments of Western Europe and America—prized discourse that could illuminate the issue at hand. Such persuasion could take the form of an argument, a debate, a discussion, or just a well-argued speech presenting the case for or against a given proposition. The end result was an education for both the audience and the speakers.

In the city-states of ancient Greece, all citizens were considered equal and everyone was expected to be able to speak on his own behalf.[9] For example, the Greek court system did not allow lawyers or individuals hired to plead a case; citizens were required to plead their own cases in the courts or, more exactly, before 201 of their neighbors—the minimum size of an Athenian jury. Similarly, the citizen of Greece was also expected to speak on the issues of the day in political assemblies. This task was not left to elected representatives. Needless to say, the average Greek citizen was interested in learning how to argue, lest he lose his possessions or risk banishment from his community on the basis of a frivolous lawsuit.

To help him learn about persuasion, the Greek citizen could hire a Sophist to provide instruction on how to argue. The Sophists were a group of itinerant teachers who gave lectures and wrote the first books on persuasion, similar in nature to the "how to" books that can be found in bookstores today. These handbooks, most of which are now lost to antiquity, described "commonplaces"—general arguments and techniques that could be adapted for a variety of persuasive purposes. One famous handbook, the *Dissoi logoi*, consisted of a series of pro and con arguments on a number of topics—ready for use by a speaker at a moment's notice.

The Sophists are perhaps best known for their "dangerous" views about the role of persuasion in society—hence the negative connotations of the word *sophistry*—meaning "trickery," or "fallacious argumentation." The Sophist viewpoint is expressed in two seemingly innocent maxims attributed to Protagoras: "Humans are the measure of all things" and "There are two sides to every issue." For the Sophist there is no absolute truth and no sure-fire means, whether through divine inspiration or human intuition, for finding this truth. The only standards are human ones, and these are always debatable. How, then, does one decide what to do? The Sophists believed that persuasion is necessary to discover the "best" course of action; by arguing and debating, many facets of an issue can be laid bare and the advantages and disadvantages of a course of action more plainly seen.

Foreshadowing much modern commentary on persuasion, Plato found the Sophist position to be outrageous. Plato believed in an absolute knowledge that could be appreciated only through the study of philosophy. Society had little need for the "word tricks" of the Sophist. Such trickery, in Plato's mind, was leading the youth of

Athens astray. The Sophist practice of arguing both sides of any issue merely clouded the understanding of what he saw as truth.

Around 323 B.C., Aristotle reconciled the view of the Sophists and the position of his teacher, Plato, in the *Rhetoric*—the first comprehensive theory of persuasion. For Aristotle, the purpose of persuasion was the communication of a point of view or position. Although the Sophists believed that persuasion was needed to discover important facts, Aristotle believed that knowledge could be gained only by logic and reason. Unfortunately, according to Aristotle, not everyone was capable of reasoning clearly about every issue. For these denser souls, the art of persuasion was needed to communicated the truth to them in such a manner that they might come to a *right* conclusion.

The tradition of "decision by persuasion" was kept alive by the early Romans. The political and court system of the Roman Republic, much like that of the Greeks, encouraged debate and political speechmaking. However, unlike the Greeks, the Romans employed professional persuaders—politicians and lawyers who made a career of arguing. The role of persuasion in Roman society was aptly expressed by one of the most famous of the Roman professional persuaders—the lawyer Cicero (106 to 43 B.C.). When asked "Has rhetoric produced more harm than good?" Cicero gave an answer that would have satisfied even Aristotle: "Wisdom without eloquence has been of little help to the states, but eloquence without wisdom has often been a great obstacle and never an advantage."[10]

The eloquent rhetoric of early Greek, Roman, and colonial American times was a far cry from the typical communication of today, with its emphasis on the use of simple slogans and images. Increasingly, the goal of modern propaganda is not to inform and enlighten but rather to move the masses toward a desired position or point of view. The persuasion landscape of today differs vastly from those of the past in some very important ways.

We live in a message-dense environment. The advertisers Al Ries and Jack Trout call ours an "overcommunicated" society.[11] The average American will see or hear more than 7 million advertisements in his or her lifetime. In contrast, the average pious Puritan attending church once a week in seventeenth century New England would hear about 3,000 sermons in a lifetime. This message-dense environment places a burden on both the communicator and the recipient of a persuasive message. The communicator must design a message that will not only be appealing but will also attract special notice in this cluttered environment. On the other hand, the recipient is so deluged by messages that it becomes difficult to devote the mental energy necessary to make sense of many of the important issues of the day.

Our age of propaganda differs in another way. Puritan sermons could last as long as two hours. Roman orators of the second century took courses to improve their memory so that they could remember all that they had to say. Early American patriots spent the entire summer of 1787 debating the U.S. Constitution and then produced, for the newspapers of the day, eighty-five articles totaling nearly 600 pages in its defense. Today, a televised political advertisement typically runs for thirty seconds or less. Magazine ads often consist of little more than a picture and a phrase. News of the day comes in short "sound-bites" and "news snippets." As the columnist George Will once put it, if Lincoln were to give his Emancipation Proclamation today, he would probably say: "Read my lips. No more slavery." Our age of persuasion is populated with short, catchy, and often visually oriented messages. Although such persuasive images are frequently successful in capturing our attention in the message-dense environment, they substitute slogans and images for well-reasoned arguments and can turn complex issues into vulgar black-and-white caricatures of reason.

Persuasion in modern times is also much more immediate. The Puritan would wait all week for a sermon and months for news from England. CNN coverage of the Tiananmen Square massacre stands in stark contrast. Despite efforts by the Chinese government to the contrary, journalists phoned in detailed reports of the violence, play-by-play descriptions of government action and student reaction, which were then quickly broadcast to an eagerly waiting but stunned world. In a similar vein, a week before the Allied bombing of Iraq in 1991, Tariq Aziz, foreign minister of Iraq, claimed to understand American politics because he got his news from CNN. The result is timely information—but, often perhaps too timely. Whereas the Puritan could spend all week mulling over the implications of last Sunday's sermon, today's TV viewer and magazine reader has little time to think about one persuasive image before another one quickly takes its place—the trees are replacing the forest.

Perhaps the major difference between our own and past eras is how we instruct our citizens about persuasion. If you were a citizen of a Greek city-state in the third century B.C., your education would include four years of rhetoric designed to teach you how to understand persuasive arguments and to construct your own. Should you miss your lessons, a Sophist could be hired to provide further instruction. Roman students of the first century took courses in persuasion from perhaps the greatest professor of rhetoric of all times, Quintilian, whose textbook on the subject was used for almost a 1,000 years. Students at Harvard College in seventeenth century America also had many opportunities to learn about persuasion. Every Friday afternoon for four years, the students would study how to argue; at least once a month they were required to demonstrate what they had learned by taking a stand, defending it, and attacking the views of others.

These cultures, unlike our own, considered an understanding of persuasion to be an essential skill needed by every citizen in order to participate fully in the affairs of state. The teaching of persuasion was a basic component of their education. In contrast, few Americans have taken a formal course on social influence. "Pop" books on the subject typically present exaggerated warnings of the dire consequences of persuasion and the mass media or simplistic "how to get ahead" instructions. Although we are bombarded daily with persuasive messages, we have little opportunity to learn about the techniques of persuasion and to understand how they work. Sadly, such a state of affairs can lead to a sense of alienation and cynicism, as many Americans become bewildered by the basic decision-making processes of their society.

For the last six decades, social psychologists such as ourselves have been studying the everyday use and abuse of persuasion.[12] They have conducted thousands of experiments to test countless hypotheses concerning the effects of a persuasive communication. Their labors have resulted in the discovery of which persuasion techniques are effective and an understanding of what makes a persuasive message so persuasive. One purpose of this book is to share this information.

In the next section (The Psychology of Everyday Persuasion), we

look at what social psychologists and other investigators have discovered about how we are persuaded: what factors determine when we
will be influenced? How do we respond, in general, to a persuasion
attempt? Then the next four sections, the heart of the book, present an
in-depth analysis of propaganda tactics commonly used today, along
with a discussion of why these tactics are so effective in securing our
compliance. After investigating the techniques of the propagandist, we
look at how our knowledge of such tactics affects persuasion, with the
goal of understanding how we can defend ourselves from influence
attacks. The final section returns to some of the issues raised in this
chapter: What is and what should be the role of persuasion in our
society? When is persuasion ethical and "good" and when is it misleading propaganda?

Our book has a second purpose as well. The persuasive appeals
directed at Demetrick James Walker, the voters of North Carolina,
rape victims, and every television viewer and magazine reader take
advantage of our basic human psychology; they often appeal to our
deepest fears and most irrational hopes, while they make use of our
most simplistic beliefs; they come to paint a picture of the world—distorted as it may be—in which we must live. It is our hope, that by
discussing the ways of persuasion, we can all better understand our
world of propaganda and deal with it sensibly and effectively.

—

THE
PSYCHOLOGY
OF EVERYDAY
PERSUASION

—

2

MYSTERIOUS INFLUENCE

The Manchurian Candidate, produced in 1962, has become something of a cult classic. The movie, starring Angela Lansbury, Frank Sinatra, and Laurence Harvey, tells the story of an American soldier captured during the Korean War and brainwashed by the Chinese. The POW is programmed by Chinese Communists to go into a hypnotic trance and to assassinate U.S. political leaders on command. The plot thickens when the Chinese Communists are able to mastermind the nomination of their own candidate for Vice-President and the brainwashed ex-soldier is commanded to kill the presidential nominee.

The Manchurian Candidate is certainly a thriller. But we wonder if its popularity is not based, at least in part, on the image it presents of social influence. Persuasion is a mysterious and powerful force. In the hands of those "in the know," it can be used to bring us to perform some strange and often despicable acts for no apparent good reason.

People indeed do strange things for seemingly no good reason. Many mysterious causes have been invented throughout history to help explain why we humans are influenced and persuaded. For example, the ancients believed that a person's fate is determined by the position of distant stars. During the Middle Ages, there was a widespread belief that a person could be possessed by demons or that behavior could be controlled by witches who cast spells over the unsuspecting.

Centuries later in the 1770s, Franz Anton Mesmer (whose name gave us the word *mesmerize*) created a secular version of witchcraft that still influences our thinking today.[1] According to Mesmer, we are not possessed by spirits or demons, but each of us possesses an "animal fluid" that serves as a major determinant of our behavior—as well as of our health and well-being. (Interestingly, the word *influence* comes from the word *fluid* and literally means "to affect fluid"). Mesmer claimed he could control human behavior and promote human potentials by passing a magnet over the body to redirect the flow of this animal fluid.

Mesmer's therapy sessions created quite a stir in eighteenth-century Europe and America. At a typical session, a leader would

17

"mesmerize" a few faithful souls either by placing magnets at key locations around their bodies or by manually massaging their bodies to stimulate the flow of the animal fluid or, later, simply through a command of voice. Those in the mesmerized state would report seeing bright lights or feeling the animal magnetism tingle their bodies or would report no pain from pinpricks, pinches, or other pain inducers. Loud clapping and ammonia passed under the nose would not wake them from the trance. Some claimed to be cured of disease. A blue-ribbon panel of the leading scientists of the day—including Antoine Lavoisier and Benjamin Franklin—was commissioned to investigate Mesmer's practices. They concluded that, "there is no proof of the existence of Animal Magnetism; that this fluid, having no existence, has in consequence no utility." The panel dismissed the claims for physical cures as "the mere product of the patient's own imaginations."[2]

Mesmer's successors were undaunted. They began a search for new and improved techniques, leading to the abandonment of magnetism and the discovery of the hypnotic trance as a technique for controlling our animal nature.[3] The first popular self-help movements in America, the Society of Harmony of the 1830s and the New Thought movement of the 1890s, made extensive use of Mesmer's theories of human nature. Thousands of Americans sought relief from all sorts of ailments—psychological and physical—by taking the "cure," which could involve anything from being placed in a hypnotic trance to receiving treatment from a magnet to the spiritual healing of Mary Baker Eddy. Similarly, today's New Age healers seek to influence behavior by rechanneling the inner self, sometimes called *chi*, by means of hypnotic trances, subliminal commands, or the power, not of magnets, but of crystals.

In nearly every age and nearly every culture, humans wonder just how they come to be influenced by others.

As noted in Chapter 1, Aristotle was the first to develop a comprehensive theory of persuasion.[4] Aristotle's theory recognized three facets of persuasion—the source (*ethos*), the message (*logos*), and the emotions of the audience (*pathos*). For each facet, Aristotle provided recommendations to the would-be communicator. For example, Aristotle recommended that the orator present himself as a good person and as one who could be trusted. Aristotle suggested that speech writers, in constructing a persuasive message, use arguments that appear to follow the rules of logic and that they use vivid historical and imaginary examples to illustrate points. The message should be tailored to fit the preexisting beliefs of the audience. Aristotle considered an understanding of the feelings of the audience to be essential. An angry person will act differently from one who is pleased. The orator must be able to direct these emotions to good use. To this end, Aristotle described how to evoke emotions in an audience—anger, friendship, fear, envy, and shame—and discussed how to put such emotions to effective persuasive use.

Aristotle recognized one other factor influencing persuasion, which he called *atechnoi*—facts and events outside the immediate control of the speaker. In a court of law, for example, Aristotle identified certain circumstances—the way the law was written, the content of a contract, the testimony of a witness—that set the stage for persuasive argument; in a sense, these circumstances establish the playing field on which argument takes place. They serve to focus the issue and to constrain the range of argument an orator might advance. As such, they are important determinants of the outcome of a case. Aristotle suggested a number of ways for dealing with these factors— challenging the validity of a law, discrediting a witness—that we might today call "putting the right spin" on the matter.

The Roman lawyer Cicero agreed with much of what Aristotle said about persuasion. Cicero, who achieved fame in ancient Roman for his successful courtroom defense of some of Rome's most notorious villains and murderers, established what he called the *officia oratoris*, the duties of the orator—to charm (establish the credibility of the orator), to teach (present a message with sound arguments), and to move (fill an audience with emotions).

One of Cicero's most important contributions was the further development of Aristotle's concept of *atechnoi* into a theory of *statis*, or status of the issue. The task of an orator or a lawyer is to provide a definition of the situation that is most advantageous for one's point of view. For example, suppose your client has been accused of murder. The first line of defense is to deny the facts—"No, my client didn't do it." If that is not possible, then challenge the definition of the action—

"Sure, she killed him, but it wasn't murder." If that fails, then question the quality of the deed—"Yes it was murder, but it was murder with good intent and performed under extenuating circumstances." When all else fails, question the right of the tribunal to try the case in the first place—"This court has no authority to judge a queen." Readers will probably see parallels between Cicero's recommendations and the conduct of many modern cases.

It is interesting to wonder what Aristotle and Cicero might have thought had they lived to see a mesmerist therapy session. As students of persuasion, both, no doubt, would have been intrigued. Neither would likely have believed the explanation of hidden fluids and magnetic influences. They would more likely have been struck by the persuasive techniques of mesmerists, because the successful mesmerist—in the words of Cicero—performed the "duties of the orator" and performed them quite well. The first task of the mesmerist was to charm the audience and establish his or her own credibility. One of the first American mesmerists, a man named Charles Poyen, often likened himself to Galileo, Columbus, and Christ in possessing a truth so important that it was beyond the comprehension of the general public. Others donned the trappings of science or religion to lend a sense of authority to their message.

The second task was to find a message that many would find acceptable—if not totally comprehensible. The mesmerist notion of an animal fluid controlled by magnets is reminiscent of the Christian concept of a soul that can commune with God as well as be possessed by the devil. Indeed, many of America's first mesmerist leaders were originally Christian clergy, and Mesmerism was thus sold as a modern, scientific religion.

The third task of the orator was to influence the emotions to affect persuasion. Many came to mesmerism looking for an answer, such as a cure for their physical disease or relief from such psychological ailments as depression and alienation. Mesmerism offered hope—an emotion that could be exploited for desired effects.

Finally, the successful mesmerist defined the situation to his or her best advantage and thus set the stage for persuasion to occur. Often through word of mouth and local newspapers, rumors were spread about the successful cures effected by mesmerism. Before a therapy session would begin, a few well-chosen "faithful" were placed in a trance to demonstrate to the initiates what mesmerism could accomplish. Audience expectations were thus shaped to accept and believe in the power of mesmerism. For Aristotle and Cicero, influence is not all that mysterious but rather follows a set of basic principles.

Nor are many aspects of persuasion considered mysterious by the professional persuaders of today. In the twentieth century, three general answers have emerged to the age-old question: What makes a persuasive message persuasive? Modern theories of persuasion rely extensively on principles developed within at least one of the three major schools of thought in psychology— psychoanalysis, learning theory, and cognitive approaches.

The psychoanalytic approach to persuasion has a unique distinction: In terms of public awareness, it is perhaps the best known theory of persuasion; in terms of its actual use by professional propagandists, it is probably the least useful. The psychoanalytic theory of persuasion was brought to the public's attention in a highly popular exposé entitled *The Hidden Persuaders*, written by Vance Packard in 1957.[5] According to Packard, advertising agencies were secretly using the principles of psychoanalysis to create ads that were amazingly powerful and successful. To produce such ads, marketers were busily engaged in finding the hidden meaning of things. One handbook on the subject, prepared by Ernest Dichter, actually listed common objects and what they mean, in theory, to the unconscious—for example, rice means fertility, removing one's gloves is erotic and intimate, soup is the magic elixir of life, and eggs mean growth and fertility.[6] Once the unconscious meaning of a thing is uncovered, an advertiser can design a campaign that appeals to our deepest motivations and thus can be quite powerful. In many respects, the psychoanalytic theory of persuasion can be seen as a descendant of mesmerism. Animal magnetism is replaced by the psychic energy of the unconscious; magnets as a means of influence are replaced by appeals to the hidden language of the unconscious or by the use of hypnotism and subliminal commands.

The claims for the power of hidden persuaders were quite strong and, if true, quite frightening. Just what are the facts concerning the use of these hidden persuaders? It is true that advertisers, during the

1950s, *did* employ consultants and others trained in psychoanalysis to help create advertising, just as Packard claimed. Every agency had its "depth man." However, by the mid-1960s most agencies had abandoned this approach, because, quite simply, it did not work. Advertisers found psychoanalytic theory to be too vague to guide their applications; the techniques used for assessing the psychoanalytic meaning of a persuasive communication—analysis of inkblots, free associations, dreams, hypnosis—were notoriously unreliable. The sensational claims of effectiveness made during the 1950s were never realized. Nevertheless, the psychoanalytic theory of persuasion continues to garner much popular attention, as evidenced by the storyline of movies such as *The Manchurian Candidate* and many television crime dramas and by the marketing success of books and tapes touting the power of subliminal influence.

In contrast, principles of persuasion based on learning theory have been used by professional persuaders, especially advertisers and political propagandists, for almost a century. Learning theory has also inspired its share of critics, as evidenced by books such as Aldous Huxley's *Brave New World* and Anthony Burgess's *A Clockwork Orange*—both of which provide a futuristic glimpse of a world completely guided by behavioristic principles.

According to learning theory, a persuasive message is persuasive when it is learned and accepted by the recipient; propaganda must be seen, understood, learned, remembered, and acted upon. Basic principles of learning theory are of use in designing effective communications. For example, as early as 1917 Walter Dill Scott[7] wrote a textbook recommending that advertisers increase the remembering of their ads by using *repetition* (repeat the ad over and over), *intensity* (use bright and loud ads), *association* (link content to the recipient's experiences), and *ingenuity* (make the ad distinctive). One of the most important determinants of learning is incentive; a persuasive message is learned and accepted if it is rewarding to do so.

Perhaps the most important and influential learning model of persuasion, based on the research of Carl Hovland and his colleagues,[8] divides the learning process into four stages. A persuasive message is persuasive when it rewards the recipient at each of the following stages of psychological processing.

1. *The message must attract the recipient's attention.* Ignored messages fail to persuade.
2. *The arguments in the message must be understood and comprehended.* In order for persuasion to occur, we need to grasp the point the speaker is making, whether it be the meaning of a simple advertising slogan or a complex set of reasons for why a nation should go to war.
3. *The recipient must learn the arguments contained in the message and come to accept them as true.* The task of the advertiser and other persuaders is to teach arguments agreeable to the cause, so that these arguments will come easily to mind at the appropriate time and place.
4. *We act on this learned knowledge and beliefs when there is an incentive to do so.*

Although the learning model of persuasion has proven itself useful in the design of many effective communications, research has shown that a communication can be persuasive even if it misses a few of the learning theory stages. Sometimes a message can be persuasive even if its arguments are not fully understood or comprehended. For example, in his autobiography the Watergate burglar G. Gordon Liddy reports that in his youth he would often be persuaded by the speeches of Adolf Hitler, which he heard in German on the radio, even though he knew only a few German phrases.[9] Sometimes a message can be persuasive even if the key arguments are *not* learned or remembered. For example, children are often persuaded by toy advertisements even though they recall very little of the content of the communication. Finally, people are also known to act on their beliefs when there is no clear personal incentive to do so—for example, a martyr dies for a cause and a patriot advocates a policy for the good of the nation.

In the late 1960s, a new approach to persuasion—termed the *cognitive response* approach—was developed to accommodate these criticisms.[10] According to this approach, the target of persuasion is not a passive receptor of influence, dutifully obeying the principles of learning theory, but an active participant in the persuasion process. The important determinant of persuasion is the thoughts running through one's head as a persuasive communication is seen and heard.

In other words, persuasion depends on how a message is interpreted and responded to by the recipient—which could vary depending on the individual, the situation, and the appeal.

The cognitive response approach has given us one of the most important rules for determining the effectiveness of a persuasive tactic: *The successful persuasion tactic is one that directs and channels thoughts so that the target thinks in a manner agreeable to the communicator's point-of-view; the successful tactic disrupts any negative thoughts and promotes positive thoughts about the proposed course of action.*

To say that persuasion is dependent on the "thoughts running through one's head as a persuasive message is received" seems straightforward. But it begs an important question: What determines the thoughts running through one's head? Where do our cognitive responses come from? What determines the way we think about a persuasive communication? This book seeks to answer these questions.

Chapters 3 and 4 look at two overarching principles that describe our cognitive responses to persuasive communications. In general, we humans seek to conserve our cognitive energy by taking mental short-cuts whenever we can, and we attempt to rationalize our thoughts and behavior so that they appear reasonable to ourselves and others.[11] Most, if not all, propaganda appeals attempt to take advantage of these two basic human tendencies.

The next four sections discuss how commonly used persuasion tactics influence our cognitive responses and thus secure compliance. We organize our presentation using an ancient framework—the one first proposed by Aristotle and developed by Cicero and described in this chapter. The first of these sections describes what we call *pre-persuasion* and what Aristotle called *atechnoi* and Cicero termed *statis*. Pre-persuasion refers to how the problem is structured and how the decision is framed. By cleverly establishing how an issue is defined, a communicator can influence cognitive responses and obtain consent without even appearing to be attempting to persuade us. The following three sections look in turn at the influence of each of Aristotle's three facets of persuasion: the source of the communication, the content of a persuasive message, and the role of emotions in persuasion. Once we understand how persuasion works, we will be in a better position to know how best to resist unwanted appeals and how to use it wisely.

Throughout this book, the reader should note a constant theme: Persuasion is no more mysterious than a household lamp. For those who do not understand the principles of electricity, a modern lamp can be a magical, often frightening device. Imagine for a moment that you know nothing about electricity and a woman comes into your home, plugs in a lamp, and the room becomes brighter. What would you think? You would probably wonder in awe: *"Who is this all-powerful goddess of light? What magical fluid or spirit resides in the lamp, hidden from view? Can this goddess with her magical fluid cure my insomnia, too?"* If you happen to touch the lamp and receive a shock, your reverence may turn quickly to fear and cynicism. In many ways, your reactions to the lamp would not be much different from the feelings of those who first saw Mesmer and his magnets or watched *The Manchurian Candidate* in fear and amazement. Suppose we told you that we were going to equip every home in a faraway land with electricity and modern electrical devices, but that we were going to keep the populace of that country ignorant of how electricity works. You would no doubt call us irresponsible and perhaps evil. How much more irresponsible would it then be to equip every home with modern propaganda and not provide instructions concerning the ways of persuasion?

3

MINDLESS PROPAGANDA, THOUGHTFUL PERSUASION

Here are a five facts that professional persuaders have learned about modern propaganda:[1]

> Ads that contain the words *new, quick, easy, improved, now, suddenly, amazing,* and *introducing* sell more products.

> In supermarkets, merchandise placed on shelves at eye level sells best. Indeed, one study found that sales for products at

waist level were only 74% as great and sales for products at floor level were only 57% as great as for those products placed at eye level.

Ads that use animals, babies, or sex appeal are more likely to sell the product than those that use cartoon characters and historical figures.

Merchandise placed at the end of a supermarket aisle or near the checkout aisle is more likely to be purchased.

Bundle pricing—for example, selling items at 2 for $1 instead of 50¢ each—often increases the customer's perception of product "value."

Why do these five techniques work? When you think about it, it makes little sense to purchase an item because it happens to be placed at the end of a supermarket aisle or on a shelf at eye level. You may not really need this conveniently located product, or the item you really want may be located on a top shelf. It makes little sense to be convinced by an ad because it uses a baby or contains certain words; such "information" is of little value in determining the quality of the product. A subtle rewording of the price does not add any value to the product. But that is the point—we consumers often don't think about the reasons we make the decisions we do. Studies show that about half of purchases in a supermarket are impulse buys and that upwards of 62% of all shoppers in discount stores buy at least one item on an unplanned basis.[2]

We often respond to propaganda with little thought and in a mindless fashion. Consider the experiments on mindlessness conducted by Ellen Langer and her colleagues.[3] Langer's collaborators walked up to persons busily using a university copy machine and said: "Excuse me: may I use the Xerox machine?" What would you do in such a situation? If you are like most people, it would depend on your mood. On some occasions you might think: *"Sure, why not? I'm a helpful person."* At other times, you might say to yourself: *"Is this person nuts or what? I got here first and have lots of work to do."* Indeed

Langer's results indicate that both types of thinking were going on—a little over half of the people complied with this request.

Now, here's the interesting part. Langer found that she could get almost everyone to agree to let another person cut in front of them at the copy machine by adding one detail to the request—a *reason* for why the machine was needed. This makes sense. It takes a cold heart to deny someone, perhaps panic-stricken with an urgent need, the simple use of a copy machine. The odd thing about Langer's study is that although some of the reasons given made no sense at all, nearly everyone let the person cut in. For example, on some occasions Langer's collaborators would say, "Excuse me: may I use the Xerox machine, because I have to make copies." When you think about it, this is a pretty silly thing to say: Why would you need a copy machine if you were not planning to make copies? It is the same as no reason at all. But that is the point. Most of the people in the study did not think about it and mindlessly complied with the request.

We can also be influenced when we are being thoughtful. For example, most of us, at one time or another, have been panhandled, that is, stopped on the street by a passerby who asks for a quarter or any spare change. A common response is to ignore the request and continue to walk *mindlessly* down the street. Recently, we were panhandled in a novel manner. The panhandler asked, "Excuse me, do you have 17 cents that I could have?" What thoughts would run through your head in this situation? When this happened to us, our immediate thought was: "*Why does this person need exactly 17 cents? Is it for bus fare? Is it for a specific food purchase? Maybe the person came up short at the market.*" Suddenly the panhandler was a real individual with real needs, not someone we could mindlessly pass by. We were persuaded to part with a handful of change. Intrigued, we later sent our students out on the streets to panhandle for a local charity. They found that almost twice as many people contributed when asked for 17 or 37 cents compared to those who were asked for a quarter or any spare change.[4]

People can be persuaded both when they are in a mindless state *and* when they are thoughtful, but exactly how they are influenced in either of these two states differs considerably. Richard Petty and John Cacioppo argue that there are two routes to persuasion—*peripheral* and *central*.[5] In the peripheral route, a message recipient devotes little attention and effort to processing a communication. Some examples might include watching television while doing something else or listening to a debate on an issue that you don't care much about. In the peripheral route, persuasion is determined by simple cues, such as the attractiveness of the communicator, whether or not the people around you agree with the position presented, or the pleasure and pain associated with agreeing with the position. In contrast, in the central route, a message recipient engages in a careful and thoughtful consideration of the true merits of the information presented. For example, in the central route the person may actively argue against the message, may want to know the answer to additional questions, or may seek out new information. The persuasiveness of the message is determined by how well it can stand up to this scrutiny.

Let's see how the two routes to persuasion could be used to process one of the most influential and controversial television ads of the 1988 presidential election. This ad, prepared by the Bush campaign, told the story of Willie Horton, a black man who had been sent to prison for murder. During the time when Michael Dukakis, Bush's Democratic opponent, was governor of Massachusetts, Horton was released on a prison furlough program. While on furlough, Horton fled to Maryland, where he raped a white woman after stabbing her male companion.

The ad was influential because it required little thought for a person in the peripheral route to get the point. A typical response elicited by the ad went something like this: *"Dukakis let Horton out of prison to rape and kill. Dukakis is weak on crime, especially those committed by bad, black guys."* Although the response is simple, it was nonetheless effective for George Bush. Michael Dukakis was painted as a weak leader who was soft on crime; by comparison, George Bush looked strong and tough, capable of protecting us from the likes of Willie Horton.

However, no one was forced to think about this ad in the peripheral route. For example, in the central route to persuasion, the viewer might have asked: *"Just how unusual is the Massachusetts prison furlough program? Do other states have similar programs? What is the success rate of such programs? Have instances like the Horton* *case happened in other states and with other governors? Can Dukakis really be held personally responsible for the decision to release Horton? How many prisoners were furloughed in Massachusetts without incident? Given that the cost of imprisoning someone for four years is approximately $88,000, or equal to the cost of four years of tuition for a student at Harvard with enough left over to buy the student a BMW upon graduation, is the furlough release program worth trying?"* In the central route, the Horton ad is potentially less effective (and might even have had the potential to damage the Bush campaign). The ad addressed few questions that a thoughtful viewer might raise.

This raises a crucial question: What determines which route to persuasion will be adopted? One factor identified by Petty and Cacioppo is the recipient's motivation to think about the message. In one experiment, Petty and Cacioppo, along with their student Rachel Goldman,[6] investigated the role of personal involvement in determining how we think about a message. Students at the University of Missouri heard a message advocating that their university adopt an exam that all students would need to pass in their senior year in order to graduate. Half of the students were told that their university's chancellor was considering adopting the comprehensive exam the following year, thereby making the issue of adopting the exam personally relevant for these students. The other half were told that the changes would not take effect for ten years and thus would not affect them personally.

To see how the personal relevance of an issue influenced thinking about a communication, Petty, Cacioppo, and Goldman prepared four different versions of the comprehensive exam message. Half of the messages were attributed to a source low in expertise—a local high school class. The other half of the messages were attributed to a source high in expertise—the Carnegie Commission on Higher Education. The researchers also varied the quality of arguments in the message, with half of the messages containing weak arguments (personal opinions and anecdotes) and the other half consisting of strong arguments (statistics and other data about the value of the exam).

This simple study can tell us a lot about the way people think about a persuasive message. Suppose someone was operating in the central route to persuasion and was carefully scrutinizing the communication. When would that person be most persuaded? Given that the person was thinking carefully, he or she would not be persuaded by weak arguments and the source of the communication would not matter much; however, a strong message that stood up to close examination would be very effective. In contrast, the content of the message would not matter much to someone who was not thinking too much about the issue; instead, someone using the peripheral route would be most persuaded by a simple device such as a source that appears to expert.

What did Petty, Cacioppo, and Goldman find? The personal relevance of the issue determined the route to persuasion. For those students for whom the issue of comprehensive exams was personally relevant, the strength of the message's argument was the most important factor determining whether or not they were persuaded. In contrast, for those students for whom the issue of the comprehensive exam was not personally relevant, the source of the communication mattered—the source high in expertise convinced; the one from the high school class failed to do so.

Petty and Cacioppo's two routes to persuasion should alert us to two important points—one about ourselves as human beings and one about propaganda in our modern world. In many ways, we are *cognitive misers*—we are forever trying to conserve our cognitive energy.[7] Given our finite ability to process information, we often adopt the strategies of the peripheral route for simplifying complex problems; we mindlessly accept a conclusion or proposition—not for any good reason but because it is accompanied by a simplistic persuasion device.

Modern propaganda promotes the use of the peripheral route to persuasion and is designed to take advantage of the limited processing capabilities of the cognitive miser. The characteristics of modern persuasion—the message-dense environment, the thirty-second ad, the immediacy of persuasion—make it increasingly more more difficult to think deeply about important issues and decisions. Given that we often operate in the peripheral route, professional propagandists have free rein to use the type of tactics described at the beginning of this chapter and throughout this book to achieve, with impunity, whatever goal they may have in mind.

We have a state of affairs that may be called the *essential dilemma of modern democracy*. On the one hand, we, as a society, value persuasion; our government is based on the belief that free speech and discussion and exchange of ideas can lead to fairer and better decision making. On the other hand, as cognitive misers we often do not participate fully in this discussion, relying instead not on careful thought and scrutiny of a message, but on simplistic persuasion devices and limited reasoning. Mindless propaganda, not thoughtful persuasion, flourishes.

The antidote to the dilemma of modern democracy is not a simple one. It requires each of us to take steps to minimize the likelihood of our processing important information in the peripheral route. This might include increasing our ability to think about an issue through education or improving our ability to detect and understand propaganda by learning more about persuasion. It may mean alerting others to the personal importance of an issue so that many more citizens are encouraged to think deeply about a proposition. It could involve restructuring the way information is presented in our society so that we have the time and the ability to think before we decide. The dilemma of modern democracy is one that we will face throughout this volume. Given the stakes, it behooves each of us to think carefully about how this dilemma can best be resolved.

4
THE RATIONALIZING ANIMAL

We humans like to think of ourselves as rational animals. However, it is more true that we are *rationalizing* animals, that we attempt to appear reasonable to ourselves and to others. Albert Camus said that humans are creatures who spend their entire lives in an attempt to convince themselves that their lives are not absurd. How do we demonstrate that our lives are not absurd? By finding ways to justify our actions, as the following example illustrates.

Marian Keech was a charismatic, middle-aged woman living in a large midwestern city who, in the early 1950s, claimed to be receiving messages from outer space.[1] One evening in September, she received a message from the planet Clarion informing her that on December 21, the world would be destroyed by a great flood. The message went on to say that a fleet of flying saucers would come from Clarion to rescue her and those close to her.

Mrs. Keech attracted a small but loyal group of followers who fervently believed in her prophecy and who made a great many sacrifices consistent with this belief—they quit their jobs; gave away their money, houses, and possessions (who needs money and possessions on the planet Clarion?); and withdrew from their friends. A few even left their spouses.

Mrs. Keech also attracted a small group of social psychologists who infiltrated the movement, pretending to be believers, because they wanted to get a precise, close-up view of what these people would do after December 21 when they discovered that their prophecy had failed—*if* indeed, it *did* fail! The social psychologists noted that Mrs. Keech and her followers were a gentle, benign, reclusive group. One of the most interesting things about them was that they shunned publicity and discouraged converts; they were content to stick to themselves. They treated the "newcomers" politely, but they made it clear that it was of no consequence to them whether or not the newcomers chose to remain a part of the group. They were confident in their beliefs, but it was a quiet, nonflamboyant confidence. Mrs. Keech and her followers refused to grant interviews to reporters and declined to publicize their beliefs in any way.

On the morning of December 20, Mrs. Keech received a message from the planet Clarion instructing her group to be prepared to be picked up precisely at midnight. They were also told to remove all metal from their clothing. The group complied; zippers and clasps were dutifully removed from trousers, skirts, and blouses. When midnight passed, the group became increasingly engulfed by feelings of anxiety and despair. By 4:00 A.M. the group was sitting in stunned silence. But then, at 4:45 A.M., Mrs. Keech's face suddenly took on a radiant glow; she had just received a message from Clarion to the effect that there was no longer any need for the flying saucers to descend—the world had been spared a cataclysm because of the unflagging faith of this small group of believers! The message went on to say that the little group, sitting all night long, had spread so much light that the God of Earth had decided to save the world from destruction. As you might imagine, the group was relieved and elated to hear this news.

What the group did next caused the *social psychologists* to become elated. Within 24 hours, the true believers—this group of quiet, reclusive, shy people—began calling newspapers and TV stations to talk about their prophecy and why it had failed. They made speeches at the drop of a hat and stood on street corners handing out leaflets trying very hard to attract followers. Apparently, the group suddenly found it of urgent importance to spread its message to as broad an audience as possible. Why?

We would suggest that, after the initial elation, the group experienced some doubts; they had given up a great deal because of their belief in the imminent end of the world. The world had not ended, and they were now devoid of their homes, jobs, and possessions—even, a few of them, their spouses. How could they be certain that they had done the right thing? How could they convince themselves that their behavior had not been absurd? By convincing others, of course! After their original prophecy failed, the group felt motivated to attract followers as a way of convincing *themselves* that the sacrifices they had made were not in vain; if they could somehow persuade *others* that their belief had saved the world, then they could allay their own doubts. In the process, they transformed themselves from believers into zealots.

In 1957, Leon Festinger—one of social psychology's most important theorists—proposed his theory of *cognitive dissonance*, which describes and predicts how we humans rationalize behavior.[2] Dissonance occurs whenever a person simultaneously holds two inconsistent cognitions (ideas, beliefs, opinions). For example, the belief that the world will end on a certain day is dissonant with the awareness, when the day breaks, that the world has not ended. Festinger maintained that this state of inconsistency is so uncomfortable that people strive to reduce the conflict in the easiest way possible. They will change one or both cognitions so that they will "fit together" better. This is especially true in situations (such as the one just described) in which a person's self-esteem is at risk.[3] In these circumstances, individuals will go to great lengths of distortion, denial, and self-persuasion in order to justify their past behavior. When our self-esteem has been threatened by our own past behavior, we all have a powerful tendency to become rationalizing animals.

The fact that we are rationalizing animals has important implications for how we receive and react to propaganda. Consider what happens when Frank, a smoker, is confronted with evidence that smoking causes cancer. Frank will be motivated to change either his attitudes about smoking or his behavior. And as anyone who has tried to quit knows, the former alternative is easier. Frank may decide that the studies are lousy. He may point to friends—"If Sam, Jack, and Kate smoke, cigarettes can't be all that dangerous." He may conclude that filters trap all the cancer-producing materials or he may try a low-tar, low-nicotine brand of cigarette. Or Frank may argue that he would rather live a short and happy life with cigarettes than a long and miserable life without them. The more a person is committed to a course of action, the more resistant that person will be to information that threatens that course. Psychologists have reported that the people who are least likely to believe in the dangers of smoking are those who tried to quit and failed. They have become more committed to smoking.

By reducing dissonance, a person defends the ego and retains a positive self-image. But self-justification can reach startling extremes; people will ignore danger in order to avoid dissonance, even when that ignorance can cause their deaths and the deaths of loved ones. We mean that literally.

California is earthquake country.[4] On May 2, 1983, an earthquake of magnitude 6.5 struck the quiet farming town of Colinga, California. Although the quake caused considerable damage and destruction to the town, there was one positive result: The state of California mandated that all cities and towns assess how local buildings would fare in a large earthquake and begin to take steps to minimize that damage. In the city of Santa Cruz (where we live), Dave Steeves, a respected engineer, was charged with the task of preparing such an earthquake audit. Steeves identified 175 buildings that would suffer severe damage in a large earthquake, many of which were located in the Pacific Garden Mall area, the picturesque downtown shopping area of Santa Cruz. This area was particularly vulnerable to earthquake damage because many of the buildings were constructed of unreinforced masonry and, in addition, were built on sandy landfill, which tends to magnify the effects of a quake.

What was the reaction of the Santa Cruz city council to Steeves's report? A rational response would have been to carefully evaluate what he had to say. Did his arguments about unreinforced masonry and sandy landfill make sense? Did he do a complete inspection of the town? Once satisfied that Steeves's argument was sound, a rational person would then have turned to a search for solutions—perhaps asking state and federal agencies for aid, alerting citizens to the danger, identifying immediate but low-cost ways of improving safety, marshaling local citizens to help with the situation and so on. Indeed, Steeves identified at least one such low-cost solution.

But this was not the reaction of the town to Steeves's news. Instead, his report was dismissed by the city council, which voted unanimously in 1987 to wait for the state of California to clarify the "nature of the state law, its options and their legal circumstances regarding the state law" and to convene a new committee to look at the issue. Steeves was called an alarmist and was charged with threatening the town with financial ruin. Many denied that a large earthquake was imminent or would even come at all. In short, Steeves's report set off an attempt at collective dissonance reduction among town leaders.

On October 17, 1989, an earthquake of magnitude 7.1 hit Loma Prieta, a mountain area just outside of Santa Cruz. Five people were killed and about 2,000 were injured in Santa Cruz County; 300 homes were destroyed and 5,000 more were seriously damaged. The Pacific Garden Mall lay in ruins. If anything, Steeves's report had erred on the side of optimism. As further testimonial to the powerful need to reduce dissonance, one city official blamed Steeves for the lack of earthquake preparedness because his report "succeeded in having the whole issue put off by scaring people."

Dissonance reduction can lead to more than just attempts to avoid disagreeable information, as in the case of the smoker and the city of Santa Cruz. The reduction of dissonance is a part of everyday life; this is used to advantage by propagandists in what we call the *rationalization trap*. The trap goes like this. First, the propagandist intentionally arouses feelings of dissonance by threatening self-esteem—for example, by making the person feel guilty about something, by arousing feelings of shame or inadequacy, or by making the person look like a hypocrite or someone who does not honor his or her word. Next, the propagandist offers one solution, one way of reducing this dissonance—by complying with whatever request the propagandist has in mind. The way to reduce that guilt, eliminate that shame, honor that commitment, and restore your feelings of adequacy is to give to that charity, buy that car, hate that enemy, or vote for that leader.

Throughout this book, we will see many variations of the rationalization trap, especially when we talk about the use of emotions in propaganda. But for now, to provide a flavor of what we mean, let's look at two examples of the trap: one involving a subtle request to give to a charity and the other dealing with the more serious issue of war propaganda.

Suppose you are at home and someone knocks at your door, asking you to contribute to a worthy charity. If you don't want to contribute, you probably wouldn't find it too difficult to come up with reasons for declining—you don't have the money, your contribution probably won't help much anyway, and so on. But suppose that, after delivering a standard plea for a donation, the fund-raiser adds one simple phrase: "even a penny will help." There goes your easy excuse. Refusing to donate after hearing this statement would undoubtedly stir up some dissonance by challenging your self-concept. After all, what kind of person is it who is too mean or stingy to come up with a penny? Your previous justifications would no longer apply. The rationalization trap is set. The request threatens your self-esteem and there is only one way to reduce this negative feeling—give to the charity.

Such a scenario was tested experimentally by Robert Cialdini and David Schroeder.[5] Students acting as fund-raisers went door to door asking for donations. Their appeal was identical except that half of the time they added the phrase "even a penny will help." The residents who were approached with the "even-a-penny" request gave contributions more often, donating almost twice as frequently as those getting just the standard plea. Furthermore, on average, the "even-a-penny" contributors were likely to give as much money as the others; that is, the statement legitimizing the small donation did not reduce the size of the contributions. Why? Apparently, not only does the lack of external justification for refusing to donate encourage people to give money, but, after they have decided *whether* to contribute, the desire to avoid appearing stingy or cheap affects their decision about *how much* to give. Once people reach into their pockets, emerging with a mere penny is self-demeaning; a larger donation is consistent with their self-perception of being reasonably kind and generous.

One of the most pernicious functions of war propaganda is make it easier for members of one nation to destroy members of another nation with psychological impunity. War causes a great deal of harm and destruction, often to innocent bystanders and children. The cognition *"I and my country are decent, fair, and reasonable"* is dissonant with the cognition *"I and my country have hurt innocent people."* If the harm is clear, then you cannot reduce your dissonance by claiming that it wasn't done or it wasn't really violence. In this situation, the most effective way to reduce dissonance is to minimize the humanity or maximize the culpability of the victim of your action—to convince yourself the victims deserved what they got.

How else can we account for the following phenomenon? Near the end of World War II, American planes dropped nuclear bombs on Hiroshima and Nagasaki. More than 100,000 civilians (including woman and children) were killed, and countless thousands suffered severe injuries. It is currently fashionable for most Americans to decry that decision. But a week after the bombs were dropped, a public opinion poll indicated that less than 5% of the American population felt we should not have used those weapons, and an astonishing 23% felt we should have used many more of them before allowing Japan the opportunity to surrender.[6]

Some of our readers might consider these events ancient history. But, more recently, during the Persian Gulf war, the people of Iraq were depicted as the unfortunate followers of Saddam Hussein, "the butcher of Baghdad." In the aftermath of the war, amidst the legitimate celebration of a stunning victory, very few Americans paused to express much regret about the killing of tens of thousands of Iraqi noncombatants by our "surgical" bombing raids—which also destroyed the infrastructure of Baghdad (including the water supply), resulting in the suffering of hundreds of thousands of innocent civilians. Almost every war in modern times has been accompanied by characterizations of the enemy as less than human.

Dehumanization succeeds in resolving any dissonance that may be aroused by our cruelty toward our enemies. However, watch out; the more we justify our cruelty, the easier it becomes. The rationalization trap becomes an escalating spiral: *"I committed an act of cruelty; I justify this act by believing that the victim deserved it. If the victim deserved that cruelty, well maybe they deserve more and maybe I am just the one to give it to them."*

In this section we have seen that the tendency to justify our past behavior can lead us into an escalation of rationalizations that can be disastrous. The irony, of course, is that, in order to avoid thinking of ourselves as stupid or immoral, we set the stage for increasing our acts of stupidity or immorality. Is there any antidote to the rationalization trap? Although it is clear that most of us will go to great lengths to justify our actions, it is just as clear that, if that is all we did, we would never learn from our experience; human beings cannot live by consonance alone.

In our everyday experience, we have seen people break out of the rationalization trap by courageously admitting to their mistakes and learning from their errors. How? Under what conditions? Ideally, when we make a mistake, it would be useful for us to be able to interrupt the ego-protective tendency to deny, distort, and to justify it; to bring ourselves to say, in effect, "OK, I blew it. What can I learn from the experience so I will not end up in this position again?" This can come about, first, through an understanding of our defensiveness and dissonance-reducing tendencies and, second, through the development of enough ego strength to recognize and face up to errors in past behavior that require correction—not justification.

We are well aware of the fact that this is easier said than done. We live in a culture where mistakes are not easily tolerated and failure is considered sinful—where children who flunk an exam are sometimes held up to ridicule and where skillful major league baseball managers are fired after one losing season. Perhaps, if we could bring ourselves to be more tolerant of the failure of others, we might be able to tolerate our own short-comings and thereby short-circuit the knee-jerk tendency to justify whatever it is that we have done.

PRE-PERSUASION: SETTING THE STAGE FOR INFLUENCE

WORDS OF INFLUENCE

The comedienne Roseanne Barr tells a joke that goes something like this. "I have a great new recipe for trail mix—two scoops of Reese's Pieces to one scoop of Peanut M&M's. The kids love it. You know it's nutritional because it's trail mix."

The joke is funny because we all know that candy cannot be turned into a nutritional foodstuff simply by calling it by a different name. Yet this is what advertisers and political pundits do everyday for their products with great success. They know that the language allows for much latitude in usage and interpretation—latitude that can be used for persuasive purposes. In such cases, *their* joke may be on us.

The social psychologist Daryl Bem provides us with an interesting analysis of how words and slogans are used in television commercials.[1] According to Bem, a well-known brand of aspirin (which we will call "Brand A") advertises itself as 100% pure aspirin; the commercial goes on to say that government tests have shown that no other pain remedy is stronger or more effective than Brand A. What the maker does not bother to mention is that the tests actually showed that no brand was any weaker or less effective than any of the others. In other words, aspirin is aspirin; all tested brands are equal—except in price, that is. For the privilege of gulping down Brand A, consumers must pay approximately three times the price of an equally effective but unadvertised brand.

Or perhaps you prefer an aspirin proclaiming it is "unsurpassed in speed—no other brand works faster," and buffered so "none is gentler to your stomach." The same government tests showed that this buffered brand works no faster than regular aspirin, nor is there any difference between the two in the frequency of stomach upset. Thus it is truly unsurpassed—but, of course, it doesn't surpass any other brand, either. This well-known brand sells briskly at five times the price of equally effective products with less familiar brand names.

Another product proclaims it uses the ingredient "that doctors recommend." By reading the label, we discover the "magic" ingredient to be good old inexpensive aspirin. Several pharmaceutical companies also market "extra-strength" varieties of "arthritic pain" formulations. You will pay a premium price for these products, although their extra strength comes only from extra aspirin (or acetaminophen, an aspirin substitute), along with a dose of caffeine. Taking additional aspirin would be less expensive, but the product sounds great in the ads: "Not one, but a combination of medically proven ingredients in an extra-strength formula."

Such blatant attempts at mass persuasion seem pitifully obvious when we are mindful and scrutinize them closely. But most of us are not always mindful and are, therefore, vulnerable to unwitting influence. Thus the cash registers ring, and in tremendous numbers we line up and buy the advertised product as if we really believed that there is a major difference among brands of aspirin.

How, then, do words gain their power, their ability to influence and persuade? Briefly put, the way an object is described and the manner in which a course of action is presented direct our thoughts and channel our cognitive responses concerning the communication. Through the labels we use to describe an object or an event, we can define it in such a way that the recipient of our message accepts our definition of the situation and is thus pre-persuaded even before we seriously begin to argue. This simple rule of persuasion was recognized by Cicero as long ago as the second century. Cicero claimed that one of the factors in his success at establishing the innocence of some of Rome's most notorious murderers was his ability to argue that their heinous crimes were not "crimes" at all, but virtuous deeds—that the victims were villains who deserved to be killed.

Psychologically, the aspirin commercials work because by saying that no other remedy is stronger, faster, gentler, or more effective, they lead us to draw, almost automatically, the (incorrect) inference that no other pain reliever is *as* strong, *as* fast, *as* gentle, *as* effective as Brand A. The product description creates the illusion that Brand A is the best, not that Brand A is just like all the rest.

In a recent experiment, two consumer psychologists demonstrated the effectiveness of message wording in the formation of consumers' attitudes toward ground beef.[2] They found that consumers' evaluations were more favorable toward a beef labeled "75% lean" than one labeled "25% fat." Is it any wonder that gasoline stations (who charge a bit more if you use a credit card) call the price of gas purchased by cash "a cash discount" and grocery stores refer to frozen fish for sale in the fresh meats department as "fresh frozen"? The word lean is more attractive then the word fat; the word fresh tends to obscure the fact that the fish is frozen.

Often the full meaning of the inference is left to the imagination of the audience. W. H. Werkmeister calls this the use of *glittering generalities*.[3] In such cases, the propagandist uses "purr" words— words that have positive connotations but are usually ambiguous in the context in which they are used. Some examples include: "A *kindlier, gentler* America" ; "Let's make America *strong* again"; "The *best* that money can buy"; "We must support our *valiant freedom fighters*." Few would disagree that kindlier, gentler, strength, the best, and fighting for freedom are good things; in most concrete situations, however, even fewer would agree on the meaning of each of these words.

Take, for example, Richard Nixon's 1968 campaign pledge to secure an "honorable peace" in Vietnam. What did this really mean? For some, an honorable peace meant immediate withdrawal and an end to an unjust war. For others it meant fighting until the United States had achieved an unconditional victory. What Richard Nixon meant by an honorable peace was left to each listener's imagination, but it was made perfectly clear that Nixon had the "right" objective regarding Vietnam.

Words can also be used to define problems and thus create personal and societal needs. In his history of American advertising, Stephen Fox argues that advertising had its greatest influence during the 1920s.[4] At that time, advertisers gave names to many of the "consumer needs" that we seek to satisfy even today. For example, the Lambert Company, makers of Listerine, popularized the term *halitosis* to refer to bad breath; most Americans didn't know they *had* halitosis until the Lambert Company made us all aware of the possibility of offense by informing us that "even your best friends won't tell you." Arthur Kudner, a copywriter at Erwin, Wasey, & Jefferson, invented the phrase *athlete's foot* (to refer to a fungus infection) and then linked it to a product, Absorbine Jr., that would presumably cure it. Everett Grady of Ruthrauff & Ryan advertised Lifebouy soap as a cure for that dreaded disease, B.O. More recently, advertisers have invented new product categories (needs) and brands to fill them, such as Nyquil, the nighttime cold medicine; 7-Up, the uncola; Miller, the "lite" beer; various brands of vaginal deodorants; and George Bush, the education president.

Advertisers, of course, are not the only ones to invent new labels as a means of propaganda. Early American patriots were able to increase revolutionary fervor by terming a minor skirmish with the British the *Boston massacre*. Adolf Hitler used the same technique to mobilize the German people by explaining Germany's economic troubles in terms of the *red menace* and the *Jewish problem*. Those opposed to abortion call their position *pro-life*, whereas those supporting a woman's right to elect an abortion call themselves *pro-choice*. The Defense Department (formerly called the War Department) uses the term *low-intensity conflict* to refer to wars the United States supported in Nicaragua and El Salvador during the 1980s; this is a curious term when one considers that these have been very intense experiences for those innocent civilians caught in the crossfire—estimated at 50,000 in Nicaragua and 70,000 in El Salvador. Similarly, those opposed to the war with Iraq talked about "bringing home our sons and daughters in body bags," whereas the military used more sanitized terms, such as *collateral damage* and *BDA* (bomb-damage assessment). Politicians interpret social problems and invent the national agenda by using such phrases as *the Cold War, the domino theory of creeping communism, perestroika and glasnost, the war against drugs, Japanese protectionism*, and, now, *the new world order*. Indeed, the use of words in such a manner is so common that William Lutz has amassed a volume of what he calls "doublespeak" and annually presents an award for the most deceptive and self-contradictory use of language by a public figure.[5]

The propaganda power of words is dramatically portrayed in George Orwell's novel *1984*, in which history is continually rewritten in the language of the day—Newspeak—to conform to the needs and desires of government leaders. As Orwell put it:

> The purpose of Newspeak was not only to provide a medium of expression for the world-view and mental habits proper to the devotees of Ingsoc, but to make all other modes of thought impossible. It was intended that when Newspeak had been adopted once and for all and Oldspeak forgotten, a heretical thought—that is, a thought diverging from the principles of Ingsoc—should be literally unthinkable, at least so far as thought is dependent on words.[6]

This novel takes on even more chilling dimensions when one realizes that Orwell's job during World War II was to write pro-British propaganda for broadcast to India.

The psychologist Gordon Allport pointed out that it is the nature of language to divide up and categorize the buzzing boom of information that comes our way every second of the day.[7] It is this inherent nature of language that gives it the power to persuade. By labeling someone a "man," a "woman," a "philanthropist," an "attractive Chinese," a "physician," an "athlete," we emphasize some particular feature of the object "human being" over many other possible ones. We then respond to these features, organizing our realities around the object label. Nouns that "cut slices"—such as we–they, black–white, rich–poor, free–soviet, male–female—serve to divide up the world into neat little packages and to imply the range of appropriate courses of action to take. As just one example, researchers have found that job announcements using the generic *he* (a pronoun that supposedly applies to both males and females) produced considerably fewer female applicants than those that use more inclusive terms.[8] Advertisers know the power of naming and select brand names for their products—such as Head & Shoulders shampoo, DieHard battery, Close-Up toothpaste, that draw attention to the brand's major selling benefit.[9]

The history of advertising and political movements attests to the fact that people tend to act on the names and labels that are given to describe an event or situation. But the power of words and labels to influence how we conceive of the world extends to other contexts as well. One of social psychology's best-documented phenomena is the *self-fulfilling prophecy*—the tendency for a definition of a situation to evoke behavior that makes the definition come true. Dozens of experiments have shown that students who are randomly labeled "smarter," *act* smarter; sane people identified as "insane" are treated as if they *are* insane and may begin to act that way; and women labeled "beautiful," behave as if they *are* beautiful.

The research of Richard Miller, Phillip Brickman, and Diana Bolin, for example, illustrates the persuasive power of a label in an educational setting.[10] In one of their studies, Miller and his colleagues attempted to persuade fifth-grade students in Chicago to be neat and tidy and not to litter—a task that most parents will recognize as quite formidable. Some of the students received lectures on the importance of being neat and tidy. These included lectures on ecology and the dangers of pollution, on why it is important to throw away lunchroom trash, and a plea from the janitor to keep things clean. Other students did not receive a lecture but were repeatedly told that they were a neat and tidy class. For example, these students were told by the janitor that they were one of the neatest classes in the school, and they were encouraged by their teacher to think about why they were so tidy.

What did the results show? Those students who received lectures did *not* improve their littering behavior. In contrast, the fifth-graders who were randomly labeled "neat and tidy" became neater and tidier, dropping three times more litter in the trash cans than did their classmates. In a second study, Miller and his colleagues repeated their results, finding that average second-graders who were labeled "math achievers" subsequently improved in math to a greater extent than their classmates who were merely exhorted to do better at math.[11] In both cases, the *name* made the *thing*; a weed by any other name may be a rose.

A study by Mark Snyder, Ellen Decker Tanke, and Ellen Berscheid illustrates that our labels and conceptions of reality can actually come to create and change that reality.[12] Put yourself in the place of a typical male in their experiment: You have volunteered to participate in an investigation of "how people become acquainted with each other," and you have been paired with a female who is located in another room, ostensibly because the two of you are assigned to the "no nonverbal communication" condition of the study. You will communicate with her on a telephone. Although you have not seen your partner, you have been given a packet of information that contains a snapshot. For half of the subjects, the snapshot was of a very attractive woman; for the others, it was of a relatively unattractive woman. How did the label "attractive female" influence the males' behavior? The males who thought they were talking with an attractive partner rated her as more poised, humorous, and socially adept than did those who thought they were talking with a less attractive woman. This is not very surprising. But what *was* startling is this: When independent observers were allowed to listen to a tape recording of only the woman's half of the conversation (without looking at the photograph), they were far more impressed by the woman whose male partner thought she was physically attractive. How did this come about? Since the male partner thought he was talking to an attractive woman, he spoke to her in a way that brought out her best and most sparkling qualities. When these independent observers listened to her conversation, they rated her as more attractive, more confident, more animated, and warmer than the woman whose partner thought her to be less beautiful. In other words, expectations had created reality.

Throughout this chapter, we have emphasized the propaganda value of words and labels—how they can be used to persuade and create social reality. But words do not have to be used to cloak reality in deception. The ability to manipulate words and concepts in our head—that is, the ability to think—is a uniquely human characteristic. It allows us to solve problems creatively without requiring the manipulation of the actual thing itself in a trial-and-error fashion. Given the flexibility of the human mind, there are many ways to label any given event. This flexibility provides the key to overcoming the propagandist's intent: When presented with a definition of the world, we can always ask, "Why this label? What other definitions of the situation would shed more light on the issue?" By looking at any given event from many different perspectives we can gain new insights to guide our decision making.

At the same time, it is important to remember that words have the power to pre-persuade. The words and labels we use come to define and create our social world. This definition of reality directs our thoughts, our feelings, our imagination and thus influences our behavior. Perhaps Joseph Goebbels, Hitler's minister of propaganda, best described the power of words:

> It would not be impossible to prove with sufficient repetition and psychological understanding of the people concerned that a square is in fact a circle. What after all are a square and a circle? They are mere words and words can be moulded until they clothe ideas in disguise.[13]

6

PICTURES IN OUR HEADS

In *Public Opinion*, the distinguished political analyst Walter Lippmann tells the story of a young girl, brought up in a small mining town, who one day went from cheerfulness into a deep spasm of grief.[1] A gust of wind had suddenly cracked a kitchen windowpane. The young girl was inconsolable and spoke incomprehensibly for hours. When she finally was able to speak intelligibly, she explained that a broken pane of glass meant that a close relative had died. She was therefore mourning her father, whom she felt certain had just passed away. The young girl remained disconsolate until, days later, a telegram arrived verifying that her father was still alive. It appears that the girl had constructed a complete fiction based on a simple external fact (a broken window), a superstition (broken window means death), fear, and love for her father.

The point of Lippmann's story was not to explore the inner workings of abnormal personality, but to ask a question about ourselves: To what extent do we, like the young girl, let our fictions guide our thoughts and actions? Lippmann believed that we are much more similar to that young girl than we might readily admit. He contended that the mass media paint an imagined world and that the "pictures in our heads" derived from the media influence what men and women will do and say at any particular moment. Lippmann made these observations in 1922. Seven decades later, we can ask: What is the evidence for his claim? To what extent do the pictures we see on television and in other mass media influence how we see the world and set the agenda for what we view as most important in our lives?

Let's look at the world we see on television. George Gerbner and his associates have conducted the most extensive analysis of television to date.[2] Since the late 1960s, these researchers have been videotaping and carefully analyzing thousands of prime-time television programs and characters. Their findings, taken as a whole, indicate that the world portrayed on television is grossly misleading as a representation of reality. Their research further suggests that, to a surprising extent, we take what we see on television as a reflection of reality.

In prime-time programming, males outnumber females by 3 to 1, and the women portrayed are younger than the men they encounter. Nonwhites (especially Hispanics), young children, and the elderly are underrepresented; and members of minority groups are disproportionately cast in minor roles. Moreover, most prime-time characters are portrayed as professional and managerial workers: Although 67% of the work force in the United States are employed in blue-collar or service jobs, only 25% of TV characters hold such jobs. Finally, crime on television is ten times more prevalent than it is in real life. The average 15-year-old has viewed more than 13,000 TV killings. Over half of TV's characters are involved in a violent confrontation each week; in reality, fewer than 1% of people in the nation are victims of criminal violence in any given year, according to FBI statistics. David Rintels, a television writer and former president of the Writers' Guild

"...No, he can't really fly...no, the bad guys don't really have a ray gun...no, this cereal really isn't the best food in the whole world...no, it won't make you as strong as a giant..."

of America, summed it up best when he said, "From 8 to 11 o'clock each night, television is one long lie."[3]

To gain an understanding of the relationship between watching television and the pictures in our heads, Gerbner and his colleagues compared the attitudes and beliefs of heavy viewers (those who watch more than four hours a day) and light viewers (those who watch less than two hours a day). They found that heavy viewers (1) express more racially prejudiced attitudes; (2) overestimate the number of people employed as physicians, lawyers, and athletes; (3) perceive women as having more limited abilities and interests than men; (4) hold exaggerated views of the prevalence of violence in society; and (5) believe old people are fewer in number and less healthy today than they were twenty years ago, even though the opposite is true. What is more, heavy viewers tend to see the world as a more sinister place than do light viewers; they are more likely to agree that most people are just looking out for themselves and would take advantage of you if they had a chance. Gerbner and his colleagues conclude that these attitudes and beliefs reflect the inaccurate portrayals of American life provided to us by television.

Let's look at the relationship between watching television and images of the world by looking more closely at how we picture criminal activity. In an analysis of "television criminology," Craig Haney and John Manzolati point out that crime shows dispense remarkably consistent images of both the police and criminals.[4] For example, they found that television policemen are amazingly effective, solving almost every crime, and are absolutely infallible in one regard: The wrong person is never in jail at the end of a show. Television fosters an illusion of certainty in crimefighting. Television criminals generally turn to crime because of psychopathology or insatiable (and unnecessary) greed. Television emphasizes criminals' personal responsibility for their actions and largely ignores situational pressures correlated with crime, such as poverty and unemployment.

Haney and Manzolati go on to suggest that this portrayal has important social consequences. People who watch a lot of television tend to share this belief system, which affects their expectations and can cause them to take a hard-line stance when serving on juries. Heavy viewers are likely to reverse the presumption of innocence, believing that defendants must be guilty of something, otherwise they wouldn't be brought to trial.

A similar tale can be told about other "pictures painted in our heads." For example, heavy readers of newspaper accounts of sensational and random crimes report higher levels of fear of crime. Repeated viewing of R-rated violent "slasher" films is associated with less sympathy and empathy for victims of rape. When television is introduced into an area, the incidence of theft increases, perhaps due partly to television's promotion of consumerism, which may frustrate and anger economically deprived viewers who compare their lifestyles with those portrayed on television.[5]

It should be noted, however, that the research just described —that done by Gerbner and colleagues and by others—is correlational; that is, it shows merely an association, not a causal relation, between television viewing and beliefs. It is therefore impossible to determine from this research whether heavy viewing actually causes prejudiced attitudes and inaccurate beliefs or whether people already holding such attitudes and beliefs simply tend to watch more television. In order to be certain that watching TV causes such attitude and believes, it would be necessary to perform a controlled experiment in which people are randomly assigned to conditions. Fortunately, some recent experiments do allow us to be fairly certain that heavy viewing does indeed determine the pictures we form of the world.

In a set of ingenious experiments, the political psychologists Shanto Iyengar and Donald Kinder varied the contents of evening news shows watched by their research participants.[6] In their studies, Iyengar and Kinder edited the evening news so that participants received a steady dose of news about a specific problem facing the United States. For example, in one of their experiments, some participants heard about the weaknesses of U.S. defense capabilities; a second group watched shows emphasizing pollution concerns; a third group heard about inflation and economic matters.

The results were clear. After a week of viewing the specially edited programs, participants emerged from the study more convinced than they were before viewing the shows that the target problem—the one receiving extensive coverage in the shows they had watched—was a more important one for the country to solve. What is more, the participants acted on their newfound perceptions, evaluating the current president's performance on the basis of how he handled the target issue and evaluating more positively than their competitors those candidates who took strong positions on those problems.

Iyengar and Kinder's findings are not a fluke. Communications researchers repeatedly find a link between what stories the mass media cover and what viewers consider to be the most important issues of the day.[7] The content of the mass media sets the public's political and social agenda. As just one example, in a pioneering study of an election in North Carolina, researchers found that the issues that voters came to consider to be most important in the campaign coincided with the amount of coverage those issues received in the local media.[8] Similarly, the problems of drug abuse, NASA incompetence, and nuclear energy were catapulted into the nation's consciousness by the coverage of dramatic events such as the drug-related death of basketball star Len Bias, the *Challenger* explosion, and the nuclear-reactor accidents at Three Mile Island and Chernobyl. Former Secretary of State Henry Kissinger clearly understood the power of the news media setting agendas. He once noted that he never watched the content of the evening news but was only interested in "what they covered and for what length of time, to learn what the country was getting."[9]

Of course, each of us has had extensive personal contact with many people in a myriad of social contexts; the media are just one source of our knowledge about political affairs and different ethnic, gender, and occupational groups. The information and impressions we receive through the media are relatively less influential when we can also rely on firsthand experience. Thus those of us who have been in close contact with several women who work outside the home are probably less susceptible to the stereotypes of women portrayed on television. On the other hand, regarding issues with which most of us have had limited or no personal experience, such as crime and violence, television and the other mass media are virtually the only vivid source of information for constructing our image of the world.

The propaganda value of the mass media in painting a picture of the world has not been overlooked by would-be leaders. Such social policy as a "get tough on crime" program, for example, can be easily sold by relating it to the prime-time picture of crime as acts committed by the psychopathic and the greedy, rather than dealing with situational determinants such as poverty and unemployment. In a similar vein, it is easier to sell a "war on drugs" after the drug-related death of a prominent basketball star or to promote an end to nuclear power after a fatal tragedy at a nuclear reactor.

It is even more important for a would-be leader to propagate his or her own picture of the world. The political scientist Roderick Hart notes that since the early 1960s, U.S. presidents have averaged over 25 speeches per month—a large amount of public speaking.[10] Indeed, during 1976, Gerald Ford spoke in public once every six hours, on average. By speaking frequently on certain issues (and gaining access to the nightly news), a president can create a political agenda—a picture of the world that is favorable to his or her social policies. Indeed, one of President Bush's key advisors is Robert Teeter, a pollster who informs the president on what Americans think and what issues should be the topic of his speeches. This can be of great importance in maintaining power. According to Jeffery Pfeffer, an expert on business organizations, one of the most important sources of power for a chief executive officer is the ability to set the organization's agenda by determining what issues will be discussed and when, what criteria will be used to resolve disputes, who will sit on what committees, and, perhaps most importantly, which information will be widely disseminated and which will be selectively ignored.[11]

Why are the pictures of the world painted by the mass media so persuasive? For one thing, we rarely question the picture that is shown. We seldom ask ourselves, for example, "Why are they showing me this story on the evening news rather than some other one? Do the police really operate in this manner? Is the world really this violent and crime-ridden?" The pictures that television beams into our homes are almost always simply taken for granted as representing reality.

Once accepted, the pictures we form in our heads serve as fictions to guide our thoughts and actions. The images serve as primitive social theories—providing us with the "facts" of the matter, determining which issues are most pressing, and decreeing the terms in which we think about our social world. As the political scientist Bernard Cohen observed, the mass media may not be successful much of the time in telling people *what to think*, but it is stunningly successful in telling its readers *what to think about*... The world will look different to different people, depending...on the map that is drawn for them by writers, editors, and publishers of the papers they read.[12]

7

SADDAM HUSSEIN: THE HITLER WE "KNOW"

Before the Persian Gulf war of 1991, the U.S. Congress debated the positive and negative consequences of going to war. Those who supported the war described Saddam Hussein as the new Hitler: They emphasized the parallels between Saddam's gassing of the Kurds and Hitler's gassing of the Jews, Iraq's invasion of Kuwait and Germany's invasion of Czechoslovakia and Poland, and Saddam and Hitler's build-up of armaments. Those who opposed the war saw the situation in Iraq as paralleling that of Vietnam: They saw both incidents as civil wars—a fight between various Arab factions and between North and South Vietnam; they worried about the U.S. military's ability to fight in difficult foreign terrain consisting of deserts and swamps; they characterized the war effort as being in support of "big business" and "big oil."

The debate over war with Iraq was really a debate over whose definition of ambiguous events was "correct." And with good reason: once it is decided how an event or person should be categorized, it becomes clear what course of action should be taken. If Saddam was truly a new Hitler, then a policy of appeasement and letting him have Kuwait would only bring additional threats to peace and ultimately a much worse war. If Iraq was another Vietnam, then U.S. intervention would lead to a long and divisive war and the country would become stuck in a quagmire with no clear victors and losers.

We "debate" how to define persons and events thousands of times a day and, although we usually do not go to war over the results, the consequences of how we interpret and define events can be quite significant. For example, we may see a political candidate as "presidential" simply because he or she shares some irrelevant mannerisms with one of our favorite politicians from the past; a college athlete may be viewed as "pro" material because he fits the mold of past successes—he's a Lynn Swann type or he reminds us of the old-style Steeler linebackers of the past; we like the new car we purchased because it is similar in style to a high-priced, sporty model that we cannot afford.

Ten years before the Persian Gulf war, Thomas Gilovich published a set of experiments looking at how irrelevant associations to the past can influence decision making.[1] In one of his studies, students majoring in political science were asked to resolve a hypothetical international crisis. In this crisis, a small democratic country was being threatened by an aggressive, totalitarian neighbor that was conducting subversive activities against the democratic regime as well as massing troops along a shared border. Embedded in the information about the crisis were irrelevant phrases designed to highlight the similarities in the hypothetical crisis to either the war against Nazi Germany or that against North Vietnam. For example, the political science majors were either told that minorities were fleeing the democratic country via boxcars on freight trains or via small boats; the impending invasion was referred to as a Blitzkrieg or a Quick-strike; the current U.S. president was from the state of New York (as was FDR) or from Texas (as was LBJ); the briefing concerning the crisis was held in Winston Churchill Hall or Dean Rusk Hall. Did these irrelevant "similarities" influence judgments about what should be done about the crisis? Amazingly, they did. Gilovich found that the students who were "primed" to see the crisis as like the one involving Nazi Germany were more likely to recommend U.S. military intervention than were those who saw it as another Vietnam.

In the end, debates on a course of action must come down to which definition of the situation is perceived to be *correct*—Is Saddam more like Hitler or is Iraq more like Vietnam? Of course, we should entertain the hypotheses that both analogies are true, that neither is true, or that perhaps other analogies also fit the situation. For example, the historian Paul Kennedy sees the U.S. military involvement in the Persian Gulf as reminiscent of Spain's foreign wars of the 1630s and

1640s.[2] One argument given by supporters of U.S. participation in the war was that the success of the war would help restore American self-confidence and break the mood of self-doubt and defeatism that had purportedly prevailed in the country since the 1960s—in other words, overcome the "Vietnam syndrome." The great Spanish minister, the Count-Duke de Olivares, made a similar argument in favor of Spain's intervention on the side of the Hapsburgs in the Thirty Years' War. Upon hearing of Spain's first battlefield success, Olivares declared it to be "the greatest victory of our times"—one that proved Spain's domestic and foreign detractors wrong; because of military prowess, Spain was still number one on the international scene. Domestically, however, Spain's industries lacked competitiveness, its streets were filled with the unemployed and the homeless, and the nation's debts were increasing at a rapid clip. A generation later, Spain was no longer a world power.

Classical theories of rhetoric look with disdain upon analogy as a form of persuasion; any given analogy is vulnerable to the attack that it is based on faulty comparisons—that the points of similarity presented in the analogy are irrelevant and inconsequential. According to classical theory, analogies should be evaluated using two rules:

1. The similarities between two things must concern pertinent, significant aspects of the two things.
2. The analogy must not ignore pertinent dissimilarities between the two things being compared.[3]

Notice what happens if we use these two classical rules to evaluate any of the three proposed perspectives on the Persian Gulf war. We immediately desire more information and facts about the present and the past: What are the economic and social conditions of the nations involved? What happened to the Hapsburg Empire, Germany, and Vietnam after each respective war was over? What were the economic and social cost of each war? In answering such questions, we can develop a more complete understanding of the situation at hand—an analysis that can inform such important decisions as whether or not to go to war.

There is another way to evaluate the validity of a communicator's definition of the situation—by the sincerity of the communicator. In other words, does the advocate of a given view of the world really believe that is the way things are, or has he or she merely adopted this viewpoint for expedient, propaganda purposes?

For example, shortly before the onset of the Persian Gulf war on October 15, 1990, President Bush stated:

> Every day now, new word filters out [of Kuwait] about the ghastly atrocities perpetrated by Saddam's forces... of a systematic assault on the soul of a nation, summary executions, routine torture... newborn babies thrown out of incubators... dialysis patients ripped from their machines... Hitler revisited. But remember, when Hitler's war ended there were the Nuremberg trials.[4]

Was he serious? Perhaps so. But given the fact that, just a short time earlier, our government was staunchly supporting Saddam in his war against Iran, it is at least conceivable that Bush was exaggerating.

If the president was engaging in hyperbole, some people believe that it is forgivable. After all, he was intent on mobilizing the nation for what might have been a long and costly war and on gaining the approval of his fellow citizens for putting hundreds of thousands of young American men and women in harm's way in order to come to the aid of a nondemocratic nation. And it worked; support for the war soared and George Bush's popularity soon reached an all-time high. During and immediately after the war, Bush's approval rating hovered around 90%.

But the use of such propaganda devices carries a price—for the communicator as well as the audience. In this case, once the American people recovered from their euphoria after the war came to a quick and (in terms of U.S. casualties) relatively bloodless end, a great many Americans began to wonder why, after having achieved total military dominance, we had allowed Saddam to remain in power with a large part of his military force intact—a force that he promptly began to use with impunity against his own civilian population.[5] Indeed, even the commander of the United Nations forces in the Persian Gulf, General Norman Schwartzkopf, was bold enough to wonder about this out loud on network television. Can you imagine the President of the United States in 1945, having won a smashing victory over Adolf Hitler, allowing Hitler to continue to govern the German people? Can you imagine the Allied forces stopping just inside the border of Germany and then turning back? Utterly impossible. If Hitler had survived he would certainly have been tried, convicted, and executed as a war criminal. Why, then, did George Bush allow Saddam Hussein free rein in Iraq? It was confusing. In a *Newsweek* poll taken on May 1, 1991, 55% of those questioned did not view the Persian Gulf war as a victory because Saddam was still in power. President Bush's popularity began to fade—but not by much. In a sense, he got away with it.

But in a deeper sense, he did not. For, in our judgment, there was a more serious price to pay. We feel that a good case can be made that George Bush never really believed that Saddam Hussein was another Hitler. His use of the analogy was a cynical attempt to strike fear and loathing into the hearts of the American people. Saddam Hussein is certainly an unsavory villain. But an unsavory villain capable of achieving stability in Iraq—a stability that President Bush and his advisors obviously considered worth the price of allowing him to remain in office. An unsavory villain that we could live with comfortably—one we had lived with and supported in the past and not unlike a great many other unsavory villains around the world whom the United States continues to support.

The cynicism evinced by Mr. Bush is more than merely unfortunate. As citizens of a democracy, we have the right to look closely at the facts so that we might arrive at our own rational conclusions about whether or not we should go to war and whether or not it is appropriate to bring Saddam to trial as a war criminal—based not on the hyperbole of a president, but on the facts of the matter. We have a right to be angry at being manipulated by a president if he depicts our enemy as another Hitler one month and as a difficult but stabilizing force the next.

It is not our intention to single out Mr. Bush for special criticism. Unfortunately, pulling the wool over the eyes of the people has been a common practice in the White House; from Lyndon Johnson's false statements of optimism during the Vietnam war ("there is light at the end of the tunnel") to Richard Nixon's stonewalling of the Watergate affair ("I am not a crook") to Ronald Reagan's statements about the Iran/Contra scandal ("I think I don't remember"), American presidents have been denying citizens the information necessary to properly analyze a situation and to act rationally. The truly unfortunate aspect of this is that most Americans have rather cynically come to take it for granted that they will be misled.

8

ASKING THE *RIGHT* QUESTIONS

Imagine that you are the President of the United States and the country is bracing itself for the outbreak of an unusual epidemic expected to kill 600 people. Your top advisors have prepared two alternative programs to combat the disease and have estimated, to the best of their abilities, the likely consequences of each program.

If Program A is adopted, 200 people will be saved.

If Program B is adopted, there is a one-third probability that 600 people will be saved and a two-thirds probability that no people will be saved.

Mr. or Ms. President, which program do you favor?

If you are like most of the participants in an experiment performed by Daniel Kahneman and Amos Tversky, you would select Program A.[1] (Seventy-two percent of their subjects selected this option). You might think to yourself, "Program A guarantees that 200 people will be saved while Program B gambles the lives of these people for only a 1 in 3 chance that more lives could be saved."

But suppose your advisors had presented the epidemic problem this way instead:

If Program A is adopted, 400 people will die.

If Program B is adopted, there is a one-third probability that nobody will die and a two-thirds probability that 600 people will die.

Which program would you now favor?

The two sets of options are the same. Program A means that 200 people will live and 400 will die. Program B results in a one-third chance that no one would die and 600 people will live and a two-thirds chance that no one will be saved and 600 people will die.

But for most people, their thinking about the epidemic is quite different. *"If I go with Program A, 400 people will surely die; I might as well gamble on B."* When asked in this second manner, 78% of Kahneman and Tversky's subjects favored Program B.

Why did such a simple rewording of the options produce such a drastic switch in answers? Kahneman and Tversky (as well as others) have noted that people dislike losses and seek to avoid them. It is more painful to give up $20 than it is pleasurable to gain $20. The first policy decision was worded so that Program B looked like the bigger loss; the second version was phrased so that Program A looked like a sure loss. It's all in how the question is *framed*.

This is, of course, just a hypothetical situation. What happens when requests are reworded in real life? Let's look at the prevention of breast cancer—a serious health threat for many women. Fortunately, early detection and diagnosis of breast cancer can greatly improve a woman's chances of surviving the disease. Unfortunately, one of the best methods for detecting breast cancer, a monthly breast self-examination, is not performed regularly by most women.

Beth Meyerowitz and Shelly Chaiken developed and distributed three pamphlets asking women to perform a routine breast self-examination regularly.[2] One pamphlet contained only instructions on how to perform a breast self-examination. The second pamphlet contained these instructions and asked women to perform the exam by emphasizing the positive consequences of self-examination (i.e., women who perform such examinations have an *increased* chance of finding a tumor at a treatable stage). The third pamphlet contained the instructions and also stressed the negative consequences of failing to perform a self-examination i.e., women who do *not* perform such examinations have a *decreased* chance of finding a tumor at a treatable stage). Meyerowitz and Chaiken found that, four months after reading the pamphlet, those women who were asked to perform the breast exam using the negative consequences were significantly more likely to perform a self-examination. How you ask can make a significant difference in a real life-and-death situation.

In both of the above examples—the epidemic decision and the communication about breast self-exams—the way the request was put influenced the way the issue was defined. In both cases, defining the issue as "losing something" was more persuasive than stating it in terms of a gain. Question-asking can be a subtle form of pre-persuasion —a carefully crafted question can be used to define the issue at hand, to suggest subtly what the "right" answer may be, and to organize the way we think about the issue. Let's look at some of the ways that an artfully worded question can produce the results we seek.

Opinion pollsters have long known that subtle changes in the wording of a question can produce dramatically different responses. For example, the percentage of Americans supporting aid for the Contras in Nicaragua from 1983 to 1986 varied from 13% to 42%, depending on how the question was worded.[3] If the question mentioned Ronald Reagan or the Contras explicitly, or used ideological labels to identify the opposing forces in Nicaragua, more Americans supported the aid. If the question mentioned a dollar amount of aid or presented both sides of the issue, fewer Americans wanted to give aid to the Contra rebels. Legitimate pollsters who seek accurate responses will go to great lengths to avoid bias in the wording of questions. Those who seek to use polls for their own advantages—to convince people that everyone else supports their policy or their political candidacy— will not be so careful.

Lawyers also know the importance of a carefully phrased question. Textbooks describing how to cross-examine a witness stress the maxim, "Never ask a question for which you don't already know the answer." Put more accurately, "Never ask a question that doesn't get the answer you want."

Elizabeth Loftus has conducted a program of research looking at how leading questions can influence eyewitness testimony.[4] In one of her studies, Loftus showed subjects a film depicting a multiple-car accident. After the film, some of the subjects were asked, "About how fast were the cars going when they *smashed* into each other?" Other

*"This is not your usual poll.
I'm here to tell you what I think."*

subjects were asked the same question, but the word *smashed* was replaced by the word *hit*. Subjects who were asked about *smashing* cars, as opposed to *hitting* cars, estimated that the cars were going significantly faster and, a week after seeing the film, were more likely to state that there was broken glass at the accident scene (even though no broken glass was shown in the film).

Leading questions can influence not only judgment of facts but also actual memory of what has happened. In another study, Loftus showed subjects a series of slides depicting an auto–pedestrian accident. In a critical slide, a *green* car drove past the accident. Immediately after viewing the slides, half of the subjects were asked, "Did the *blue* car that drove past the accident have a ski rack on the roof?" The remaining subjects were asked this same question but with the word *blue* deleted. The results showed that those subjects who were asked about the "blue" car were more likely to claim incorrectly that they had seen a blue car (even though in the slide it was green). A simple question had distorted their memory.

It is not only what is asked but also the order in which it is asked that influence our decisions and choices. Suppose your head is throbbing and your stomach is acting up. You need a strong pain reliever that will not adversely affect your stomach. Displayed below are your available options and how they rate on various attributes of a pain reliever:

	SPECIAL-GRIP BOTTLE	EASY ON THE STOMACH	PAIN-RELIEF STRENGTH
Brand W	yes	good	very good
Brand X	yes	good	good
Brand Y	yes	poor	excellent
Brand Z	no	excellent	excellent

Before you rush out to the store, you see the following ad for Brand W on television: All four pain relievers are lined up in a row. The announcer asks, "Which of these pain relievers gives you a special grip-bottle?" Brand Z is removed before your eyes. "Which of these brands won't upset your stomach?" Out goes Brand Y. "Which brand gives you the most pain relief?" Brand X is forcefully removed. "The choice is—Brand W."

Or is it? Suppose the last two questions were asked in reverse order? Our choice would be much different—Brand Z would be our *best* buy and Brand W the *worst*. Given your throbbing head and your upset stomach, you may wish to give more weight to these two attributes than the special-grip bottle. Again, Brand Z is your pain reliever.

With all of the information on the different pain relievers conveniently displayed, it is easy to see how the order in which questions are asked and the order in which information is received can distort and bias the decision-making process. Unfortunately, for many of our decisions, we rarely have all of the information at once—either because it is unavailable or we do not have the time or energy to secure it. In such cases, the order in which we seek and obtain information can influence our decisions in subtle but important ways.

Question asking can be a powerful persuasion device because questions structure our decision-making process. They do this by directing our thoughts about the issues at hand and by implicitly specifying the range of possible answers. Consider the question, "Do you support the constitutional right to bear arms?" The question directs our thoughts and attention to the constitutionality of gun ownership as opposed to other concerns, such as the right to a safe neighborhood. The question also implicitly defines the issue as guns versus no guns and excludes middle-of-the road proposals such as gun registration, waiting periods, and restricted access to certain types of arms (such as Saturday night specials, automatic assault weapons, or nuclear arms). The Constitution also guarantees free speech, but not the right to yell *fire* in a crowded movie house.

If you doubt the power of a question to pre-persuade, observe how politicians handle themselves at press conferences and on public affairs programs. They know that questions can direct attention and change public opinion. That is why, when a question is not to a politician's liking, he or she will try to dodge it. Suppose a politician is on record as favoring gun control. The stinging question about supporting the Constitution can be avoided by rephrasing it ("It's a good question; just what will I do about the crime in our streets?"), by postponing it ("Let's first clear up a few important issues"), by glossing over it in a way that appears to answer the question ("You know I support the Constitution of the United States and the people's right to live in safety as they see fit"), or by diverting attention by asking yet another question ("But do you believe in the right of every American to live in safety?").

So far in this section, we have seen how the definition of an issue—whether it be through choice of words, images, analogies, or just by asking the "right question"—serve as a form of pre-persuasion.

In the next chapter, we look at how context—the "other" issues and objects that we can consider—influences perception and, thus, our subsequent behavior.

THE POWER OF "DECOYS"

A trip with your local real estate agent can illustrate the powerful impact of a decoy. At the realtor's office, you are shown pictures and descriptions of many homes—beautiful split-levels, roomy ranches, an old Victorian. After determining your needs, the agent drives you to some homes "you might find of interest." The first stop is a tiny two-bedroom house sitting on a narrow lot. The house needs a new coat of paint; the interior is in disarray; the linoleum in the kitchen is buckling; the living room carpet is worn; the master bedroom is so small that an average-sized bedroom suite just won't fit. When the realtor tells you the asking price, you exclaim, "Holy cow! Who'd be dumb enough to pay so much for this shack?" Probably not you, and probably not anyone else. But that dilapidated house may influence you to buy another house more readily and to buy it at a much higher price than you might normally be willing to pay.

How can this come about? We can clarify the process by looking at an experiment we conducted with our colleagues Peter Farquhar, Sarah Silbert, and Jennifer Hearst.[1] In our study, students were asked to make decisions such as the following:

> Which would you select (a or b)?
> a. *Nutri-burger*: a tofu burger that is very good on nutrition but only average on taste
> b. *Tasti-burger*: a hamburger that is very good on taste but only average on nutrition.

For some decisions, a *decoy* was given as an additional option. A decoy is an alternative that is inferior to other possible selections. For example:

Which would you prefer (a, b, or c)?

a. *Nutri-burger*: the tofu burger described above

b. *Tasti-burger*: the hamburger described above

c. *Bummer-burger*: a hamburger that is only good on taste and only average on nutrition.

In this case, the decoy is option c—the hamburger that is only *good* on taste (as opposed to very good). No reasonable person would select this inferior burger. If you wanted a lunch that tasted great, you would select Option b, the very good-tasting Tasti-burger. If you wanted nutrition, you would go for the Nutri-burger. Indeed, in our study the decoy was almost never selected.

But that doesn't mean that its presence as an option wasn't influential. Our study investigated decisions about nine common consumer products; we found that, on average, including a decoy increased the probability of people's selecting the products that were similar (but superior) to the decoy such as the Tasti-burger (the very good hamburger) over the Nutri-burger by 6.7%. Does 6.7% seem like a small amount? To put this in perspective, a 1% change in market share for a small brand manufactured by a company like Procter & Gamble or General Motors could mean an annual increase in sales of more than $10 million. In short, extrapolating into the real world, our decoys might have produced a $67-million effect!

How did this relatively worthless decoy change our students' choices? The answer in a nutshell: contrast effects. To contrast means to make differences apparent. When an object is contrasted with something similar but not as good, or not as pretty, or not as tall, it is judged to be better, prettier, taller than would normally be the case. If a man of normal height (say 5 feet 11 inches) is in the company of midgets, he seems very tall. If he is a member of a professional basketball team, he seems very short. Such was the case with "Tiny" Archibald, who played basketball for the Boston Celtics. "Tiny" stood 6 feet, 1 inch tall. In Jonathan Swift's classic novel Gulliver's Travels, the hero, a man of normal height, was considered a giant when traveling among the residents of Lilliput and a dwarf when traveling among the residents of Brobdingnag.

As a scientific example of contrast effects, let's look at an experiment by Douglass Kenrick and Sara Gutierres, who asked males to rate the attractiveness of a potential blind date before or after watching the television show "Charlie's Angels".[2] The males rated the woman as less attractive after they saw the show than before. Presumably, the gorgeous Angels provided a stringent context for rating attractiveness; the blind date appeared to be far less physically attractive when compared to the Angels than to women in general.

In our study on consumer decision making, two contrast effects occurred that made the Tasti-burger look more attractive. The presence of a decoy made the very good tasting Tasti-burger appear to be even better tasting and the average-tasting Nutri-burger to be even poorer tasting. In other words, the decoy "spread apart" the Tasti- and Nutri-burgers on the dimension of taste. With this change in the perception of tastiness, the choice became much clearer for our subjects.

Now we can see how that visit to the dilapidated house can influence our purchase. Perhaps the next house we look at is *not* really ideal. But compared to that last one—what an improvement! The yard and the master bedroom are bigger. The interior is in good shape. We won't need to paint it for at least three years. And the price is only slightly higher than what they were asking for that old shack. What a deal! We'll take it right away—before the owners have a chance to change their mind!

Decoys come in a variety of shapes and sizes. A used car dealer may place an old clunker on the lot to "improve the appearance" of the other autos. A presidential candidate may select a vice-presidential running mate of lesser stature to enhance the positive perception of his or her own presidential qualities. That blind date looks a lot better compared to the loser your uncle is trying to fix you up with. Seven hostages in Beirut doesn't seem so bad compared to the kidnapping of an entire embassy in Iran.

The lesson to be learned from research on decoys is that the *context* makes a difference. Judgment is relative, not absolute. Depending on the context, objects and alternatives can be made to look better or worse. Often we do not pay much attention to the influence of context, much less question the validity of the alternatives presented. This greatly enhances the power of "context-makers," such as politicians, advertisers, journalists, and sales agents. The context they set can pre-persuade us by influencing our perceptions and judgments; we are thus lulled into decisions that we would not normally make.

10

THE PSYCHOLOGY OF FACTOIDS

On September 1, 1944, the *Daily Journal-Gazette* carried a startling story of a "gas attack" on the citizens of Mattoon, Illinois. The headline read: ANESTHETIC PROWLER ON LOOSE. The story described how a local woman and her daughter had been gassed by an intruder. Apparently, a sickish, sweet-smelling gas had been sprayed into their open bedroom window. The gas made both the woman and her daughter ill and paralyzed their legs for a couple of hours. Although police found no sign of the intruder, when the woman's husband arrived home from work a few hours after the incident, he saw a man run from the window.[1]

This would not be the gasser's last strike. A short time later, Mattoon's at-large anesthetist attacked another couple, with the husband becoming sick to his stomach and the woman unable to walk. Four days later, another woman reported finding a cloth on her porch, which, when she smelled it, burned her mouth and lips so badly that they bled. In the week that followed, 21 more incidents were reported to the police. All the victims reported symptoms such as nausea and vomiting, paralysis of the legs, dryness of mouth and throat, and burns about the mouth.

The local police were stymied. They beefed up patrols. The state police were called in as reinforcements. Analysis of the crime scenes and cloths that carried the gas turned up nothing. Physicians, after examining the victims, were unable to isolate the chemicals used in the attack.

To this day, the gasser of Mattoon remains at large. He has never been captured nor brought to justice for one simple reason—the elusive anesthetist never existed except in the minds of the citizens of Mattoon. The gasser was a factoid.

The novelist Norman Mailer, who coined the term factoid, defines it as "facts which have no existence before appearing in a magazine or newspaper."[2] We define factoid as an assertion of fact that is not backed up by evidence, usually because the fact is false or because evidence in support of the assertion cannot be obtained. Factoids are presented in such a manner that they become widely treated as true. In our workplaces and neighborhoods, they are known as rumors and gossip. In courts of law, factoids are called hearsay and inadmissible evidence. In the mass media, they are called libel, slander, innuendo, and the reporting of currently circulating rumors, gossip, and hearsay as news.

Factoids are common.[3] On October 30, 1938, Orson Welles presented a radio dramatization of *The War of the Worlds*, the H. G. Wells classic that describes the takeover of Earth by invaders from Mars. The broadcast, coming during a time of concern over the events in Europe, set off a panic—people all over the United States were praying, crying, and fleeing frantically from what they thought was an invasion from Mars. Some tried to rescue loved ones; others telephoned friends with the news and to say their last good-byes. In the 1960s, rumors circulated that the Beatle Paul McCartney was dead. Music fans around the world scoured album covers and music lyrics (forward and backward) looking for (and finding) clues of Paul's death. In the late 1970s, consumers boycotted Procter & Gamble's products because of a rumor that the thirteen stars in the company's logo were a tribute to the devil. In the late 1980s, the nation's attention was riveted on a hunt by Boston police for the black man who murdered Carol Stuart, a white woman. The search, which eventually resulted in the jailing of a prime suspect, was instigated by a 911 call placed by Charles Stuart from his car phone reporting that his wife Carol was just killed by a black youth. A recording of the phone call was repeatedly played on national television news shows. It was subsequently discovered that Charles had killed his own wife. Today, entire newspapers, magazines, and television programs, under the guise of "news," are devoted to inventing and circulating believable rumor.

In politics, the art of innuendo in the United States goes back to the birth of the nation in what were called "whispering campaigns." For example, rumors circulated that Thomas Jefferson was an atheist and had debauched a well-born Virginia belle, that Martin van Buren was the illegitimate son of Aaron Burr, that Andrew Jackson had lived with his wife before marriage, and that John Quincy Adams had acted as a panderer for a Russian nobleman. The tradition continues into the modern era. In the 1970s, Richard Nixon's campaign staff hired "dirty tricksters" to spread rumors about leading Democratic candidates— rumors that many political analysts believe were at the heart of the withdrawal of front-running Edmund Muskie from the presidential race. Factoids continue to be transmitted even today by presidential and congressional "leaks," by mud-slinging in election campaigns, and by journalist's reports based on information from "well-placed" sources.

The use of factoids is also a common practice in campaigns against other nations. Adolf Hitler and his propaganda minister Joseph Goebbels mastered the art of what has been termed "the big lie." According to Nazi propaganda theory, one effective way to persuade the masses is to develop and repeat falsehoods—for example, "the German people are a master race; Europe is menaced by the Jewish conspiracy." Such big lies are difficult to prove false. For example, the fact that there is no evidence that a Jewish conspiracy exists is just further evidence regarding the cleverness of Jews. The big lie is then supported by many small, but often irrelevant, facts to make the big lie all that more believable—for example, some Jews own banks and Marx, the founder of communism, was Jewish. The big lie technique continues to be used by many governments today. As just one example, Iranian government officials circulated the story that the Iraqi invasion of Kuwait had been masterminded by the United States as a pretext for the U.S. invasion of the Persian Gulf region.

But do factoids really influence our judgments and beliefs? After all, some of them are often just plain unbelievable. Much research continues to show that the reaction of the citizens of Mattoon is not an isolated example; factoids can have a powerful effect on belief and human action. Let's look at some of that research.

During the past decade, Daniel Wegner and his colleagues have conducted a series of experiments looking at people's reactions to innuendo.[4] In their studies, participants were asked to rate the favorability of political candidates on the basis of a newspaper headline. For example, participants read either a directly incriminating headline (BOB TALBERT LINKED WITH MAFIA), a questioning incrimination (IS KAREN DOWNING ASSOCIATED WITH A FRAUDULENT CHARITY?), a denial of unseemly behavior (ANDREW WINTERS NOT CONNECTED TO BANK EMBEZZLEMENT), or a neutral headline (GEORGE ARMSTRONG ARRIVES IN CITY).

The results showed, not surprisingly, that candidates linked with a directly incriminating headline were perceived more negatively. Strikingly, however, merely questioning a candidate's association with an undesirable behavior or simply denying that the candidate performed an undesirable behavior also resulted in negative perceptions of the candidate—just slightly more positive than those evoked by a direct incrimination. It appears that simply questioning a candidate's connection with unseemly activities can be enough to damage that candidate's public image. What's more, the source of the innuendo made little difference: The candidates were still rated negatively even if the source of headline was a newspaper lacking in credibility (the *National Enquirer* or the *Midnight Globe* as opposed to the *New York Times* or the *Washington Post*). Negative political advertising and slur campaigns often do indeed pay off.

Other researchers have found that unsubstantiated evidence in a court of law can have an impact on juries, even when the judge explicitly tells the jury to ignore the factoid.[5] For example, in one experiment, Saul Kassin and his colleagues found that the credibility of an expert trial witness could be damaged merely by asking accusatory questions, such as, "Isn't it true that your work is poorly regarded by your colleagues?" The expert's credibility was damaged regardless of whether the accusation was denied or withdrawn by the lawyer after an objection was raised. Stanley Sue and his colleagues found that evidence prejudicial to a defendant would result in more convictions even when the evidence was ruled inadmissible. Numerous studies have found that negative pretrial publicity, such as reports of a confession, a failed lie detector test, the defendant's prior record, details of the case, and other information that was not admitted into trial testimony, can have a serious impact on jury decision making.

Factoids can influence not only political and judicial but also consumer decision making. For the past decade, a flier called the "Leaflet of Villejuif" has been circulating in France and other European nations.[6] The leaflet, typed on ordinary typewriters and then photocopied, urges parents to protect their children by boycotting popular brands of food and beverage such as Coca-Cola, Schweppes, Canada Dry, and others because they contain cancer-causing agents.

Surveys of the French population have found that about half of all housewives have read or heard about the leaflet and that it is likely to be affecting their behavior. In a study of 150 housewives who received the leaflet, 19% stated that they had stopped buying listed brands and another 69% stated that they planned to do so. In a survey of primary school teachers and physicians who had heard of the leaflet, almost all of the teachers and nearly half of the physicians agreed with what the leaflet stated. Only a few teachers or physicians (less than 10%) attempted to check out the validity of the claims, although many schools stopped providing the offending brands at meals out of fear of doing harm to children.

What is so remarkable about the persuasiveness of the "Leaflet of Villejuif" is that the claims it makes are completely false. For example, the additive identified by the leaflet as the most serious cancer-causing agent is E330. E330 is the European Common Market code for harmless citric acid, an ingredient found in many nutritional fruits such as oranges. Further, the leaflet also identifies other ingredients as "harmless" and therefore good for you, even though some of these ingredients are actually known carcinogenic agents. In other words, the leaflet not only contains false and misleading information, it also contains harmful information. After a year or two of circulation, the original source of the leaflet was changed from "a hospital in Paris" to the "Hospital of Villejuif," a hospital internationally recognized for its advanced research on cancer. The hospital at Villejuif has denied any association with the leaflet and has repeatedly denounced its fraudulent claims. Despite these efforts, the leaflet continues to be passed from one person to the next and continues to be believed.

As Mark Twain once put it, "A lie can travel halfway around the world while the truth is putting on its shoes." Why are factoids so persuasive? We can suggest three reasons.

First, few attempts are made to verify the truth of a factoid. We often hear rumor and gossip directly from trusted friends whom we are not in a habit of questioning. We also turn to the "news"—whether on television or in other mass media—expecting, quite frankly, "the news" and are often not prepared to debunk each and every presented "fact." Factoids often just sneak by our persuasion defenses. We rarely think to ask, "Is this factoid really true? Who gains by repeated telling of this factoid?" Even when we seek to verify a factoid, it is often difficult, since many rumors deal with "secret information," "secret conspiracies," and "esoteric knowledge" that is hard to critically evaluate and scrutinize.

Second, we accept factoids because they often meet one or more psychological needs. For example, many factoids are entertaining and thus capture our attention—it is fun to look for clues that Paul McCartney is dead. More seriously, the very best factoids help us rationalize and justify our most fundamental worries and concerns. The "Leaflet of Villejuif" confirms the belief held by many that big corporations have conspired to kill us for profit. Accepting as true a damaging factoid about a well-known person can make us feel better about ourselves by showing us that the great "Mr. So and So" has his faults, too. Believing that a black youth killed Mrs. Stuart helps confirm many people's mistaken ideas about the nature and character of black Americans. Spreading a factoid may also enhance our self-images by showing that we are in the "know" about secret information and by helping us address some of our most threatening fears. As a factoid is spread, it is often "modified and elaborated" to better serve our psychological needs.

Finally, and perhaps most importantly, factoids function as a form of pre-persuasion; they create social reality. Factoids serve as bits and pieces that are used to construct our picture of the world. As such, factoids direct our attention and suggest how we should interpret the world. For example, consider a citizen of Mattoon who wakes up one morning with an upset stomach or a pair of tired, aching legs (as undoubtably someone in the town will do). What will he or she think? *"It must be the gasser. That's why I feel this way."* That person may go on to interpret other random occurrences, such as a passing cat or a gust of wind, as supporting the notion of a visit from the gasser. *"You know, I did hear the porch creak and what sounded like a rapping at the window last night."* The rumor is thus given credence and then spread, going on to help others create their social worlds. Even when the factoid is shown to be false, it can still direct attention and thinking. For example, a political candidate falsely accused of embezzling must spend his or her time refuting and denying the charge instead of proposing substantive new programs in an attempt to win the election. And, as we saw in the research by Daniel Wegner and colleagues, such denials are usually doomed to fail—because they often serve to remind the casual reader of the original accusation.

Given that factoids can be so persuasive, it is understandable that a number of attempts have been made to limit their influence, with varying degrees of success. For example, during World War II, the U.S. government was particularly worried about how rumors and gossip could undermine the war effort. A well-placed rumor could raise unrealistic expectations of a quick victory or could dash all hopes of ever winning the war, thereby damaging morale. Further, spreading rumors about troop movements and the like could alert the enemy to Allied plans.

During the war, the U.S. government attempted to persuade citizens that repeating rumors was unpatriotic and could handicap the war effort—as the old saw went, "Loose lips sink ships." Citizens were instructed to treat rumors as Nazi propaganda. Rumor-control clinics were also created to identify harmful rumors and to take measures to defuse them. For example, one government pamphlet recommended that harmful rumors be referred to the appropriate government agency (e.g., Army, Navy, FBI, etc.), which would then present a logical and factual refutation of the rumor. In order to stand a chance of succeeding, such refutations should not overstate the case, should embed the rumor in a negative context (or damn it, state it, and then damn it again), and should not repeat verbatim particularly memorable rumors.

Another attempt to regulate the influence of factoids, at least in the courts, is the development of evidence law. Since the rise of jury trials in twelfth-century England, judges have been fearful that untrained, lay jurors would be misled by false testimony and would succumb to improper appeals to their emotions and sympathies.[7] As a means of lessening the impact of such information, courts have developed rules of procedure that specify who can present evidence, what evidence can be admitted, how evidence is to be introduced, and how a jury is to deliberate about the evidence. For example, evidence may be excluded from a court of law because it is hearsay or secondhand and therefore of questionable validity, because it is not relevant to the case and its value to the court is outweighed by the risks of prejudicial impact, because it is the opinion of an ordinary witness and not fact, or because it is from a privileged communication (such as that between attorney and client or husband and wife).

Evidence law is still evolving and generates much controversy even today. On the one hand, evidence law can be frustrating to those seeking an efficient means of convicting criminals. Trial procedure and rules of evidence often present obstacles to the prosecution in arguing a case, thereby giving the impression that evidence law is designed to protect the criminal. One the other hand, evidence law is one of the most important safeguards for insuring the right of both the innocent and guilty to a fair trial, one that is devoid of innuendo and hearsay. We would argue for even stronger evidence rules, noting that while some rules, such as changing the location of a trial if there is considerable prejudicial pretrial publicity, are usually helpful in insuring a fair trial, other procedures, such as ruling that a piece of prejudicial evidence is inadmissible and instructing a jury to ignore it, do not prevent a jury from being unfairly influenced by that evidence. Regardless of one's own views on the matter, the controversy over evidence law should further underscore the importance of factoids in the persuasion process.

If the control of factoids is difficult in a relatively well-controlled environment such as a court of law, it is all the more complicated in the mass media.[8] Attempts to diminish the effects of factoids in the mass media are relatively recent. The first deceptive advertising cases in the United States occurred in the late 1950s and early 1960s. One of the most important cases was brought by the Federal Trade Commission (FTC) against Colgate-Palmolive, the makers of Rapid Shave. In one of their television commercials, an actor was shown squirting Rapid Shave onto sandpaper and then, moments later, shaving it clean with just one stroke. When the FTC attempted to repeat this demonstration, they found that sandpaper could not be shaved clean unless moisturized for an hour. Indeed, the makers of the original ad had used plexiglas covered with sand, not sandpaper. The courts ruled that this ad was deceptive—it led consumers mistakenly to believe that Rapid Shave could shave even the toughest textures quickly—and Colgate-Palmolive was ordered to cease showing the commercial.

However, just stopping a deceptive advertisement may not be enough. We have seen that a belief in a factoid can linger for a considerable length of time. Such deceptive advertising can unfairly place business competitors at a disadvantage and can confuse and mislead consumers. During the 1970s, the FTC argued that manufacturers who make misleading claims must not only cease making the claims but correct and dispel any false beliefs created by the advertisement. For example, Profile Bread claimed to be a "diet" bread having fewer calories than other breads. (In reality, it had the same number of calories—but slices were cut thinner to reduce the number of calories per slice by seven). Profile Bread was ordered to spend at least one-fourth of its advertising budget for a year to correct this belief. Other firms, including other bakers, Ocean Spray (makers of a brand of cranberry juice), and various manufacturers of analgesics were similarly ordered to spend a percentage of their advertising budgets to correct false beliefs. What did the manufacturers do? Some merely stopped advertising for a year—one-quarter of $0 is $0 spent on corrective advertising. Others spent the money to buy ads that not many would read, for example, classified ads in the daily newspaper. In response, the FTC required subsequent deceptive advertisers to take specific steps to dispel false beliefs. In particular, Warner-Lambert, makers of Listerine, was required to dispel the myth that

*"$8,500? But you said that deceptive ad
would cost me $1,200!"*

Listerine kills cold-producing germs by spending $10 million to promote the following statement: "Contrary to prior advertising, Listerine will not prevent colds or sore throats or lessen their severity." The FTC also issued guidelines on how to spend the money.

However, correcting mistaken beliefs may not be the most efficient method for dealing with factoids; perhaps a better approach is to nip them in the bud before they become factoids. During the 1970s, the FTC attempted to do this through its program on ad substantiation. This program required advertisers in selected industries to submit to the FTC evidence that would substantiate their advertising claims. The response of automakers was typical: They sent hundreds upon hundreds of technical documents that were nearly impossible to understand. Later, the FTC amended its procedures to require more focused and readable documents.

In the 1980s, however, much of the FTC's attempt to control factoids was abandoned as America elected a new president who emphasized a free market as opposed to the use of "big-government" regulation. During the Reagan years, the FTC's budget was cut by 41%, whereas the overall federal budget increased by 31%. The result was a cutback of almost half the FTC staff. Other advertising regulatory bodies followed suit, with the major networks cutting many of their employees responsible for policing television advertising. Today, the major regulator of advertising is the industry-sponsored Association of National Advertisers, which *has* asked its members on a number of occasions to stop certain advertising practices.

The relaxing of government controls has reopened the door to blatant abuses. As we are writing this, we have in front of us a full-page ad from General Motors boasting about being the automaker that pioneered air bags. Sounds wonderful. The fact of the matter is that while GM *did* do some of the early research on air bags, they then spent vast sums of money during the next several years trying to fight attempts by consumer groups to make air bags mandatory.

Consumers worried about commercial (and political) factoids do have one recourse—themselves. Both *Consumer Reports* and *Advertising Age* publish lists of advertisements that have been found to make false or misleading claims. Consumers can also ask manufacturers to substantiate their claims. This is exactly what students in one of our courses did. They culled magazines and television to identify ninety-nine advertising claims and then wrote to the manufacturers of the products asking for any information that would substantiate their claims. The responses they received would startle even the most cynical critic of advertising. Just under 50% of the companies responded to the request. Of those responding, only five companies sent information that adequately substantiated their claims. The great majority sent more advertising. Indeed, for every page of materials directly related to the claim, the students received eighty-six pages of additional unrelated advertising and promotional materials.

Although the students did not find the answers to their ad-substantiation questions, their project is still of considerable value. First, it provides yet more evidence for a basic point of this chapter—factoids are abundant in the age of propaganda. Second, the students' project suggests a method for dealing with potential factoids. Suppose consumers and voters began questioning and confronting the makers of factoids directly. It is just possible that many of our advertisers and politicians would be forced to begin replacing factoids with facts.

COMMUNICATOR CREDIBILITY: REAL AND MANUFACTURED

THE CREDIBLE COMMUNICATOR

Picture the following scene: Your doorbell rings; when you answer it, you find a middle-aged man in a rather loud, checkered sports jacket. His tie is loose, his collar is frayed, his pants need ironing, he needs a shave, and his eyes keep looking off to the side and over your head as he talks to you. He is carrying a small can in his hand with a slot in the top, and he is trying to convince you to contribute a few dollars to a charitable organization you have never heard of. Although his actual pitch sounds fairly reasonable, what is the possibility of his succeeding in prying you loose from your money?

Now let's turn back the clock a few minutes: You open your door in response to the bell, and standing there is a middle-aged man in a conservative business suit, well tailored and well pressed. He looks you squarely in the eye, introduces himself as a vice-president of the City National Bank, and asks if you would contribute a few dollars to the same charitable organization, using exactly the same words as the fellow in the loud, checkered jacket. Would you be more likely to contribute some money?

We were struck by the likely response to such a substitution several years ago when the poet Allen Ginsberg appeared on one of the late-night talk shows. Ginsberg, one of the most popular poets of the "beat" generation, was at it again; his poem "Howl" had shocked and stimulated the literary establishment in the 1950s. On the talk show, having just finished boasting about his homosexuality, Ginsberg was talking about the generation gap.

The camera panned in. He was fat, bearded, and looked a trifle wild-eyed (was he stoned?); long hair grew in unruly patches from the sides of his otherwise bald head; he was wearing a tie-dyed T-shirt with a hole in it and a few strands of beads. Although he was talking earnestly—and, in the opinion of some, very sensibly—about the problems of the young, the studio audience was laughing. They seemed to be treating him like a clown. In all probability, the vast majority of the people at home, lying in bed watching the poet from between their feet, were not taking him seriously either—no matter how sensible his message, no matter how earnestly he delivered it.

His appearance and his reputation were, in all probability, overdetermining the audience's reaction.

The scientist in us longed to substitute the conservative-looking banker in the neatly pressed business suit for the wild-eyed poet and have him move his lips while Ginsberg said the same words off camera. Our guess is that, under these circumstances, Ginsberg's message would have been well received.

No need. Similar experiments have already been done. Indeed, speculations about the effects of character and prestige on persuasion are ancient. More than 300 years before Christ, Aristotle wrote:

> We believe good men more fully and more readily than others: this is true generally whatever the question is, and absolutely true where exact certainty is impossible and opinions are divided. It is not true, as some writers assume in their treatises on rhetoric, that the personal goodness revealed by the speaker contributes nothing to his power of persuasion; on the contrary, his character may almost be called the most effective means of persuasion he possesses.[1]

It required some 2,300 years for Aristotle's observation to be put to a scientific test. This was accomplished by Carl Hovland and Walter Weiss.[2] What these investigators did was very simple: They presented large numbers of people with a communication that argued a particular point of view—for example, that building atomic-powered submarines was a feasible undertaking (this experiment was performed in 1951, when harnessing atomic energy for such purposes was merely a dream).

Some of the people were informed that the argument was made by a person possessing a great deal of public credibility; for others, the same argument was attributed to a source with low credibility. Specifically, the argument that atomic-powered submarines could be built in the near future was attributed to J. Robert Oppenheimer, a highly respected and nationally known atomic physicist, or to *Pravda*, the official newspaper of the Communist Party in the Soviet Union—a publication not famous in the United States for its objectivity and truthfulness.

Before reading the arguments, the participants were asked to fill out a questionnaire that revealed their opinions on the topic. They then read the communication. A large percentage of those people who believed the communication came from J. Robert Oppenheimer changed their opinions—they then believed more strongly in the feasibility of atomic submarines. Very few of those who read the identical communication attributed to *Pravda* shifted their opinions in the direction of the communication.

This same phenomenon has received repeated confirmation by several different investigators using a wide variety of topics and attributing the communications to a wide variety of communicators. Careful experiments have shown that a judge of the juvenile court is more likely than most other people to sway opinion about juvenile delinquency, that a famous poet and critic can sway opinion about the merits of a poem, and that a medical journal can sway opinion about whether or not antihistamines should be dispensed without a prescription.

What do the physicist, the judge, the poet, and the medical journal have that *Pravda* doesn't? Aristotle said we believe "good men," by which he meant people of high moral caliber. Hovland and Weiss used the term *credible*, which removes the moral connotations present in the Aristotelian definition. Oppenheimer, the juvenile court judge, the poet, and the medical journal are all credible—that is, they are not necessarily "good," but they are both *expert* and *trustworthy*.

It makes sense to allow yourself to be influenced by communicators who are trustworthy and who know what they are talking about. It makes sense for people to be influenced by Ralph Nader when he is voicing an opinion about consumer safety, and it makes sense for people to be influenced by someone like Dr. C. Everett Koop, the Surgeon General during the Reagan presidency, when he is talking about the use of condoms to prevent AIDS. These are expert, trustworthy people.

But not all people are equally influenced by the same communicator. Indeed, the same communicator may be regarded by some people as possessing high credibility and by others as possessing low credibility. Moreover, certain peripheral attributes of the communicator may loom large for some people; such attributes can serve to make a given communicator either remarkably effective or remarkably ineffective.

The importance of peripheral attributes in persuasion was forcefully demonstrated in an experiment we performed in collaboration with Burton Golden.[3] In this study, sixth-graders received a speech extolling the usefulness and importance of arithmetic. The speaker was introduced either as a prize-winning engineer from a prestigious university or as someone who washed dishes for a living. As one might expect, the engineer was far more effective at influencing the youngsters' opinions than the dishwasher. This finding is consistent with previous research; in and of itself, it is obvious and not very interesting.

But, in addition, we varied the race of the communicator: In some of the trials the communicator was white, and in others, black. Several weeks prior to the experiment, the children had filled out a questionnaire designed to measure the degree of their prejudice against black people. The results were striking: Among those children who were most prejudiced against blacks, the black engineer *was* less influential than the white engineer, although both delivered the same speech. Moreover, among those children who were the least prejudiced against blacks, the black engineer was *more* influential than the white engineer.

It seems unreasonable that such a peripheral attribute as skin color would affect a person's credibility. It might be argued that, in a purely rational world, a prestigious engineer should be able to influence sixth graders about the importance of arithmetic regardless of the color of his or her skin, but apparently this is not a purely rational world. Depending upon listeners' attitudes toward blacks, they were either *more* influenced or *less* influenced by a black communicator than an otherwise identical white communicator.

Clearly, such responses are maladaptive. If the quality of your life depends on the extent to which you allow a communication about arithmetic to influence your opinion, the expertise and trustworthiness of the communicator would seem the most reasonable factors to heed, and it would seem foolish to take into account factors irrelevant to the issue (such as skin color).

But, although such responses are maladaptive, it should not be very astonishing to anyone who has ever watched commercials on television. For example, Bill Cosby has starred in a series of commercials in which he playfully interacts with children. He tells the children how delicious a particular brand of pudding is, and together they chat, laugh, and enjoy their snacks. He also reminds the audience that the product not only "tastes good," but is "good for you," because it's made with milk. What makes Cosby an expert on children and nutrition? For several seasons on "The Cosby Show," he has played Dr. Cliff Huxtable, a pediatrician who is also a warm, funny, and insightful father to five children.

Similarly, Karl Malden has starred in a series of commercials in which Americans traveling in a foreign country either lose all their money or have it stolen. The tourists are distraught, humiliated, traumatized, panicky. At the end of the commercial Karl Malden appears and, in an authoritative voice, warns us not to carry money while traveling and recommends "American Express Traveler's Cheques—don't leave home without them." What makes Karl Malden an expert on vacation financing? Nothing, but he is perceived as somewhat of an expert on *crime*. For several television seasons, Malden portrayed Lieutenant Mike Stone in "The Streets of San Francisco," a popular detective show.

Though Cosby and Malden probably do not know a great deal more about nutrition, crime, or even traveler's checks than the average viewer, they almost certainly gain credibility and trust when they are identified with their particular roles.

The fact that we humans often use the credibility of a communicator to guide us in the acceptance or rejection of a message opens the door once again for mindless propaganda. Although it makes sense to believe the credible source when his or her expertise and trustworthiness are directly related to the issue at hand, it is often easier to *feign* credibility than to actually *achieve* it. One of the important tasks of media research is to keep tabs on the "reputation and credibility" of public figures such as movie stars, sports figures, and other public "personalities." Advertisers want to know which celebrity figures are most believable, who among the stars is most liked by the public, who has been on the cover of leading magazines, and who has been overexposed. The answers to such questions determine the celebrity's value as a spokesperson for the advertiser's product. Credibility has become a commodity not only to be feigned but also to be bought and sold on the open market.

When Aristotle wrote his description of the effects of "good character" on persuasion, a debate was raging in Greece. Many people, such as Socrates and Plato, saw those engaged in persuasion, such as professional speechmakers and the Sophists, as deceitful and untrustworthy persons. Rhetoric was a worthess art practiced by worthless people. In order to justify a place for persuasion in society, Aristotle argued that not only *should* a persuader be of good character for moral reasons but also that the trustworthy source *would* be more effective than the speaker lacking in character. Modern research on persuasion has supported Aristotle's belief in the effectiveness of the trustworthy communicator—with a few notable exceptions to be discussed later. Modern propaganda practices, with their ability to manufacture credibility and buy and sell it as a commodity, raise anew the ethical concerns prominent in Aristotle's times.

12

BREAKFAST OF CHAMPIONS, JUNK FOOD FOR THE SELF

The celebrity endorsement has been a common feature of America's advertising landscape for decades. In the 1950s, future president Ronald Reagan described the revolutionary collars of Arrow shirts and the high-quality tobacco of Chesterfield cigarettes. In the 1960s, pro quarterback Joe Namath urged vieweres to "take it off" with Noxema shaving cream. In the 1970s, Rodney Dangerfield, Bob Uecker, and a collection of madcap football players told us about the less-filling, great taste of Miller Lite beer. In the 1980s, Priscilla (the wife of Elvis) Presley told us to go ahead and buy that new car, because it really isn't our father's Oldsmobile. Now in the 1990s, we know that "Bo knows" tennis shoes.

The use of such celebrity representatives may seem quite irrational and bizarre. After all, when we think about it in a rational manner, who is an expert on the topic of razor blades or shaving cream? Well, perhaps a barber; maybe a dermatologist or a cosmetologist. Who is it that tells us what blades or lather we should use? Most often, it is a professional football player.

Throughout the 1950s and 1960s, one of the most persistent peddlers of breakfast food was former Olympic decathlon champion Bob Richards, who was probably far more effective at selling Wheaties than some learned professor of nutrition, no matter *how* expert he or she might have been. In the 1970s, Richards was replaced by another gold medal decathlon champion, Bruce Jenner. How effective are these sports stars? Well, when Jenner was finally replaced in the 1980s, the Wheaties people again decided not to use a nutritionist and hired Mary Lou Retton, an Olympic gymnastics gold medalist. She was later replaced in the 1990s by basketball star Michael Jordan. This would suggest that whoever handles advertising for Wheaties is convinced of the effectiveness of famous athletes.

Is this conviction justified? Will people be influenced by an ad just because a prominent celebrity is involved? Even if we admire the skills and talents such individuals display on the movie screen or the playing field, can we really trust them to be telling us the truth about the products they endorse? After all, we all know that the star peddling shaving cream, beer, or breakfast cereal is getting paid handsomely for his or her time. Indeed, the multimillion-dollar deals celebrities such as Madonna, Michael Jackson, and Bill Cosby cut with various sponsors have become part of the common knowledge touted in the news magazines. So we know better. Surely we cannot be influenced by such blatant hypocrisy. Or can we?

Our guess is that most people would be quick to say, "No; maybe *other people* might be persuaded to run out and buy something because a movie star or sports figure tells them to, but certainly I wouldn't trust even my favorite celebrity's advice on how to spend my hard-earned cash." But can people really predict their own behavior?

Not necessarily. Although most of us might not *trust* movie actors and sports stars, that does not necessarily mean we wouldn't buy the products they endorse. Another significant factor determining the effectiveness of spokespersons is how attractive or likable they are, regardless of their overall expertise or trustworthiness.

Several years ago, we and our colleague Judson Mills did a simple laboratory experiment demonstrating that a beautiful woman—simply because she was beautiful—could have a major impact on the opinions of an audience on a topic wholly irrelevant to her beauty and, furthermore, that her impact was greatest when she openly expressed a desire to influence the audience.[1] There is a sense in which people act as if they are attempting to please someone they find attractive, even though that person may never know about it. A later experiment not only replicated the finding that more likable communicators are more persuasive but went on to show that attractive sources are *expected* to support desirable positions.[2]

Are we condemned to follow the desires of the beautiful and the famous? Richard Petty, John Cacioppo, and David Schumann have demonstrated that there is at least one circumstance in which we do not follow the dictates of the socially attractive—when we are motivated to *think* about the issue at hand.[3] That is, the attractiveness of the source has less of an impact when we operate in the central, as opposed to the peripheral, route to persuasion. In their experiment, subjects received one of four different ads for a fictitious new product, "Edge Disposable Razors." Two ads featured photographs of well-known and well-liked sports celebrities, and two ads featured middle-aged citizens from Bakersfield, California. Further, two ads contained six cogent and compelling arguments for Edge Razors (e.g., the handle is tapered and ribbed to prevent slippage) and two ads contained six specious and vague statements (e.g., it is built with the bathroom in mind).

The researchers varied subjects' motivation to think about Edge Razors by telling half of them that, at the end of the study, they would be allowed to select a gift from among several brands of disposable razors. The results showed that, for subjects motivated to think about the communication by the prospect of choosing a gift razor, the quality of the message's arguments, not the attractiveness of the source, was the most important determinant in the subjects' ratings of Edge Razors. The other subjects were strongly influenced by the source of the message, rating Edge Razors as superior when the ad contained sports personalities as opposed to citizens of Bakersfield, California.

The Petty, Cacioppo, and Schumann findings notwithstanding, it is still somewhat disconcerting that under most circumstances attractive communicators can wield such influence. Again, we all know that the football player holding up his can of shaving cream is clearly trying to influence us—the shaving cream company is not paying him all that money not to sell shaving cream. Moreover, he seems to be operating in his own self-interest; when we take a good look at the situation, it's clear the only reason he's up there with the shaving cream is to make a buck.

The effectiveness of attractive sources in selling products and changing our beliefs indicates that we hold our beliefs for other reasons in addition to our desire to be correct and to size-up the world accurately. We hold our beliefs and attitudes in order to define and make sense of our *selves*. By shaving with the right razor or eating the right cereal, we are saying, "I am just like that ballplayer; I am part of the attractive in-group." By purchasing the "right stuff," we enhance our own egos and rationalize away our inadequacies as we "become" just like our favorite celebrity.

Advertisers know all too well that we believe what we believe, and buy what we buy, in the service of our self-image. They imbue their products with a "personality." Marlboro cigarettes are macho. Dr. Pepper soft drink is unconventional. A BMW automobile is yuppie. Calvin Klein is chic. To claim the desired persona, all we need to do is to purchase and display the right products.

Political pundits and consultants are increasingly learning that appeals to our self-image make good politics. Candidates for political office are given attractive personalities; images are created by making speeches about the American flag, by posing in an Army tank, and by being photographed with schoolchildren in prayer. All we need to do to be patriotic, to be strong and tough, to be holy, is merely to cast a vote for the right candidate. It would be sad indeed if we lost our 200-year-old tradition of democracy because, like the unthinking subjects of Petty, Cacioppo, and Schumann, we were never motivated to scrutinize the candidate's self-image and evaluate the substance of his or her message.

13

HOW DO YOU PERSUADE IF EVERYONE KNOWS YOU ARE UNTRUSTWORTHY, UNBELIEVABLE, AND DISLIKED?

When you think about it, the professional propagandist has a difficult task. We commonly respond to persuasive messages by questioning the speaker's bias and noting how his or her self-interest is being served. This general skepticism can serve a useful purpose for the target of the appeal. By identifying a message as biased, the audience can prepare to defend its position and either to scrutinize carefully the contents of the message or to reject it out of hand, depending on the circumstances. But from the propagansist's perspective, this constitutes a formidable obstacle to securing compliance. Accordingly, the propagandist finds it important not to *appear* to be a propagandist. In order to be successful, the communicator must appear unbiased and trustworthy. In this chapter we will look at two general strategies for making the untrustworthy, the unbelievable, and the disliked look trustworthy, believable, and liked.

The Chinese rhetorician Han Fei-Tzu, who advised rulers in the third century B.C., told the following story to illustrate how a ruler can improve the perception of his credibility.[1] The Duke of Wu wished to invade the country of Hu. The Duke pulled aside one of his most trusted counselors and asked him to argue in public that the Duke should attack Hu, which the counselor then did. The Duke immediately put the counselor to death as a dramatic way of reassuring the ruler of Hu that he had no intention of attacking. Assured that the Duke was a trustworthy leader—after all he just put one of his most trusted advisors to death—Hu disarmed. The Duke of Wu immediately launched a surprise attack and the country of Hu was captured.

One of the morals of Han Fei-Tzu's story is that communicators can make themselves seem trustworthy by apparently acting against their own self-interest. If we are led to believe that communicators have nothing to gain and perhaps something to lose by convincing us, we will trust them and they will be more effective. When the Duke of Wu put his counselor to death, he appeared to be arguing against his own self-interest—"No! Invading Hu—even though it may result in benefits to my country—is wrong. I believe this so strongly that I will put my favorite advisor to death for merely suggesting it." The problem—for the citizens of Hu—was that the Duke's position was an illusion; he had arranged it so that it would appear he was acting and arguing against his own self-interest. This leads us to the second moral of Han Fei-Tzu's story: When it comes to persuasion, appearances can be deceiving.

The strategy of acting or arguing against you own self-interest can be used to increase the perception of your trustworthiness without actually putting your best friend to death. An illustration may be helpful. Suppose a habitual criminal, recently convicted as a smuggler and peddler of cocaine, was delivering a talk on the harshness of the American judicial system and the overzealousness of its prosecutors. Would he influence you? Probably not. Most people would probably regard him as biased and untrustworthy. The cocaine peddler occupies a position clearly outside of the Aristotelian definition of a "good person." But suppose he was arguing that criminal justice was too *soft*—that criminals almost always beat the rap if they have a smart lawyer, and that even if criminals *are* convicted, the sentences normally meted out are too lenient. Would he influence you?

The evidence from one of our own experiments suggests that he probably would. In a study conducted in collaboration with Elaine Walster and Darcy Abrahams, we presented our subjects with a newspaper clipping of an interview with Joe "the Shoulder" Napolitano, who was identified in the manner described above.[2] In one experimental condition, Joe "the Shoulder" argued for stricter courts and more severe sentences. In another condition, he argued that courts should be more lenient and sentences less severe. We also ran a parallel set of conditions in which the same statements were attributed to a respected public official.

When Joe "the Shoulder" argued for more lenient courts, he was totally ineffective; indeed, he actually caused the subjects' opinions to change slightly in the opposite direction. But when he was arguing for stricter, more powerful courts, he was extremely effective—as effective as the respected public official delivering the same argument. This study demonstrates that Aristotle was not completely correct—a communicator can be an immoral person and still be effective, as long as it seems clear that the communicator has nothing to gain (and perhaps something to lose) by persuading us.

Why was Joe "the Shoulder" so effective in the experiment? Let's take a closer look. Most people would not be surprised to hear a known convict arguing in favor of a more lenient criminal justice system. Their knowledge of the criminal's background and self-interest would lead them to expect such a message. When they receive the opposite communication, however, these expectations are disconfirmed. To make sense of this contradiction, the members of the audience might conclude that the convict had reformed, or they could entertain the notion that the criminal is under some kind of pressure to make the anti-crime statements. In the absence of any evidence to substantiate these suppositions, however, another explanation becomes more reasonable: Maybe the truth of the issue is so compelling that, even though it apparently contradicts his background and self-interest, the spokesman sincerely believes in the position he espouses.

Evidence for this phenomenon comes from an experiment by Alice Eagly and her colleagues, who presented students with a description of a dispute between business interests and environmental groups over a company's polluting of a river.[3] The students then read a statement about the issue. In some conditions the spokesman was described as having a business background and was said to be speaking to a group of businessmen. In others, his background and audience were varied, thereby altering the subjects' expectations of his message. The results supported the reasoning above: When the message conflicted with their expectations, listeners perceived the communicator as being more sincere, and they were more persuaded by his statement.

It is hard to imagine a more convincing spokesperson for an anti-smoking campaign than someone whose fortune was made off the habits of millions of American smokers. In fact, Patrick Reynolds, who inherited $2.5 million from the R. J. Reynolds Tobacco Company founded by his grandfather, has taken a strong public stand against smoking and has recently gone so far as to urge victims of smoking-related illnesses to file lawsuits against tobacco companies![4]

Similarly, among the most effective opponents of the nuclear arms race in recent years have been several professionals who have taken stands that seemingly contradict their backgrounds. These communicators—for example, J. Robert Oppenheimer, a respected nuclear physicist who, for many years, cautioned against the further development of nuclear technology; Carl Sagan, a trusted astronomer who has warned the world about nuclear winter; and Admiral Elmo Zumwalt, a former naval commander who campaigned for a halt to certain military developments—have been perceived as highly credible precisely because of the discontinuity between their messages and the apparent interests of their professions. First of all, they are experts. Second, since they have nothing to gain (and perhaps collegial esteem to lose) it seems that only the compelling need for disarmament led them to speak out. Not only do we tend to take more notice of unexpected events, but we also attribute more credibility to speakers who appear to resist the pressures of their colleagues and who take stands in opposition to their backgrounds.

Today, one of the nation's most respected authorities on health issues is the former U.S. Surgeon General, Dr. C. Everett Koop. That was not the case when Koop was first appointed to the position in the early 1980s by President Reagan. Koop is an evangelical Christian whose position on abortion and contraceptives caused many Americans, especially those with a more liberal bent, to worry that Koop would use his position to advance his own view of morality. As the full meaning of the AIDS epidemic began to be discovered, Dr. Koop made a dramatic recommendation: obviously the best way to avoid the AIDS virus is sexual abstinence or monogamy; however, if you plan to be sexually active you should use a condom. Koop's recommendation resulted in a firestorm from those on the Right and, especially, evangelical Christians. They believed that Koop's recommendation to use condoms promoted promiscuity. The firestorm did not end there. In the last days of his appointment, Koop released a report stating that there was no evidence that an abortion causes emotional harm to the woman—although Koop himself still believed that abortion was morally wrong. The report dismayed many in the Reagan administration, who had hoped to use evidence of emotional harm as an argument against abortion. However, C. Everett Koop turned out to be a man of impeccable integrity who had earned his reputation as a trustworthy source.

The Chinese philosopher Mencius, who lived in the fourth century B.C., provides us with another technique for increasing the perception of trustworthiness.[5] Mencius had gained fame as a wise counselor. The king sent a polite note asking Mencius to come to court so that he might advise the king. Mencius replied that he was not well and was unable to come to court. The next day he walked conspicuously around town. The king was outraged and sent several men to find out why Mencius showed so little respect and to beseech him once more to come to court. Mencius would not receive the men and left to visit a friend. The king could stomach Mencius's impertinence no more and accused him of disloyalty. Mencius replied that far from being disloyal and disrespectful, he had shown the most loyalty and respect for the king in all the land. He could be useful to the king only if the king absolutely trusted his integrity and independence of mind. If the king suspected that he might do or say things merely to please, his counsel would be ignored.

Mencius's actions illustrate another way of increasing the perception of credibility: The apparent trustworthiness of a person can be *increased* and the apparent bias of the message *decreased* if the audience is absolutely certain the person is not trying to influence them. To illustrate, let us bring this discussion into the twentieth century. Suppose a stockbroker calls you up and gives you a hot tip on a particular stock. Will you buy? It's hard to be sure. On the one hand, the broker is probably an expert, and this might influence you to buy. On the other hand, the stockbroker has something to gain by giving you a tip (a commission), and this could lower her effectiveness. But suppose you accidently happened to *overhear* her telling a friend that a particular stock was about to rise. Because she was obviously not *trying* to influence you, you might be more readily influenced.

This is exactly what was discovered in an experiment by Elaine Walster and Leon Festinger.[6] In this study, a conversation was staged between two graduate students in which one of them expressed his opinion on an issue. The situation was arranged so that an undergraduate student was allowed to overhear this conversation. In one experimental condition, it was clear to the undergraduate that the graduate students were aware of his presence in the next room; therefore, the undergraduate knew anything being said could conceivably be directed at him with the intention of influencing his opinion. In the other condition, the situation was arranged so that the undergraduate believed the graduate students were unaware of his presence in the next room. In this latter condition, undergraduates' opinions changed significantly more in the direction of the opinion expressed by the graduate students.

There are many tactics for making it appear that you are not really trying to influence someone. A few years back, the brokerage firm of E. F. Hutton ran a series of commercials in which, when one person began to pass on some stock advice from E. F. Hutton, a sudden hush fell over the room and everyone strained toward the speaker to better "overhear" the tip. The implication is clear: Everyone is getting in on advice that was not intended for them, and the information is all the more valuable as a result. Another example of this phenomenon is the "hidden camera" advertisements on television; if we are convinced a person has been caught unaware, we do not attribute a persuasive intent to the message. Believing the person is acting spontaneously, we are more persuaded by his or her testimony. Finally, politicians are notorious for claiming that, unlike their opponents, they are above "politics" and are merely taking the position that they do because they have the best interest of the public at heart. When communicators do not appear to be *trying* to influence us, their potential to do so is increased.

Throughout this book, we look at how clever propaganda tactics can be used to manipulate our beliefs and behavior. Indeed, in the next chapter we will look at the wholesale manufacture of source credibility. The second moral of Han Fei-Tzu's story—that appearances can be deceiving—is often all too true; but the acceptance of this moral can breed an unhealthy cynicism.

For this reason, it is good to pause and reflect on the behavior of people such as Dr. C. Everett Koop. In an era in which political self-interest appears to dominate—where, for example, congressional leaders opposed to excessive military spending are in favor of shutting down military bases except, of course, for the ones in their district—it is refreshing to run into a public servant of high integrity. When Koop, as Surgeon General, was confronted with the AIDS crisis, he conducted a thorough investigation so that he could render an expert judgment. At great risk to his career and at the cost of alienating his friends and supporters, Dr. Koop spoke what he knew to be true. The cost to Dr. Koop's career for his honesty should not be downplayed. Although he made it clear that he would like to continue in public service and would enjoy a promotion to Secretary of Health and Human Services, Koop was not reappointed by the Bush Administration. His accomplishments should not be taken lightly either. There are untold Americans—perhaps the people who live next door to you, perhaps your own son or daughter, perhaps even yourself—who will not die of AIDS but will go on to live long and productive lives as a result of Dr. Koop's actions. In this age of propaganda, Dr. Koop's behavior reminds us that there is still a place for Aristotle's communicator of good character.

14

THE MANUFACTURE OF CREDIBILITY

Imagine the following hypothetical situation: Two men are running for the Senate. One of the candidates has far less money to spend on his campaign than the other. Accordingly, in order to get maximum free exposure, he consents to numerous interviews, gives frequent news conferences, and appears often on panel-type programs on television. The interviewers on these occasions are seasoned reporters who frequently ask him difficult questions, occasionally hostile ones. The candidate finds himself forever on the defensive. Sometimes the camera catches him at an unflattering angle or in the act of scratching his nose, yawning, or fidgeting. Watching at home, his mother is surprised at the bags under his eyes and at how tired and old he looks. Sometimes, when faced with a tough or unexpected question, he has difficulty finding the right response; he hems and haws and sounds inarticulate.

His opponent with the well-stocked campaign chest does not need to appear in such forums. Instead, he spends vast amounts of money videotaping spot commercials. Because he pays the camera crew and the director, his countenance is captured only from the most flattering angles. His personal makeup artist works hard to mask the bags under his eyes and to make him appear young and dynamic. His mother, watching him at home, never saw him looking so well. The interviewer asks him questions prepared and rehearsed in advance, so that his answers are reasonable, concise, and articulate. If the candidate does happen to stumble over a word or to draw a blank, the cameras are stopped and the scene is shot over and over again until it portrays him in the best light.

This situation is no nightmarish projection into the future; it closely approximates what occurred, on a much more important and dramatic scale, during the 1968 presidential election. In an extraordinary behind-the-scenes account of Richard Nixon's campaign, journalist Joe McGinness reported on the adeptness with which Nixon's advisors controlled the image of the candidate that was projected to the American people.

In reporting these events, McGinness claims that television is a powerful means of seducing voters to vote for *images* of candidates rather than the candidates themselves. Or, as one Nixon staffer put it: "This is the beginning of a whole new concept...This is the way they'll be elected forevermore. The next guys up will have to be performers."[1]

This proved to be a prescient statement indeed—for in 1980 a seasoned movie and television personality was swept into office, and reelected by a landslide in 1984. Moreover, he managed to retain his *personal* popularity, despite the fact that public opinion polls indicated most Americans felt he was not doing a good job.

When Nixon's staffer made his prediction, he was referring specifically to a television program that was arranged to look as though candidate Nixon was spontaneously answering questions phoned in by voters. In reality, he was giving carefully rehearsed answers to questions prepared by his staff. When a voter asked a question on the telephone, Nixon's staff simply reworded it in the form of a prepared question, attributed the question to the voter, and allowed Nixon to recite his prepared answer.

When McGinness's book made its appearance, many people were shocked and appalled at what they considered to be unethical and dishonest behavior. On the other hand, the overwhelming majority of

*"I understand the Republicans have retained a
top-notch make-up man."*

voters either did not care or thought Nixon's deceptiveness was merely
an indication that he was a clever, shrewd politician. Richard Nixon's
popularity remained high throughout his first term in office, and in
1972 he was reelected in one of the most lopsided landslides in the
nation's history, despite the fact that, at the time, it was known that a
group of individuals financed by the Committee to Reelect the President had been caught breaking into the offices of the Democratic
National Committee in a building called Watergate.

How extensive is the use of advertising to create seductive images
of political candidates? According to Kathleen Hall Jamieson,
American presidential candidates have always tried to create images
of themselves that would appeal to voters—at least since the 1828

victory of Andrew Jackson over John Quincy Adams.[2] However, it was not until 1952, when Dwight D. Eisenhower hired as key campaign advisors two ad agencies (BBDO and Young & Rubicam) and received volunteer help from a third (the famed advertiser Rosser Reeves of the Ted Bates agency), that professional ad agencies were used extensively in presidential campaigns. Today ad agencies, political pollsters, and media consultants are a common political fixture and can be found among the highest echelon of political advisors.

How effective are media advisors in electing a candidate? Nixon's victory in 1968 could be interpreted as indicating that such deceptive programming was effective in spite of its blatant manipulativeness. On the other hand, one astute observer, John Kenneth Galbraith, has commented that Nixon may have won in 1968 in spite of these devices. Jamieson offers another perspective: Spending a large amount of money does not guarantee success in a campaign; success depends on how *well* you spend it. If you are fortunate enough to have a large wad of cash to spend, it will not insure your election, unless, according to Jamieson, you use it to run a campaign that presents a clear, consistent image of your candidacy and an appealing vision for the nation. Obviously, if you don't have a big bankroll, you are going to have a difficult time presenting any image, much less a consistent one, and, needless to say, you will be at a disadvantage.

But if you did have that wad of cash, who could you hire and what could they do for you? First, you would want to hire a pollster such as President Bush's pollster, Robert Teeter. Teeter regularly surveys public opinion and then translates it into advice for the president. Some of Teeter's advice to Bush: Give hard-hitting speeches favoring the war on drugs, harsher jail sentences for criminals, and the need for educational reform—this is what Americans want to hear. Avoid speaking on the abortion issue because many voters themselves have mixed views on the topic. At periodic intervals blame the Democratic Congress for the stalemate that prevents the country from moving forward. Bush did ignore one of Teeter's recommendations—don't violate the "read my lips, no new taxes" pledge.[3] Nevertheless, Bush's overall approval rating has hovered around 70%—one of the highest ratings ever—throughout his term of office. Indeed, for a short six-month period during the preparation, conduct, and aftermath of the Persian Gulf war, Bush's approval rating even soared above 90%.

Second, you would want to hire a public relations expert such as Roger Ailes, who served as advisor to both the Reagan and Bush campaigns, or Robert Dilenschneider, CEO of the PR firm of Hill and Knowlton who has given advice to such organizations as Metropolitan Edison on how to handle public reactions to the Three Mile Island incident, the Chilean government on how to calm fears about a scare that their grapes were laced with cyanide, and Columbia University on how to deal with the student protests of the 1960s. In Roger Ailes's mind, what makes a great speaker? As he states in his book, *You Are the Message*:

> If you could master one element of personal communications that is more powerful than anything we've discussed, it is the quality of being *likable*. I call it the magic bullet, because if your audience likes you, they'll forgive just about everything else you do wrong. If they don't like you, you can hit every rule right on target and it doesn't matter.[4]

Some of Ailes's specific advice for making yourself likable: Say what the audience thinks, make others feel comfortable, and control the atmosphere (the situation) for your best advantage.

Here is some of the general advice Dilenschneider gives in his bestselling book, *Power and Influence*, for increasing your credibility:[5] Set easy initial goals and then declare victory (this will create the perception that you are a strong leader); use setting to support image (Reagan designed his presidential podium to look powerful but soft and understated; interviews should be done in settings that fit the message); choose the negatives that will be written about you (most journalists seek a balanced report; provide the reporter with negatives that you can then refute and thus look good); and understand how people see things, then appeal to what they prefer.

The advice of Ailes and Dilenschneider is a far cry from Aristotle's prescription that a communicator be of good character. Credibility is manufactured, not earned. Credibility is created by carefully managing the situation so that the star of the event, the communicator, looks just the way he or she is suppose to look—likable, credible, strong, expert, or whatever image is needed at the time. Once the image is created in the form of a celebrity or a politician, then it can be bought and sold like a commodity to advance any cause that has the resources to purchase the "rights" to the image.

The manufacture of credibility can lead to a cult of personality. Instead of thinking about important issues for ourselves, we turn to credible-looking leaders for their solutions. This strategy would make some sense if the people we turn to do indeed possess the required expertise. Sadly, it is often the case that "credibility" has been subtly manufactured and sold for propaganda purposes. And the media often serve as unwitting handmaidens in this charade. Consider, for example, the post-debate "analyses" served up by many of the TV network pundits, who, instead of talking about the issues, seem to prefer to discuss such superficialities as which candidate "looked more presidential" or appeared to handle complex issues "more adroitly." Such reporting contributes to the cult of personality and promotes propaganda at the expense of persuasion.

15
PRIZEFIGHTER SLAYS 11 WITH ONE LOOK : THE INFLUENCE OF MASS MEDIA MODELS

The checkout stand at the local supermarket is lined with newspapers claiming to have "the largest circulation of any paper in America" and to be "America's fastest growing weekly." Recent issues contained prophecies for the 1990s.[1] The psychics predict that Princess Di will divorce Charles to become a nun; a mysterious virus will turn Barbara Bush's hair bright red; a meteorite will plow into the White House Rose Garden; Mikhail Gorbachev will buy a beach home near the Reagans in Bel-Air, California; the AIDS virus will be shown to have been developed by religious fanatics as a plot to wipe out gays; deep-sea explorers will discover a sunken Spanish galleon full of gold and artifacts from an alien spaceship. Of course, most of us doubt that many of these predictions will come to pass.

However, there is a sociologist at the University of California at San Diego named David Phillips who can, with remarkable accuracy, foretell some striking future events.[2] Phillips's latest startling prediction: Within 4 days of the next nationally televised heavyweight championship prize-fight, at least 11 innocent United States citizens who would not normally have died will be murdered in cold blood. The reason: People learn from the behavior of those they see and admire on television.

Here's how Phillips came to make his startling prediction. He first gathered an exhaustive list of past heavyweight championship prizefights and examined the fluctuation of daily homicide rates before and after each fight. After correcting for the influence of seasons, days of week, holidays, and other trends, he discovered that homicide rates rose significantly on the third and fourth days after the fights. Sadly, homicide rates did not decrease at any time after the fight to compensate for the immediate effects of the bout. Thus one can safely conclude that most of these eleven murdered individuals would not have died in this manner had there not been a publicized prizefight.

What is even more haunting about Phillips's research is that the type of person killed just after the prizefight is likely to be similar to the fighter beaten in the bout. That is, if a young black male was beaten, then murders of young black, but not white, males increased. Similarly, if a young white male was beaten, more young white, but not black, males were murdered. Furthermore, the effects of prizefights on homicides increased with the amount of fight publicity: The more people who knew about the fight, the greater the number of homicides.

Phillips has found that mass media models can influence other behavior as well. In March 1986, four teenagers in New Jersey made a suicide pact and then carried out their plan. Within a week of this multiple suicide, two teenagers in the Midwest were found dead under similar circumstances. Media reports no doubt spotlighted the confusion and grief surrounding teenage suicide. But did the media's coverage of these tragedies actually inspire copycat suicides? According to Phillips, the answer is a qualified "yes."

How can he be sure? Phillips and his colleagues studied suicide rates among teenagers following network television news or feature stories about suicide. Their research tracked fluctuations in teenage suicides by comparing suicide rates before the stories with rates after the stories. Within a week of the broadcasts, the increase in teenage suicides was far greater than could be explained by chance alone. Furthermore, the more coverage major television networks devoted to suicide, the greater the subsequent increase in suicides among teenagers. These increases held even when the researchers took other possible causes into account. Thus the most likely explanation for the increase in teenage suicides following media publicity is that such publicity actually triggers subsequent copycat suicides.

"I love the whole thing. In fact, one day I'm going to take up either animated cartooning or violence."

The effects of mass media models on violence and other social behaviors have been known for several years. In the early 1960s, the noted psychologist Albert Bandura began an extensive laboratory program looking at television models and aggression.[3] In a typical study, children would watch, on a television monitor, an adult beating a Bobo doll—a large, plastic doll with a weight at the base. When punched, the doll falls backwards and then springs upright. In the Bandura-produced television show, models would punch, kick, fling, hit with a mallet, and scream at a Bobo doll. The children would then have the opportunity to play with various attractive toys, including a Bobo doll. The results repeatedly showed that children were likely to do what they had previously seen; those exposed to the violent model were more likely to strike, hit, and punch the bobo doll.

Much subsequent research supports Bandura's initial findings. Aggressive models have been shown to influence the aggression of both males and females, children and adults; to influence behavior in and out of the laboratory; and to teach aggression regardless of whether the model is a cartoon character or a real person and whether the aggression is an isolated act or part of a complex plot, such as a television crime story. Watching aggressive models has led people to kick a Bobo doll, electrically shock a classmate, verbally assault a stranger, and harm a small animal.

Fortunately, modeling works in two directions; that is, the power of mass media models can also be used to teach pro-social behavior. For example, social models have been used to increase people's likelihood of helping a stranded motorist with a flat tire and to increase the amount of donations dropped into a Salvation Army kettle.[4] Similarly, models have been used to teach nonviolent responses and to lower levels of aggression in a violent situation.[5]

But teaching is not the same as preaching; models persuade far more effectively than words. In a series of insightful studies, James Bryan and his colleagues exposed children to adult models who *preached* either greed or charity or *practiced* either greed or charity.[6] The results: Children were more influenced by what the model *did* than what the model *said*. This finding takes on increased importance in an era when the mayor of Washington, D.C., lectures children about the evils of drugs and subsequently is caught using cocaine, or when televangelists engage in illicit sexual behavior or pocket money from the collection plate.

The power of models to persuade has not been lost on advertisers. Thirty-second spots are full of chubby people losing weight with the right diet aid; housewives impressing their husbands with clean houses brought about by an advertised cleanser; boyfriends and girlfriends being rewarded with love, affection, and prestige for just one smile polished by a special toothpaste; young couples achieving the good life with the use of a major credit card. These models do more than just sell products; they also reinforce values (e.g., thin is good) and teach lifestyles (e.g., housewives as husband pleasers, yuppies have the good life).

Politicians use models, too. One effective technique is to create a *bandwagon* effect—the impression that everyone is for the candidate. Politicians do this by staging large rallies attended by what appears to be a multitude of supporters in the hopes of convincing the as-yet-uncommitted voter. Success in the polls—an indication of popular support—is essential if the candidate hopes to secure campaign contributions.

Mass media models are effective for two primary reasons. First, they teach new behavior. For example, a young child learns the "specifics" of how to shoot and kill a "suspect" by watching television crime shows such as "Miami Vice" or "Hunter." A newly married couple discovers that the good life can be purchased on credit by watching others on television use a credit card. A teenager learns about the attractiveness of committing suicide from a news report.

Of course, just because someone *knows how* does not necessarily mean that he or she will *do it*. Most of us know how to beam someone down to the surface of an alien planet from watching "Star Trek" or to protect Superman from kryptonite by using a lead shield, but it is unlikely we will ever engage in such behavior. What, then, causes us to behave like our media models? One important factor is that we believe the rewards received by a model for a given behavior will also come to us. That is why advertisers often use models "just like us" and place them in familiar situations such as at home, work, school, or the supermarket.

This brings us to the second reason why mass media models are persuasive: They serve as a cue to indicate that a certain behavior is *legitimate* and *appropriate*. After watching a prizefight, it appears to be okay to "punch someone's lights out;" hearing about a teenage suicide says that this may be a reasonable way to deal with life's problems or that those who have wronged us will now be forced to grieve for us; watching a housewife mop the floor convinces us that this is an appropriate lifestyle for women (but not necessarily for men). A steady diet of mass media models can shape and twist our understanding of what is right and wrong with the world.

What characteristics make a mass media model *most* persuasive? The accumulation of much research shows that a model is most effective when he or she is high in prestige, power, and status, is rewarded for performing the behavior to be learned, provides useful information on how to perform the behavior, and is personally attractive and competent in facing life's problems. In other words, the model is a credible and attractive source. Think for a moment about an advertisement that uses models to persuade. We bet that the models in these ads possess most, if not all, of these attributes.

The immediate persuasiveness of mass media models is clearly known by professional persuaders, although the subtle, but nonetheless important, effects of such models are often ignored by everyone. For example, if it were known that in three or four days eleven people would die, perhaps trapped underground, perhaps at the hands of foreign terrorists, the nation would mobilize. The major networks would send camera crews and reporters. CNN would carry around-the-clock coverage. The story would dominate the front pages of newspapers. The person who predicted such an event would become an overnight celebrity, being asked to appear on the Carson show, invited to give his or her opinions on morning talk shows, and perhaps, receive his or her own cubicle on the "Hollywood Squares."

But Phillip's prediction is *not* about eleven people whom the nation will come to know personally by media coverage of the event. The eleven people who will be murdered as a result of the next publicized prizefight will be, for the most part, nameless faces known only to their loved ones. They will not die in exotic places and lands, but in their own neighborhoods. They will not die of supernatural causes, of a freak accident of nature, or at the hands of a ruthless dictator. Indeed, the cause of their deaths will not be known immediately, if at all. But they will certainly die, and they will die as a result of the simple fact that mass media models are persuasive.

THE MESSAGE
AND HOW IT IS
DELIVERED

16
PACKAGES

The cereal aisle at the local supermarket is the battleground for many a weekly war of words. The battle usually goes something like this: Seven year-old Rachel spots her favorite cereal, Lucky Charms, picks up a box from the shelf and quietly delivers it to the shopping cart. Her mom looks at the box in disgust. It is bright red. A leprechaun is sprinkling shining stars (must be sugar) over pink and purple marshmallow bits. On the back of the box she reads that a special pair of glasses is enclosed to be used in spotting hidden leprechauns.

Mom sternly announces, "Rachel, put that junk back on the shelf. It's loaded with sugar and nothing but empty calories."

Rachel replies, "But mom, it tastes good. The other stuff tastes yukky."

Being a smart mom, she offers Rachel another choice and a little inducement, "Why not this one? It's 100% Natural. It's good for you. You'll be a big girl."

Rachel looks at the box. It is small, but heavy. The front features a bowl of light brown cereal set against a wood-grain background and a couple of stalks of unprocessed grains. On the back of the box is a lot of small print.

Rachel exclaims, "Yukko! I don't want to be a big girl."

How would you resolve the great breakfast cereal standoff? Would you side with the mother and opt for nutrition even though Rachel may not eat it? Or would you feel that Rachel, even at this young age, should be making her own decisions regardless of the consequences? Our recommendation may surprise you. The fight is for naught. Tell Rachel and her mom to buy the Lucky Charms because, quite truthfully, it is more nutritional than the "natural" cereal.

Every year Americans spend roughly $6.9 billion on breakfast cereals. In 1981, *Consumer Reports*, a highly respected source of consumer information, conducted a test of some of these breakfast cereals.[1] Their researchers fed young rats, which have nutritional requirements remarkably similar to humans, an exclusive diet of water and one of thirty-two brands of breakfast cereals for a period of fourteen to eighteen weeks. They found that the rats grew and remained quite healthy on a diet of such cereals as Cheerios, Grape-nuts, Life, Shredded Wheat, and Lucky Charms. On the other hand, fifteen ready-to-eat cereals such as Captain Crunch, Corn Flakes, Product 19, and Quaker's 100% Natural either prevented the rats from growing or were judged to be not sufficiently nourishing to support life.

A comparison between Lucky Charms and 100% Natural shows that Lucky Charms is lower in calories but slightly higher in sodium and sugar than 100% Natural, although the differences probably do not matter very much. 100% Natural, like many granola-style cereals, is higher in saturated fats, which raise blood cholesterol levels. Whereas Lucky Charms contains no saturated fat, a cup of 100% Natural is equivalent in fat content to about a half a rack of greasy spare ribs.[2]

What caused the disagreement between Rachel and her mom? It is clear that they used the cereal package (not the cereal) as what is technically called a *heuristic*—a simple cue or rule for solving a problem. In this case, the problem for mom was to select a nutritious cereal; for Rachel the problem was to get a cereal that is fun and tasty. The bright colors, the cartoon character, and the kids' game on the box of Lucky Charms suggest that this cereal is for kids—and we all know that kids' food is junk food. On the other hand, the earth tones and pictures of unprocessed grains on the 100% Natural box indicate that this cereal is "all-natural" (even the brand name agrees). Nature is good and wholesome; this cereal must be nutritious. In both cases, the cereal packages were designed so that Rachel and her mom would infer certain attributes about the products—qualities that may or may not be present. Armed with these conclusions, the choice of which cereal to purchase can proceed without much additional thought; persuasion occurs in the peripheral route.

Marketers have been using packages to guide consumer decision making for nearly a century. Since the 1890s, Quaker Oats has been boxing rolled oats in a container with a picture of a religious Quaker to suggest the purity and consistency of their breakfast cereal. In 1898 a man named C. W. Post reinforced the image of a healthy breakfast food by enclosing a copy of the pamphlet "The Road to Wellville" in each box of Grape-Nuts cereal. Sales took off. Packaging is such a success-ful heuristic device that generic and store brands often try to take

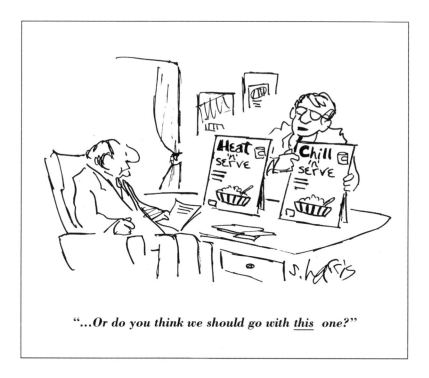

"...Or do you think we should go with this one?"

advantage of it by making their packages—the color of their labels, the shape of the container, and so on—resemble the bestselling national brands.

Other heuristics are also used to encourage consumers to infer product quality and thus buy a particular brand. Three of the most important are price, store image, and brand name. Each heuristic comes with its own rules for inferring product quality. For example, the higher the price, the better the quality—which is probably true when it comes to such products as Yugos and Rolls Royces, but not necessarily the case for wines, medicines, sport sneakers, prepackaged foods, and a host of other products. The same pair of jeans looks better in a high-class department store than in the local discount mart. Nationally recognized brand names are deemed superior to store brands and generics. In addition, advertisers spend vast sums of money to link their brand name to a brand-specific proposition, such as "Michelob is classy" or "Bud is for the everyday working Joe," to guide our supermarket visit.

Persons can be packaged, too. The first information that we typically pick up about a person—gender, age, race, physical attractiveness, and social status—is usually associated with simple rules and stereotypes that guide thought and behavior. Gender and racial stereotypes tell us "just how men and women differ" and "what a particular member of an ethnic group is like." Much research has demonstrated that beautiful people are assumed to be more successful, more sensitive, warmer, and of better character than less physically appealing persons and that we often act in accord with those assumptions. Persons of high social stature, often inferred by dress and mannerisms, are respected and held in high esteem. Is it any wonder that "get-ahead" self-help books often describe how to take advantage of these heuristics by urging their readers to "dress for success," that is, to wear the *right* clothes to create the *right* image or to use the *right* cosmetics to enhance their attractiveness?

Heuristics can also be used to judge whether a persuasive communication is worthy of acceptance and belief. In the prior section of the book, we looked in detail at one such heuristic—the source of the message. We saw that, in general, the more credible, attractive, or expert the source, the more effective is the communication; we also saw that we are more likely to use the source to guide our opinions if we are operating in the peripheral, as opposed to central, route of persuasion.

There are other persuasion heuristics. For example, the advertisers John Caples and David Ogilvy argue that advertisements are most effective when they contain long, compelling copy—in other words, a long message with many arguments. Obviously, such a message would be more effective than a short message containing weak arguments—*if the message is read.* But what about cases where the message is only skimmed or not read at all? According to research in social psychology, when people are not thinking very carefully about an issue, long messages, regardless of whether they contain weak or strong arguments, are most persuasive.[3] It appears that we operate on the principle that "message length *equals* message strength." If the message is long, it must be important.

If you have watched commercial programming, those half-hour "shows" that feature knives, blenders, cleansers, and sandwich makers for sale, you have seen another persuasion cue in action. These shows inevitably feature a "daring" demonstration of the product—a knife cutting up an old tennis shoe and then slicing a tomato perfectly, a blender making mayonnaise from scratch, or a magic powder removing a difficult stain. What is the audience's reaction? At first there is murmuring, as disbelief fills the air with tension. And then the audience, acting as one, bursts into loud, thunderous applause.

The thunderous clapping and cheering serves as a *social consensus* heuristic—a cue that says "everyone accepts the conclusion of this message, so you should too!" Recognition of the power of the applause-makes-right heuristic leads politicians to schedule major talks in favorable settings, television producers to insert canned laughter and applause, advertisers to use testimonials and portray their products as being in great demand. Once again, the evidence shows, social consensus heuristics are most likely to have an impact when people are unmotivated to think about a message's meaning.[4]

Another common persuasion heuristic is based on the confidence of the speaker—the more self-assured and confident a communicator appears, the more likely that we will accept what is said. Research on trial testimony in courts of law, for example, has found that juries are more likely to believe testimony when it is given by an eyewitness or expert who exudes confidence. Similarly, nonverbal behavior that suggests confidence in the message, such as a low rate of speech errors, an authoritative tone of voice, and a steady body posture, are positively related to persuasion.

Another frequently used persuasion tactic is to load a speech with the "correct" symbols and buzzwords as a means of informing the recipient that the message is acceptable and worthwhile. For example, car dealers and politicians often appear with the flag or invoke God, as if to say, "My position is patriotic and religious, so it is worthy of acceptance." Of course, history reveals that just about any scoundrel can wrap him- or herself in the flag—usually for personal profit, not for the nation's best interest.

Often the symbols and buzzwords are tailored to a specific audience. One craze that is currently sweeping some regions of the country is "PC"—political correctness. PC is a fast-changing set of symbols, phrases, and actions that, when properly used, lets everyone know that the message is right and the communicator is doing the right thing. To gain acceptance, one should not wear fur in public; one should always say "he or she"—never the generic "he"; one should eat free-range chicken, not formula-fed, assembly-line chicken; one should never eat veal; one should use cloth, not disposable, diapers; one should demand paper bags at the grocery store—never plastic; above all, one should not provide a critique intolerant of PC.

Never mind that some of the rules are contradictory and ineffective. For example, if fur is unacceptable, why not forgo leather? It has been argued that paper bags, unless they are recycled, produce more environmental waste than plastic and that cloth diapers result in more pollution in their manufacturing and cleaning than do disposables and greatly disadvantage working and single parents. But that is the nature of heuristics—they aren't meant to be thought about, lest they appear as silly as applauding a sliced tomato.

Consider the case of McDonald's.[5] In the early 1970s, environmentalists launched a campaign criticizing McDonald's for its use of paperboard packaging. Ray Kroc, McDonald's founder, commissioned the Stanford Research Institute to conduct a study comparing the environmental impact of different forms of packaging. The study concluded that when all aspects of the issue were considered—from manufacturing to disposal—polystyrene is better for the environment than paper. When paper and cardboard are used for food, they must be coated with a plastic film, making them nearly unrecyclable. The manufacture of polystyrene uses less energy and conserves more natural resources than does the production of paper, and polystyrene takes up less room in landfill and is recyclable. The infamous McDonald's clamshell was born.

In the 1980s, environmentalists raised another, quite legitimate, concern: the manufacturing of polystyrene releases chlorofluorocarbons, which contribute to the destruction of the earth's ozone layer. In 1987, McDonald's directed its polystyrene suppliers to eliminate chlorofluorocarbons from their manufacturing process. However, the clamshell had become a symbol of environmental irresponsibility and McDonald's, in response to pressure groups, ceased using it in the early 1990s, returning to unrecyclable, plastic-coated paper wrappers. Ironically, McDonald's image of being "concerned about the environment" has suffered because it was responsive to environmental concerns. One of McDonald's competitors, which did not respond to earlier pressures to adopt the clamshell, actually ran ads claiming that they had always used cardboard out of concern for the environment. In truth, many American households and businesses would find it difficult to compete with McDonald's record on the environment. McDonald's earmarks 25% of its capital budget ($100 million) for purchasing recycled building materials (thus helping to create this industry), allocates $60 million to purchase recycled paper products, and recently announced forty-two initiatives aimed at holding down the volume of garbage at its restaurants by more than 80%. The destruction of the environment is a complex problem, requiring more than just symbolic finger-pointing and heuristic thinking to resolve.

Of course, as we have stressed earlier, persuasion does not have to be peripheral and decisions do not have to be based on heuristics. Rachel's parents could carefully read the ingredients on the cereal box, subscribe to a consumer magazine, or consult nutrition textbooks. Similarly, we could base our judgment of what a politician is saying not on buzzwords, audience reactions, and source demeanor, but on the actual content and implications of the message itself.

This raises an important question: What conditions are most likely to lead to heuristic rather than rational decision making? Research has identified at least five such conditions.[6] Heuristics are most likely to be used when we not have *time* to think carefully about an issue, when we are so *overloaded with information* that it becomes impossible to process it fully, or when we believe that the issues at stake are *not very important*. Heuristics are also used when we have *little other knowledge or information* on which to base a decision and when a given heuristic *comes quickly to mind* as we are confronted with a problem.

A moment's thought will reveal that the persuasion landscape faced by Rachel and her parents contains many of the features that lead to heuristic decision making. If they are like most Americans, Rachel and her family are feeling increasingly pressed for time, since their leisure time has eroded considerably in the last ten years. As consumers, they face a message-dense environment complete with a choice of, for example, more than 300 different brands of cereal currently on the market. They probably have had little consumer education or training. They have been, however, the recipients of millions of advertisements, each repeating and repeating a brand image, so that this image will quickly come to mind in the aisles of the local supermarket. Given this state of affairs, it is a wonder that *all* decisions are not made heuristically.

One of the dilemmas of modern life is that with decreasing leisure time, increasing information, and increasing choices, we must rely more and more on heuristic decision making. Although relying on heuristics is sometimes a useful way of dealing with the onslaught of the message-dense, decision-rich environment, basing our decisions primarily on heuristics can present some problems.

First, the heuristic cues that we possess may be false. There is little reason to assume that brand images and ethnic stereotypes have a reliable basis in fact. Relying on such heuristics may result in the purchase of an unwanted product and the missed opportunity to hire a qualified employee or fall in love with that special person. Furthermore, a rule may be appropriate in certain situations, but be misapplied in others. For example, spontaneous, legitimate audience applause can signal that this is an entertaining show worthy of our attention. Canned laughter does not.

Another serious problem is that heuristics can be easily faked and manipulated. Cereal boxes can be redesigned to look increasingly wholesome. Laughter and applause can be dubbed into a broadcast. Politicians can be coached to exude winning mannerisms. Physical attractiveness can be improved with makeup and surgery. Speeches and advertisements can be peppered with buzzwords and symbols. Anyone with a little cash can buy a new blazer and a sincere tie. The essence of propaganda is a well-designed package.

What can be done to lessen our dependence on faulty heuristics? One attempt to forestall these concerns is to enact legislation to insure that the cues that we do use—for example, phrases on product labels such as "low calorie," "low sodium," or "100% nutritious"—are accurate and are applied correctly. In recent days, the Federal Trade Commission has attempted to establish guidelines for the use of such labels as "low fat" and "environmentally safe." (Currently, they can mean just about anything.) This, along with other efforts to improve the quality of product information, is a step in the right direction. However, such efforts are unlikely to succeed in stamping out heuristic thinking. After all, no government, no matter how vigilant, can protect us from our own prejudices. In the long run, we must depend on our own knowledge of propaganda tactics and our own efforts to treat important issues as if they were truly important.

17
SELF-SELL

World War II was a war not only of bombs and bullets but of words and propaganda as well. The Nazi's propaganda offensive was first outlined by Adolf Hilter in *Mein Kampf* and then executed by Joseph Goebbels and his Ministry of Propaganda. The United States relied on a loose collection of social psychologists and other social scientists to develop its campaign, to boost the nation's morale, and to diffuse the impact of Nazi propaganda.

One of the unlikely combatants in this propaganda war was the U.S. Department of Agriculture's Committee on Food Habits, headed in part by the famed anthropologist Margaret Mead. Its mission during the wartime emergency was to maintain the health of the American people despite shortages of certain types of high-protein foods. One specific project was to increase the consumption of meat products that, in the United States, had often been thrown away or used as pet food—meats such as beef hearts, kidneys, intestines. To do so, the committee made us of a tactic that is now ubiquitous in attempts at persuasion.

Any parent who has ever tried to get a child to eat green vegetables can appreciate the difficulty of convincing a nation that beef hearts, kidneys, and intestines are nourishing and tasty, much less to get people to actually eat them. To accomplish the task, the Committee on Food Habits called on Kurt Lewin, the father of social psychology and himself a recent refugee from Nazi Germany.

How did Lewin do it? Well, he *didn't*—not directly. What Lewin *did* do was to get people to persuade themselves to eat these intestinal meats. To demonstrate the effectiveness of participatory, self-generated persuasion, Lewin conducted a simple experiment to convince housewives (who at the time made most of their family's food decisions) to eat intestines and other undesirable meats.[1]

Half of the housewives received an intriguing lecture on the merits of intestinal meats. The forty-five-minute lecture emphasized the importance of eating these meats for the war effort; it stressed the meats' health and economic advantages; and mimeographed recipes were distributed. The lecture concluded with a testimonial from the speaker about the success of serving intestinal meats in her own family.

The other housewives spent their forty-five minutes persuading themselves in a group discussion. This discussion began with a short introduction by the leader on the problem of maintaining health during the war. The leader then enlisted the help of the housewives by asking them, "Do you think that housewives like yourselves could be persuaded to participate in the intestinal meat program?" The group discussion covered many of the same arguments as the lecture but produced much more dramatic effects. Of the housewives who had heard the lecture, only 3% served intestines. In stark contrast, 32% of the housewives who had engaged in self-persuasion served their families intestinal meats.

Subsequent persuasion research has shown that self-generated persuasion—whether induced by group discussion, by getting someone to role-play an opponent's position, or by asking a person to imagine adopting a course of action—is one of the most effective persuasion tactics ever identified. Indeed, one recent set of studies found that just thinking about how to transmit a persuasive message to others will result in changes in attitude that persist at least twenty weeks.[2]

And why shouldn't the tactic be extremely effective? The technique of self-generated persuasion combines many of the facets of successful persuasion discussed throughout this book. It gains its power from providing subtle social cues and directions that ask the target of influence, in effect, to "think up as many positive cognitive responses about the issue as you can and, if you do happen to come up with some counterarguments, to be ready to refute them." The resulting message will come from a source that you almost always consider credible, trustworthy, respected, and liked—yourself. The act of generating arguments is an act of commitment to the cause. After all, they're your ideas, aren't they?

World War II may be over, but the use of self-sell in propaganda is certainly not. Larry Gregory, Robert Cialdini, and Kathleen Carpenter conducted a series of experiments illustrating the effectiveness of a form of self-persuasion called "self-imagining" in selling consumer products.[3] In one of their studies, salespersons went door-to-door in Tempe, Arizona, selling subscriptions to cable television. Some of the potential customers were informed of the advantages of cable TV (e.g., cheaper and less hassle than going out to a movie, you can spend more time with your family). Others were asked to "take a moment and imagine how cable television will provide *you* with broader entertainment." They were then induced to imagine how they would use and enjoy each benefit of cable television. The results showed that 19.5% of those merely receiving information about cable television subscribed to the service, whereas a whopping 47.4% subscribed when asked to imagine using the service.

The self-generated persuasion technique fits the American values of participation, self-reliance, and deciding for one's self. Ironically, while the technique trades on the value of self-reliance, in reality we are being manipulated into a course of action that is often of primary benefit to the manipulator.

A trip to a car dealership (like one we recently took) will illustrate the point. Much of the friendly salesman's banter is targeted at getting the potential customer to think about possessing that car and to come up with his or her own reasons for doing it right *now*:

"Sir, can I get you to do me a favor? I know we just met. These babies are selling like hotcakes and my boss keeps bugging me to find out just why people like yourself love 'em so much. What should I tell him?"

As we inch closer to the car and an actual test drive, the salesman persistently asks personal questions (Where do you live? What do you do? What music do you like?). When a seat is taken at the wheel, the salesman states, "The car looks good on you; and I don't tell that to everyone."

During the test drive, the pitch continues. "Did you get a look at the back seat? Plenty of room to pick up those professor friends of *yours* at the airport." "Hmmmm, who left this classical station on the

radio? I normally listen to rock. Let's switch it over to *your* station."
"Really punch that pedal, professor. I want you to see how it'll handle
those inclines on your commute from Forest Hills."

The test drive over, the salesman dramatically delivers his lines,
"Professor, I'm going in to see the boss and try to get you the best deal
on your car." The keys to the car are pressed into the flesh of the palm
and the hand gently closed. We are left alone in the showroom, tightly
holding a key to our beautiful car—left alone to think, to dream, to
imagine owning that car.

This nice, friendly social interaction seems quite cunning and
blatantly manipulative once we know the principles and power of
self-influence. But what can be done about it? Here's what we did. It
would be difficult for anyone not to imagine owning that car. You've
just daydreamed about it for almost half an hour. But what also can be
imagined is getting that car at a rock-bottom price and driving it home
to show friends and neighbors and hearing them exclaim: "That car?
At that price? What a deal!" Imagining this latter scenario led to a
stalemate that eventually produced a lengthy negotiation (almost two
hours) in which each party dug in his heels.

This tiresome negotiation was getting nowhere slowly. Why not try
self-generated persuasion tactics ourselves? "Hey, Bill [the salesman]. I
notice this dealership gives an award for the salesperson of the month.
Just how do they decide who gets this award and can you get me a sales
rep who really wants to win that thing?" Bill took the bait. He wheeled
around in his chair, leaned back, and began a fifteen-minute free association about the award. A few minutes later, we were writing a check as a
deposit on a very good deal.

Car dealers are not the only merchants who have discovered
self-generated persuasion. Mass media advertisers have developed
their own set of variants. One effective type of commercial is the "slice
of life" ad that allows us to dream with characters, much like ourselves, as they successfully solve life's problems using, of course, the
advertiser's brand. Some ads require us to complete the incomplete
jingle as in, "Where's the...[beef]?" and "You can take Salem out of the
country, but you...[can't take the country out of Salem]." Marketing
promotions and contests often ask us to, "Tell us why you like
Acme-brand widgets in 50 words or less?" Politicians send out

questionnaires and surveys asking for our opinions in "helping to plan the next election campaign." Perhaps you can further convince yourself of the effectiveness of self-generated persuasion by generating even more examples of self-generated persuasion.

18

NAKED ATTICS AND NEIGHBORHOOD WAR HEROES : ON VIVIDNESS IN COMMUNICATION

Several years ago, a local community was about to vote on whether or not to fluoridate the water supply as a means of combating tooth decay. An information campaign that seemed quite logical and reasonable was launched by the proponents of fluoridation. It consisted largely of statements by noted dentists describing the benefits of fluorides and discussing the evidence on the reduction of tooth decay in areas with fluoridated water, as well as statements by physicians and other health authorities to the effect that fluoridation has no harmful effects.

The opponents used an appeal that was much more vivid and emotional in flavor. By vivid appeal, we mean a message that is (1) emotionally interesting (it attracts our feelings), (2) concrete and imagery-provoking, and (3) immediate (it discusses matters that are personally close to us). For example, one antifluoridation leaflet consisted of a picture of a rather ugly rat, along with the inscription "Don't let them put rat poison in your drinking water." The referendum to fluoridate the water supply was soundly defeated.

Of course, this incident does not demonstrate conclusively that vivid appeals are superior, mainly because the incident was not a scientifically controlled study. We have no idea how the people would have voted on fluoridation if no publicity had been circulated, nor do we know whether the antifluoridation circular reached more people, whether it was easier to read than the proponents' literature, and so forth.

A stunning and scientific demonstration of the power of vivid arguments to persuade comes from the area of energy conservation. If home owners could be induced to make their homes more efficient (by adding insulation, weatherstripping, and the like), it could result in a savings of about 40% of the energy that is now wasted. This would not only be in the national interest, reducing dependence on Persian Gulf oil, but would also result in substantial financial savings for the individual home owner.

Since 1978, the government has required utility companies to offer the consumer a free home audit, wherein a trained auditor carefully examines one's home, recommends what needs to be done to make it more energy-efficient, and offers the consumer an interest-free loan to get the work done. What a deal! The problem is that, while a great many home owners have requested a home audit, only 15% of them have actually followed the recommendation of the auditor—even though it was clearly in their best financial interests to do so.

Why? In order to answer this puzzling question, we and our students, Marti Hope Gonzales and Mark Costanzo, interviewed several home owners and found that most of them had a hard time believing that something as small as a crack under a door or as "invisible" as the paucity of insulation in the attic could be very important.[1] Armed with this information, we conducted a workshop in which we trained several auditors to communicate in more graphic, more vivid terms. For example, instead of simply saying "You would save money if you weatherstripped your doors and put some additional insulation in the attic," the auditors were trained to say something like this:

> Look at all the cracks around that door! It may not seem like much to you, but if you were to add up all the cracks around each of these doors, you'd have the equivalent of a hole the circumference of a basketball. Suppose someone poked a hole the size of a basketball in your living room wall. Think for a moment about all the heat that you'd be losing from a hole that size— you'd want to patch that hole in your wall, wouldn't you? That's exactly what weatherstripping does. And your attic totally lacks insulation. We professionals call that a "naked" attic. It's as if your home is facing winter not just without an overcoat, but without any clothing at all! You wouldn't let your young kids run around outside in the winter time without clothes on, would you? It's the same with your attic.

Psychologically, cracks around the door may be seen as minor, but a hole the size of a basketball feels disastrous. Similarly, insulation is something people don't often think about—but the idea of being naked in winter grabs attention and increases the probability of action.

The results were striking. Auditors trained to use compelling images increased their effectiveness fourfold: Whereas previously only 15% of the consumers had the recommended work done, after the auditors began to use more vivid communications, this increased to 61%.

Why do vivid appeals work? Vivid messages affect our cognitive responses in at least three possible ways. First, vivid information attracts *attention*. It helps the communication stand out in the message-dense environment. Second, vividness can make the information more *concrete* and *personal*. We saw earlier the persuasive power of self-generated arguments and images. Finally, a vivid presentation can make the material more *memorable*. This is especially important if we do not reach an immediate conclusion but base our later judgments on information that comes readily to mind.

Our cognitive response analysis also suggests that vivid information may sometimes fail to convince—and do so in a quite dramatic fashion. Just because a message is vivid does *not* insure that it will induce positive thoughts and thus be effective. A case in point is the now infamous Dukakis tank ad used during the 1988 presidential campaign. In this ad, the Dukakis campaign staff sought to make Michael Dukakis's commitment to a strong national defense vivid in the minds of voters by showing him in an army tank. The ad was attention-getting, and it did succeed in reducing the issue to one concrete, memorable symbol. The end result was not very persuasive, however. Instead of the reaction hoped for by the Dukakis campaign (i.e., he surely is tough on defense), many viewers responded with thoughts such as, "*Gee, he looks silly in that tank.*" The vividness of the appeal just made it all the worse for Dukakis.

Nevertheless, a vivid presentation can make a strong argument even more persuasive; it may also make a more dubious appeal ring true. Consider the following example. Suppose you are in the market for a new car and the single most important thing you are looking for is reliability and longevity. That is, you don't care about looks, style, or mileage—what you do care about is the frequency of repair. As a reasonable and sensible person, you consult *Consumer Reports* and learn that the car with the best repair record is clearly a Toyota. No other car even comes close. Naturally, you decide to buy a Toyota.

But suppose the night before you are to make the purchase, you attend a dinner party and announce your intention to one of your friends. He is incredulous. "You can't be serious," he says, "my cousin bought a Toyota last year and has had nothing but trouble ever since. First the fuel injection system broke down; then the transmission fell out; then strange undiagnosable noises started to come from the engine; finally, oil started to drip from some unknown place. My poor cousin is literally afraid to drive the car for fear of what will happen next."

Let's suppose the ranking made by *Consumer Reports* was based on a sample of 1,000 Toyota owners. Your friend's cousin's unfortunate experience has increased the size of the sample to 1,001. It has added one negative case to your statistical bank. Logically, this should not affect your decision. But a large body of research by Richard Nisbett and Lee Ross (from whose work this example was "borrowed") indicates that such occurrences, because of their vividness, assume far more importance than their logical, statistical status would imply.[2] Indeed, such occurrences are frequently decisive. Thus it would be very difficult for you to rush out and purchase a Toyota with the example of the plight of your friend's cousin firmly fixed in your mind. All other things being equal, most people are more deeply influenced by one clear, vivid, personal example than by an abundance of statistical data.

Vivid examples and case studies are also used by politicians to get us to buy their programs and policies. In *Eloquence in an Electronic Age*, communications researcher Kathleen Hall Jamieson addresses the question of why Ronald Reagan was considered, by both foe and admirer, to be a great communicator.[3] The Reagan presidency produced no major addresses—no speeches as eloquent or as memorable as Washington's farewell address, Lincoln's Gettysburg address, Franklin D. Roosevelt's first inaugural address or his fireside chats, or Kennedy's inaugural address or *Ich bin ein Berliner* speech. In their stead were a series of catchphrases such as "Make my day" and "There you go again."

Jamieson argues that Reagan's communication style differed greatly from that of past presidents. Previous presidents used the devices of classical rhetoric to advance their causes—well-constructed arguments, the contrasting of possible options, argument by metaphor. Reagan relied on dramatization and storytelling to make his points. His speeches persuaded by creating visual images, by personalizing the central themes of his administration, and by involving us in a dramatic narrative of American life. Let's look at two sets of Reagan's speeches, his first inaugural address and his State of the Union addresses to Congress, to see what Jamieson means.

Reagan delivered his first inaugural address in an unusual location—from the west front of the Capitol building, the first time that this locale had been used for such a purpose. In this speech, one of the points Reagan sought to make was that America's involvement in the Vietnam war was just and honorable. There are a number of ways to argue for this proposition. One could provide the listener with a list of reasons for the war: It helped stay the spread of communism; it was designed to prevent the overthrow of a democracy and the rise of yet another totalitarian regime; it was ostensibly supported by the people of South Vietnam, and so on. The war could also be contrasted with other options available at the time. Such was *not* Reagan's style.

Instead Reagan, from his location at the Capitol, spoke these words:

> Standing here, one faces a magnificent vista, opening up on the city's special beauty and history. At the end of this open mall are those shrines to the giants on whose shoulders we stand.

The television cameras panned those monuments. Reagan proceeded to point out the sights of Washington, D.C.—the Washington monument, the Jefferson memorial, the Lincoln memorial, and finally, across the Potomac River, the hills of Arlington National Cemetery, where rows of simple white crosses and Stars of David mark those who gave their lives for their country. Reagan continued:

> Their lives ended in places called Belleau Wood, the Argonne, Omaha Beach, Salerno, and halfway around the world on Guadalcanal, Tarawa, Pork Chop Hill, the Chosin Reservoir, and in a hundred rice paddies and jungles of a place called Vietnam.

By including the Vietnam war dead in a succession of symbols and images exemplifying the best of American heroism, Reagan had transformed the war in Vietnam into a just and honorable mission with a single vivid image.

Perhaps Reagan's most memorable speeches were his addresses to Congress. In these speeches, Reagan would describe the personal acts of service performed by private citizens. The members of Congress would applaud, and the viewing public would be filled with pride at the accomplishments of their fellow citizens. Reagan gained national acceptance of his policies.

For example, to gain acceptance of the U.S. invasion of the island of Grenada, Reagan singled out Sergeant Stephen Trujillo. During the attack on Grenada, Trujillo had saved the lives of many of his fellow soldiers. As Congress applauded Trujillo's valor, Reagan quickly noted, "you [Trujillo] set a nation free," thereby justifying America's invasion.

To convince the nation that poverty was not a major social problem, Reagan frequently used rags-to-riches and neighbor-helping-neighbor stories. On one occasion, he singled out Jean Nguyen, a Vietnamese refugee who was now, after a successful academic career, graduating from West Point. On the same night, he also singled out Clara Hale, a black woman and founder of a home for the infants of drug-addicted mothers. Hale served as a concrete example that poverty and drug abuse were problems for private citizens, not for the federal government, to solve and that Reagan's policies did not systematically disadvantage black Americans.

We can analyze Reagan's arguments concerning the lack of poverty in this country in much the same way as we looked at our friend's story about the problematic Toyota. Near the beginning of the Reagan years, one out of every nine American children lived in poverty. At the end of his term, that figure was one in four children. It would be a simple matter, depending on our propaganda purposes, to find vivid examples of either children living in poverty or children whose parents had gotten themselves out of such circumstances. Such human examples may make our arguments more persuasive, but they do little to address the issue of poverty in America. This would require a detailed look at how various government policies have affected indicators of poverty. The Communist leader, Joseph Stalin anticipated the current use of vividness in the tactics of propaganda when he perceptively remarked: "The death of a single Russian soldier is a tragedy. A million deaths is a statistic."[4]

Throughout American history, vivid, personal appeals have moved the soul of the nation—such novels as Harriet Beecher Stowe's *Uncle Tom's Cabin*, Upton Sinclair's *The Jungle*, John Steinbeck's *The Grapes of Wrath*, and Kurt Vonnegut's *Slaughter House Five* are just a few examples. But although novels have been effective, it is television's ability to present vivid, emotional images that is unsurpassed.

Some communications scholars believe that anti-war sentiment during the Vietnam war—America's first televised war—was due in part to the constant stream of war images cast onto the nation's television screens. The U.S. military, having learned its lesson in Vietnam, went to great lengths to restrict the flow of vivid images of the Persian Gulf war to Americans watching on their TV sets at home. Indeed, government officials saw to it that only images that supported U.S. involvement in the Persian Gulf, such as a U.S. guided missile surgically striking an Iraqi command headquarters or an Iraqi Scud missile being shot out of the sky, consistently made it to our television screens. Americans protested when CNN aired footage, supplied by Peter Arnett, of harm to Iraqi civilians caused by U.S. bombing raids.

In recent years, Americans have been angered by watching blindfolded hostages on exhibition in Iran, impassioned by the sight of young servicemen's coffins on an airplane tarmac, and moved to compassion by scenes of devastation after hurricane Hugo and the Santa Cruz earthquake. And today, still more vivid and moving images are being televised to replace last week's vivid and moving images. The power of television to dramatize warrants our concern and scrutiny, so that compelling and sometimes vivid arguments are not replaced by merely vivid, moving tales.

19

WHY DO THEY KEEP REPEATING THE SAME ADS?

In 1882, Harley T. Procter of Cincinnati, Ohio, began to market his new soap, which he called Ivory, with newspaper and magazine ads proclaiming that "it floats" and is "99 44/100% pure." In 1922, Gerald Lambert, son of the founder of Lambert and Lambert, hired the Chicago ad agency William and Cunnyngham to improve the sluggish sales of Listerine—at the time, a product used as an antiseptic in surgery and to fight throat infection. The resulting campaign: "Even your best friend won't tell you. Listerine is good for halitosis." Five decades later, in 1954, a delegation from the Philip Morris tobacco company asked the famed Chicago adman Leo Burnett to help solve a marketing problem—to develop an ad campaign that would sell filter cigarettes (regarded at the time to be feminine) to men. The next year, Burnett released his first ads for Marlboro cigarettes featuring a virile, macho cowboy riding the range with cigarettes in hand.[1]

What do these three advertisements have in common (in addition to having sold millions of products)? These ads have been seen, in one form or another, countless times by generations of countless Americans. Repetition of ads, slogans, and selling points is a common feature of the landscape of twentieth-century American advertising. Yet, in surveys about what people think about advertising, one of the most common and consistent complaints is that it is annoying to see the same old stuff over and over again. If repetitive advertising is so irritating, why do advertisers continue to do it?

From a business perspective, frequent exposure of an advertisement helps to meet multiple marketing objectives in a cost-efficient manner. Repeatedly exposing consumers to an ad is a good way to introduce a new product or to remind customers of the value of an older brand. Often repeat exposure is an unintended consequence of attempting to present an ad to multiple target audiences (the members of which may overlap). With the high cost of creating and producing new advertising ideas and slogans, it makes sense to stick with proven winners. As a further inducement to repeat an ad, advertising agencies typically receive 15% of media costs as their fee. So the more times an ad is run, the larger the billing. However, the accomplishment of such marketing objectives and cost benefits would amount to very little if message repetition did not do one thing more and do it very well—persuade you to buy the product.

The Greek storyteller Aesop once advanced the notion that familiarity breeds contempt. Although Aesop's moral may apply to the social gatherings of foxes and lions, it certainly does *not* describe the persuasive effects of familiarity brought about by repeated exposure to advertising. The modern-day Aesop writing about advertising would probably conclude the opposite: *Familiarity breeds attraction and liking.*

How familiarity can result in sales can be seen in a typical trip to the grocery store in search of a laundry detergent. We go to the detergent section and see a staggering array of brand names. Because it doesn't much matter which one is purchased, we may simply reach for the most familiar one—and chances are it is familiar because we've heard and seen the name on television commercials over and over again. If this is the case, then sudden increases in television exposure should produce dramatic changes in familiarity and, perhaps, in sales.

Let's look at the data. Several years ago, the Northwest Mutual Life Insurance Company conducted a nationwide poll to find out how well the public recognized its name. It came out thirty-fourth among insurance companies. Two weeks and $1 million dollars worth of television advertising later, the company repeated the poll. This time it came out third in name familiarity.

Of course, familiarity does not necessarily mean sales, but the two are frequently linked. Thus, A&W root beer boosted its share of the market from 15% to 50% after six months of television advertising. By switching channels on a Saturday morning, a child can watch Ronald McDonald in up to a dozen colorful, fast-paced commercials each hour; perhaps this is one reason why the chain continues to sell billions of hamburgers.

Robert Zajonc of the University of Michigan has demonstrated in a laboratory setting that, all other things being equal, the more a person is exposed to an item, the more attractive it is.[2] In three separate studies, Zajonc presented nonsense words, Chinese ideographs, and photographs of students taken from a college yearbook. The items were repeated from zero to twenty-five times. The results showed that attraction to the item increased with the number of exposures. Much subsequent research has supported Zajonc's basic finding: More exposure results in increased liking.

But is voting for a presidential candidate the same kind of decision as choosing a laundry detergent or a breakfast cereal or evaluating nonsense words and Chinese ideographs? The answer may very well be "yes." After the 1972 U.S. congressional primaries, Joseph Grush and his colleagues examined the amount of money candidates spent on political advertising during the elections and found that a large majority of races were won by big spenders.[3] Subsequently, Grush found again that candidates who spent the most money in the 1976 Democratic presidential primaries typically received the most votes. In both studies, however, those who tended to gain the most from media exposure were candidates who were relatively unknown to the voters prior to their campaigns. But, in presidential elections in which candidates are highly familiar, massive media blitzes are less influential.[4] Nevertheless, even minimal impact may be large enough to swing some close races.

The power of repetition in propaganda was well understood by Joseph Goebbels, the head of the Nazi propaganda ministry. His propaganda crusades were based on a simple observation: *What the masses term truth is that information which is most familiar.* As Goebbels put it:

> The rank and file are usually much more primitive than we imagine. Propaganda must therefore always be essentially simple and repetitious. In the long run only he will achieve basic results in influencing public opinion who is able to reduce problems to the simplest terms and who has the courage to keep forever repeating them in this simplified form despite the objections of intellectuals.[5]

The repetition of simple messages, images, and slogans can create our knowledge of the world, defining what is truth and specifying how we should live our lives.

Consider something as simple as the Marlboro man, an image we have probably seen hundreds of times but one that we probably have not thought much about. What does this cowboy teach us? First, that smoking is for the rugged, self-confident individual (as opposed to being a health hazard). Second, that American men should be macho (as opposed to, say, caring and sensitive). And finally, that you can be rugged and macho simply by smoking Marlboros—it is that easy. A lifetime of exposures to black Americans as Uneeda Slicker boys and Aunt Jemima, to Hispanics as Frito Banditos, and women as either endlessly arguing about the benefits of a brand of paper towels or sexily draped on the hood of an automobile can reinforce and maintain pervasive social stereotypes.

This problem does not seem to worry all advertisers. What they do worry about is annoying the viewers to the point where they refuse to listen to the advertising and to buy the product. Recall that many American consumers find repetitive advertising to be irritating. Such annoyance can diminish and even reverse the effects of repetition, but this reversal is often short-lived. For example, Rick Crandall, Albert Harrison, and Robert Zajonc showed subjects the same Chinese ideographs over and over again.[6] Immediately after the repetitive presentation, subjects did not rate these ideographs as any more attractive than less familiar ones, presumably because the frequent exposures were boring and tedious. However, after a week's delay, the repeatedly presented Chinese ideographs gained in attractiveness. Apparently the annoying effects of repetition wore off faster than the familiarity-induced attraction.

Even so, advertisers know that repeated exposure can lead to what is known as "wear-out"—when an ad loses its effectiveness because consumers find repeated exposures to be tedious and annoying. Wear-out effects are most likely to occur with ads that attract much attention, such as humorous ads and informational messages. Advertisers attempt to eliminate wear-out by using a technique known as "repetition-with-variation." In this technique, the same information or theme is repeated many times, but the presentation format is varied. For example, the Marlboro man is posed at different angles and is seen in different settings, or the halitosis-fighting power of Listerine is demonstrated at work, in the home, and on a date.

Does repetition-with-variation work? A study conducted by David Schumann illustrates the effectiveness of repetition-with-variation for overcoming wear-out effects and identifies an important condition in which variation does not succeed in producing attraction.[7] In this study, participants watched a simulated television show, complete with advertising for a fictitious pen called the "Omega 3." Half of the participants viewed the *same* ad for the Omega 3 pen presented either one, four, or eight times, whereas the other participants watched either one, four, or eight *different* ads for the Omega 3—in other words, repetition-with-variation. (These differing ads contained the same information about the Omega 3 but varied irrelevant features such as wording, print type, and setting). Schumann also varied whether the ad was processed using the central or peripheral route by encouraging some participants to think about the Omega 3 advertising with a promise that, at the end of the study, they could select a gift from among several brands of ballpoint pens. Other participants were told that they would receive a free bottle of mouthwash as a gift and were thus not motivated to think about ballpoint pens and the Omega 3.

What did Schumann find? Let's look first at the effects ad repetition had for those participants who were not motivated to think much about the pens—a state we often find ourselves in when watching television and its advertisements. When the same ad was repeated, the participants' opinion of the Omega 3 pen became more favorable with four repetitions, but less favorable after eight—in other words, a wear-out effect occurred. However, when a different ad was repeated, the participants' opinion of the Omega 3 became more favorable with every exposure. Repetition-with-variation had reduced the tedium and eliminated the wear-out effects.

On the other hand, for those participants who were motivated to think about pens, wear-out occurred when both the *same* and *different* ads were repeated. Specifically, opinions of the Omega 3 pen became more favorable with four repetitions but *less* favorable after eight. For thinking participants, even repetition-with-variation could not counter the annoying effects of repeat exposure. In this case, the extra exposures provided an opportunity to scrutinize and critique the advertisement's message.

The rub, of course, is that we see and hear many, many persuasive messages each day, and we see and hear them over and over again. It is difficult to think deeply about each and every one of these communications. After all, how often do we think, in depth, about the meaning of the Marlboro man or the significance of the fact that Ivory soap floats? Repetition is thus left to create its own truths.

20
IF YOU HAVE NOTHING TO SAY— DISTRACT THEM

When confronted with a persuasive communication, especially one that runs counter to important beliefs, we tend, whenever feasible, to invent counterarguments on the spot. This tendency serves us very well: It prevents our opinions from being unduly influenced. This resistance can serve to defeat the propagandist's purpose, especially when the arguments for the cause are weak and specious and therefore easily refuted.

But professional persuaders, aware of our tendency to counterargue, have discovered a way to overcome some of this resistance. Advertisers have an old motto: "If you don't have anything to say, sing it!" In other words, a mild distraction (provided by a song, an irrelevant picture, etc.) can serve to disrupt counterarguing and increase the effectiveness of a persuasive message.

The song that was most on the lips of the typical American in the 1940s was not a great tune by Irving Berlin, Cole Porter, or Rodgers and Hammerstein. It was a ditty that was as meaningless as it was simple: "Rinso *white*! Rinso *white*! Happy little washday song!" Rinso, a laundry detergent, was no better or worse than its competitors—but the song, ah, the song. In the 1970s, Coca-Cola hit the charts with, "I'd like to teach the world to sing." Today, Pepsi has spent millions to have Ray Charles serenade us with "You've got the right one, baby—Diet Pepsi—uh-huh, uh-huh."

What effect does a song have on persuasion? Does it make people feel happy, with this happiness somehow increasing the persuasiveness of the message? Perhaps sometimes.[1] Research has shown that the major impact of a song or other distraction may be that it disrupts counterarguing.

*"When she finishes singing the commercial,
ask her about tourist class."*

An early experiment by Leon Festinger and Nathan Maccoby was the
first to demonstrate the validity of the advertiser's motto.[2] In this experiment, two groups of students who belonged to a college fraternity were
required to watch a film that presented arguments about the evils of
college fraternities. The arguments were intended to be powerful and
were widely discrepant from the beliefs of the audience. As you might
imagine, the students were motivated to counterargue this message. In
one version of the film, a young professor delivered the attack on fraternities. In the other version, the young professor was replaced by an
entertaining beatnik artist working on an abstract-expressionist painting.
The students still heard the arguments against fraternities but watched an
entertaining and distracting film as they listened.

Festinger and Maccoby reasoned that because this group was engaged in two tasks simultaneously—listening to the arguments against fraternities and watching an entertaining film—their minds would be so occupied that they would have a limited capacity to think up arguments to refute the message. The members of the control group, on the other hand, were not distracted by the entertaining film; therefore, they should be better able to devote some of their thoughts to resisting the communication by thinking up counterarguments. The results of the experiment confirmed this reasoning. The fraternity men who were distracted by watching the film underwent substantially more opinion change against fraternities than did the fraternity men who were not distracted.

How do advertisers try to disrupt our counterarguing of their messages? Sometimes they literally sing, as with the Rinso commercial and many like it. Another class of distraction techniques is the extensive use of creative license in the layout and presentation of an advertisement. For a print ad in a magazine or newspaper, examples of such *artsy* techniques would include pictures of attractive models or unique objects that command attention, reverse white-on-black print, strange layouts that confuse the reader, and typefaces that are difficult to read. For television, artsy could mean a commercial with many short scene changes (similar to an MTV video), the use of strange camera angles, the playing of fast, rhythmic music in the background, and the inclusion of offbeat characters and yelling, screaming spokespersons. All of these techniques can serve to provide a mild distraction and thus prevent counterarguing. The trick for the advertiser is to provide just enough of a distraction to disrupt counterarguing but not so much that it eliminates the reception of the message.[3]

But not all advertisers agree with the "sing it" dictum. In his advice to fellow advertisers, David Ogilvy[4] calls this kind of creative license "art-directoritis" and urges his colleagues to avoid it. Ogilvy claims, based on his own observations and years of advertising experience, that the techniques associated with art-directoritis often fail to achieve their desired effects. How does this square with what we know about distraction and persuasion?

Ogilvy achieved his fame as an advertiser in the 1950s with a series of influential print ads for Hathaway shirts, Rolls-Royce, and Schweppes tonic. Although for different products, the ads employed a similar style. Each ad contained an interesting picture featuring the product. A headline would tell readers why the product was of special value for them, and lengthy copy would explain the reason for this assertion. For example, one ad showed a picture of a Rolls-Royce with the headline: AT 60 MILES AN HOUR THE LOUDEST NOISE IN THIS NEW ROLLS-ROYCE COMES FROM THE ELECTRIC CLOCK. The copy listed thirteen unique benefits of owning a Rolls. Similarly, a more recent ad for Acura automobiles merely shows the car and states that for three consecutive years, the Acura has been number one in surveys of owner satisfaction. In this kind of situation, when one can state compelling, cogent arguments, Ogilvy is right. An artsy ad would distract the reader from the cogent arguments and might actually *decrease* persuasion. But that is only half of the equation. For weak arguments or when one fears counterarguments, well...the persuader can always sing it.

Our speculation has been confirmed by a neat little experiment by the social psychologists Richard Petty, Gary Wells, and Timothy Brock.[5] In their study, students were distracted by asking them to monitor a television screen for X's while they listened to one of two messages arguing for an increase in their tuition. One message consisted of weak, easily counterargued arguments, whereas the other consisted of strong, hard-to-refute arguments. Distraction *increased* the effectiveness of the weak message (because it disrupted counterarguing) but *decreased* the impact of the strong communication (because it disrupted the ability to pay close attention to the cogent arguments being made).

Recently television advertisers have introduced a new, more subtle technique that can serve to distract and disrupt message processing—time compression. To save media costs, advertisers can, for example, "compress" a thirty-six-second television ad into a thirty-second time slot by running the ad at 120% of its normal speed. Psychologically, time compressed ads are harder to argue against. Metaphorically speaking, the advertiser is persuading at 100 miles an hour while you maintain the speed limit and try to defend yourself at 55 miles an hour. You are bound to lose.

A series of studies by consumer psychologist Danny Moore and his colleagues[6] confirm this relationship between time compression, distraction, and persuasion. Specifically, they found that participants were less able to develop counterarguments to a time-compressed message and that time-compressing a message consisting of strong arguments reduced persuasion whereas it increased the persuasive impact of a message containing weak arguments.

In sum, advertisers (and other influence agents) use a variety of tactics to distract us from processing and counterarguing a message. This distraction, if it is mild, can lead to more persuasion when our natural inclination is to argue—for example, if the message is weak or disagreeable. The end result, of course, is just a little more mindless propaganda and a little less thoughtful persuasion.

21
IF YOU WANT TO GAIN AN INCH, ASK FOR A MILE—SOMETIMES!

Suppose you are talking to an audience that strongly disagrees with your point of view—for example, an anti-abortionist presenting a speech to a pro-choice lobby or an automaker trying to convince a nation that the car they believe to be quite worthless is, in reality, excellent. Will it be more effective to present the arguments in their most extreme form or to modulate the message by presenting it in such a way that it does not seem terribly different from the audience's position?

For example, suppose you believe people should exercise vigorously every day to stay healthy; any physical activity would be helpful, but at least an hour's worth would be preferable. Your audience consists of couch potatoes who seem to believe that switching TV channels with the remote is sufficient exercise for the average person. Would you change their opinion to a greater extent by arguing that people should begin a rigorous daily program of running, swimming, and calisthenics or by suggesting a briefer, less taxing regimen? In short, what is the most effective level of discrepancy between the opinion of the audience and the recommendation of the communicator? This is a vital issue for any propagandist or educator.

Let's look at this situation from the audience's point of view. Most of us have a strong desire to be correct—to have "the right" opinions and to perform reasonable actions. When someone disagrees with us, it makes us feel uncomfortable because it suggests our opinions or actions may be wrong or based on misinformation. The greater the disagreement, the greater our discomfort.

How can we reduce this discomfort? One way is by simply changing our opinions or actions. The greater the disagreement, the greater our opinion change would have to be. This line of reasoning, then, would suggest that the communicator should argue for the daily program of rigorous exercise; the greater the discrepancy, the greater the opinion change needed.

Several investigators have found that this "linear" relation does hold true. A good example of this relation was provided by an experiment by Philip Zimbardo.[1] Each of the women recruited as participants for the experiment was asked to bring a close friend with her to the laboratory. Each pair of friends was presented with a case study of juvenile delinquency, and then each of the participants was asked, separately and in private, to indicate her recommendations on the matter. Each women was led to believe her close friend disagreed with her, either by a small margin or by an extremely large margin. Zimbardo found that the greater the apparent discrepancy, the more the women changed their opinions toward what they supposed were the opinions of their friends.

However, a careful look at the literature also turns up several experiments disconfirming this line of reasoning. For example, Carl Hovland, O. J. Harvey, and Muzafer Sherif argued that, if a particular communication differs considerably from a person's own position, it is, in effect, outside of one's "latitude of acceptance," and the individual therefore will not be much influenced by it.[2] They conducted an experiment and found a curvilinear relation between discrepancy and opinion change. By "curvilinear," we mean that, as a small discrepancy increased somewhat, so did the degree of opinion change; but as the discrepancy continued to increase, opinion change began to slacken; and finally, as the discrepancy became large, the amount of opinion change became very small. When the discrepancy was very large, almost no opinion change was observed.

To see how it differs from the Zimbardo study, let's take a closer look at this mid-1950s experiment. The communication was based on a red-hot issue of the day, one the participants felt strongly about: whether their state of Oklahoma should remain "dry" or go "wet." The voters of the state were virtually equally divided on this issue, and the participants in the study were a representative sample: Some of the subjects felt strongly that the state should remain "dry" and continue to prohibit the distribution and sale of alcoholic beverages, others felt strongly it should go "wet," and the rest took a moderate position.

The members of each group were presented with communications supporting one of the three opinions, so that, in each group, there were some who found the communication close to their own position, some who found it moderately discrepant from their own position, and some who found it extremely discrepant from their own position. Specifically, some groups were presented with a "wet" message, which argued for the unlimited and unrestricted sale of liquor; some with a "dry" message, which argued for complete prohibition; and some with a moderately "wet" message, which argued for legalization of some drinking, but with certain controls and restrictions.

Unlike the Zimbardo study, Hovland, Harvey, and Sherif found that the greatest opinion changes occurred when there was a *moderate* discrepancy between the actual message and the opinions of individual members of the groups.

What an exciting state of affairs! In science, when there are a substantial number of research findings pointing in one direction and a similarly substantial number of research findings pointing in a different direction, it does not necessarily mean someone has to be wrong; rather, it suggests there is a significant factor that has not been accounted for—and this is indeed exciting, for it gives the scientist an opportunity to play detective.

We beg the reader's indulgence here, for we would like to dwell on this issue—not only for its substantive value, but also because it provides an opportunity to showcase one of the more adventurous aspects of social psychology as a science. Basically, there are two ways of doing the dectective work necessary to find the missing factor. We can begin by assembling all the experiments that show one result and all those that show the other result and (imaginary magnifying glass in hand) painstakingly scrutinize them, looking for the one factor common to the experiments in group A and lacking in group B; then we can try to determine, conceptually, why this factor should make a difference. Or, conversely, we can begin by speculating conceptually about what factor or factors might make a difference, then glance through the existing literature with this conceptual lantern in hand to see if the experiments in group A differ from the experiments in group B on this dimension.

Let's follow this second mode and speculate about what factor or factors might make such a difference. We can begin by accepting the notion discussed above: The greater the discrepancy, the greater the discomfort for the members of the audience. But this does not necessarily mean the members of an audience will change their opinion.

There are at least four ways in which the members of an audience can reduce their discomfort: (1) They can change their opinion; (2) they can induce the communicator to change his or her opinion; (3) they can seek support for their original opinion by finding other people who share their views, in spite of what the communicator says; or (4) they can derogate the communicator— convince themselves the communicator is stupid or immoral—and thereby invalidate that person's position.

In a great many situations, including those in these experiments, the message is delivered either as a written statement (as a newspaper or magazine article, for example) or by a communicator who is not approachable by the audience (as on television, on the lecture platform, and so on). Also, the subject is often either alone or is part of an audience whose members have no opportunity to interact with one another. Under these circumstances, it is virtually impossible for the recipients of the communication either to have immediate impact on the communicator's opinion or to seek immediate social support. This leaves the recipients two major ways of reducing this discomfort—they can change their opinion or they can derogate the communicator.

Under what circumstances would an individual find it easy or difficult to derogate the communicator? It would be very difficult to derogate a liked and respected personal friend; it would also be difficult to derogate someone who is a highly trustworthy expert on the issue under discussion. But if the communicator's credibility were questionable, it would be difficult not to derogate him or her. Following this line of reasoning, we suggest that, if a communicator's credibility were high, the greater the discrepancy between the communicator's opinions and the audience's opinions, the greater the influence exerted on the opinions of the audience. However, if the communicator's credibility were not very high, he or she would be, by definition, subject to derogation.

This is not to say that the communicator with lesser credentials could not influence the opinions of the audience. Such a communicator would probably be able to influence people to change their opinions if his or her opinions were not too different from theirs. But the more discrepant such a communicator's position is from those of the audience, the more the audience might begin to question the communicator's wisdom, intelligence, and sanity. The more they question, the less likely they are to be influenced.

Let's return to our example involving physical exercise: Imagine a 73-year-old man, with the body of a man half his age, who had just won the Boston Marathon. If he told us that a good way to stay in condition and live a long healthy life was to exercise vigorously for at least two hours every day, we would believe him. Boy, would we believe him! He would get much more exercise out of us than if he suggested we should exercise for only ten minutes a day.

But suppose a person somewhat less credible, such as a high school track coach, were delivering the communication. If he suggested we exercise ten minutes a day, his suggestion would be within our own latitude of acceptance and he might influence our opinion and behavior. But if he advised us to embark on a program of vigorous exercise requiring two hours every day, we would be inclined to write him off as a quack, a health freak, a monomaniac—and we could comfortably continue being indolent. Thus we would agree with Hovland, Harvey, and Sherif: People will consider an extremely discrepant communication to be outside their latitude of acceptance—but only if the communicator is not highly credible.

Armed with these speculations, we, with two students—Judith Turner and J. Merrill Carlsmith—scrutinized the existing experiments on this issue, paying special attention to the ways in which the communicator was described.[3] Lo and behold, we discovered that each of the experiments showing a direct linear relation between discrepancy and opinion change happened to describe the source of the communication as more credible than did those whose results showed a curvilinear relation.

We next constructed an experiment in which we systematically investigated the size of the discrepancy and the credibility of the communicator. In this experiment, women were asked to read several stanzas from obscure modern poetry and to rank them in terms of how good they were. Each woman was then given an essay to read purporting to be a criticism of modern poetry that specifically mentioned a stanza she had rated as poor. For some subjects, the essayist described this particular stanza in glowing terms—thus creating a large discrepancy between the opinion of the communicator and the opinion voiced by the subjects in this experimental condition. For some subjects, the essayist was only mildly favorable in the way he described the stanza—thus establishing a moderate discrepancy between the essayist and the subjects. In a third condition, the essayist was mildly scornful in his treatment of the stanza—thus placing the recipients of this communication in a situation of mild discrepancy. Finally, to half of the women in the experiment, the writer of the essay was identified as the poet T. S. Eliot, a highly credible poetry critic; to the other half of the subjects, the essay writer was identified as a college student.

The subjects were subsequently allowed to rank the stanzas once again. When T. S. Eliot was ostensibly the communicator, the essay had the most influence on the students when its evaluation of the stanza was most discrepant from theirs; when a fellow student of medium credibility was identified as the essayist, the essay produced a little opinion change when it was slightly discrepant from the opinion of the students, a great deal of change when it was moderately discrepant, and only a little opinion change when it was extremely discrepant.

The conflicting results are accounted for: When a communicator has high credibility, the greater the discrepancy between the view he or she advocates and the view of the audience, the more the audience will be persuaded; on the other hand, when a communicator's credibility is doubtful or slim, he or she will produce maximum opinion change at moderate discrepancies.

In this chapter, we have taken a slightly different approach to the topic of persuasion from that found in the rest of the book—here we saw it not from the propagandist's or the target's point of view, but from the perspective of a scientist. In other words, we sought to answer the question of what works, when, and how. This does not mean that the principles we discussed are not without their propaganda purposes—the politician, the advertiser, the salesclerk will all modulate their positions so as best to fit with those of the audience. We took this perspective, however, to provide a peek behind the scenes at how the principles of persuasion discussed throughout this book have been identified. The social psychologist's knowledge of persuasion has not developed from idle, armchair speculation. Each little fact about persuasion is often the result of extensive study and research, often performed by many researchers over many years. Such research is a vital antidote to the propaganda of our times. All of us owe it to ourselves to study the ways of persuasion, the good and the bad, so that we might better resist unwanted propaganda and better harness the types of persuasion that lead to fairer and better decisions.

22

PROTAGORAS' IDEAL: ONE-SIDED PUFFERY VERSUS TWO-SIDED DEBATE

The Greek historian Herodotus tells the following tale about the origins of the Persian war. In 480 B.C., Xerxes, the Persian leader, had decided to go to war against the Greek city-states in retaliation for their humiliating defeat of the Persians ten years earlier at Marathon. Artabus, Xerxes' uncle, argued against the war on the grounds that the Greek army and navy could easily defeat Persia. He began his speech with these words.

> O king, it is impossible, if not more than one opinion is uttered, to make choice of the best; a man is forced to follow whatever advice may have been given him; but if opposite speeches are delivered, then choice can be exercised. In like manner pure gold is not recognized by itself; but when we test it along with baser ore, we perceive which is the better.[1]

Artabus' words, at first, fell flat. Xerxes was filled with rage and publicly condemned Artabus for his disloyalty to Persia. However, after a period of "cooling off," Xerxes came around to Artabus' position and canceled the attack.

But then a strange event occurred. In the dead of night, Xerxes was visited repeatedly in a dream by a ghostly figure urging war. Haunted by the vision, Xerxes reversed himself once more. The Persians went to war against the Greeks and, after some initial victories, were soundly defeated. The Persian Empire went into decline, and the Greek city-states experienced their Golden Age. The moral of the story was not lost on Herodotus' Greek compatriots: Basing a course of action on irrational considerations results in disaster; full discussion and debate offers the possibility of choosing wisely in public affairs.

When it comes to persuasion, the early Greeks possessed a vision of the ideal. The sophist Protagoras believed that there are two sides to every issue. His fellow citizens agreed; they thought that persuasion happened best when all parties concerned knew both sides of the issue at hand. By juxtaposing one argument against an opposing one, the issue is made clear; the advantages and disadvantages of the available courses of action are revealed.

Aristotle made Protagoras' belief in the advantages of a two-sided message a component of his theory of effective communication.* The confrontation of opposites is a fundamental process of reasoning. As Aristotle put it, a two-sided message as

---

* Of course, consistent with Protagoras' belief that there are two sides to every issue, some Greeks argued that one-sided persuasion was best. Plato in his dialogues *Gorgias* and *Protagoras* chided the Sophists as "word tricksters and hucksters" who obscured the path to the one truth, or what has since become known as the Platonic ideal.

a form of speech is satisfying, because the significance of contrasted ideas is easily felt, especially when they are thus put side by
side, and also because it has the effect of a logical argument; it is by
putting two opposing conclusions side by side that you prove one of
them false.[2]

The influence of the Greek love for two-sided debate is still felt
today—somewhat. Rhetoric textbooks extol the communication that
explores carefully the pros and cons of an issue. The American
legal system is based on the ideal that each party to a litigation
should present its best case with a jury of peers deciding which side
of the issue will prevail. Contrast this with the first seventy-plus
years of the Soviet system, in which there was one truth embodied
in the Party and the State served as judge, jury, prosecutor, and
defense.

In our own century, the journalist Walter Lippmann argued that
opposing viewpoints are essential to democracy;[3] we learn most
from those who tell us what we don't know or don't find agreeable.
Reminiscent of the early Greeks, Lippmann believed that it was
only through listening to various positions on an issue that truth
could be found.

But Protagoras' ideal is a long way from the type of persuasion
one finds in the mass media today. The typical ad is one-sided and
consists of little information, much puffery, and many exaggerated
claims. "This pain reliever is gentler, faster, best." "Brand X will
take fat off fast." "You can't beat the taste of Brand Y." "Only
presidential candidate Z will strengthen defense, increase domestic
spending, and balance the budget (Congress willing)." For the most
part, debate and comparison are missing from today's persuasion
landscape.

Consider the simplest form of "debate"—one that hardly approaches the Greek ideal: the comparative advertisement, that is, an
ad that explicitly compares two or more brands of products on at least
one attribute. Studies have found that only 7% to 25% of all advertising in the major media is comparative in its claims.[4] Until recently, it
wasn't even possible for advertisers to present comparative ads. In the
early 1960s, major ad agencies and television networks strongly dis-

couraged comparative ads and the mentioning of a competitor's brand name on the grounds that it was unsporting. In 1964, NBC dropped its ban on such advertising, but the other two networks did not follow, thereby requiring an advertiser wishing to use a comparative campaign to create two separate ads—one for NBC and one for ABC and CBS. In the early 1970s, the Federal Trade Commission (FTC) threatened lawsuits over restraint of trade to force ABC, CBS, and the major advertisers to reverse their policy. The result, according to advertising historian Stephen Fox,[5] was an increase in comparative advertising and the development of a new philosophy of advertising termed *brand positioning*.[6]

According to the philosophy of brand positioning, market share can be gained by linking a product to one specific selling point or consumer benefit. One of the best ways to position a brand in the consumer's mind is to compare it with a competitor, especially if that competitor is well known. Some highly successful examples: 7-Up doubled its sales by calling itself the uncola in contrast to Coke; Tylenol became the number-one aspirin substitute by pointing out that "aspirin can irritate the stomach lining, trigger asthmatic or allergic reactions, and cause small amounts of gastrointestinal bleeding;" Scope improved its market share by claiming that Listerine produces *medicine breath*; Avis gained valuable ground on Hertz by arguing that because they were number two, they would try harder.

In all of these positioning ads, a comparison is made that makes the advertised brand appear superior. Of course, other contrasts can be made that would make it look inferior. For example, number-one Hertz may not need to overexert itself since it is already delivering what the consumer wants. Although brand positioning is comparative, it frequently makes comparisons on only a few advantageous dimensions and thus falls short of the Greek ideal of a full discussion of the pros and cons of an issue.

Given the complexity of many public issues, one would hope that the speeches of politicians and government officials would resemble more the ideals of Protagoras than the practices of consumer advertisers. Alas, the structure of modern mass media does not always facilitate the ideal. It is difficult to contrast opposing

viewpoints in a thirty-second advertisement or a network news sound-
bite. Indeed, the 1988 presidential campaign looked more like an
advertising campaign positioning brands than a classical debate. Bush
and Dukakis each attempted to draw simple contrasts by positioning
their opponents as the "ACLU liberal" and the "rich boy who became
a wimp," while larger issues such as the budget deficit, education,
child welfare, and foreign policy, to name just a few, were not critically
discussed.

In all fairness to Mr. Dukakis, he did attempt, early in the campaign, to discuss some issues in detail. In one such attempt, he
proposed a new plan to make a college education more affordable.
However, the news media elected to cover the anti-abortion hecklers

in the audience when Dukakis first presented his plan, as opposed to covering the substantive details. Apparently, the networks felt that hecklers make for more entertaining news.

Is it possible ever for a two-sided argument to be more persuasive than a one-sided message? Or to put it more bluntly, what factors make a one-sided argument so effective that they seem to be the tactic of choice for most modern propagandists. To sharpen our understanding of the uses and abuses of one- and two-sided communications, let's examine the conditions under which each is most persuasive.

Suppose you are about to make a speech attempting to persuade your audience that more spending on education is necessary or that the budget deficit should be reduced through cuts in domestic spending. Would you persuade more people if you simply stated your view and ignored the arguments against your position, or would you be more persuasive if you discussed the opposing arguments and attempted to refute them?

Before trying to answer this question, let's look closely at the factors involved. If a communicator mentions the opposition's arguments, it might indicate that he or she is an objective, fair-minded person; this could enhance the speaker's trustworthiness and thus increase his or her effectiveness. On the other hand, if a communicator so much as mentions the arguments on the other side of the issue, it might suggest to the audience that the issue is a controversial one; this could confuse members of the audience, make them vacillate, induce them to search for counterarguments, and ultimately reduce the persuasiveness of the communication.

With these possibilities in mind, it should not come as a surprise to the reader that there is no simple relation between one-sided arguments and the effectiveness of the communication. It depends to some extent upon how well informed the audience is and on the audience's initial opinions on the issue.

Research generally finds that the more well informed the members of the audience are, the less likely they are to be persuaded by a one-sided argument and the more likely they are to be persuaded by an argument that brings out the important opposing arguments and then attempts to refute them.[7] This makes sense: A well-informed person is more likely to know some of the counterarguments; when the communicator avoids mentioning these, the knowledgeable members of the audience are likely to conclude that the communicator is either unfair or is unable to refute such arguments. On the other hand, an uninformed person is less apt to know of the existence of opposing arguments. If the counterargument is ignored, the less-informed members of the audience are persuaded; if the counterargument is presented, they might get confused.

The message-dense nature of the mass media often makes it difficult to respond intelligently to what we receive. It takes considerable mental effort to process effectively the stream of one short message after another. Advertisers have observed that consumers frequently find comparative advertising confusing; they mistake one brand for another, leading to a situation in which the advertiser is publicizing the competition. For this reason, comparative advertising is rarely used by the leading brand (why give a new upstart free publicity?); it is used mostly by a challenger that might gain from being confused with the leader. For example, in the domain of fast-food burgers, Burger King and Wendy's often compare themselves with the market leader, McDonald's, which never mentions its competitors. Pepsi often mentions Coke; the reverse is almost never true. In the domain of political campaigns, attack advertising is most often used by the challenger, not the incumbent, and by a candidate who is behind or slipping in the polls.[8] In the confusing, message-dense environment of the mass media, one-sided messages make sense for all but a few propagandists.

Another factor influencing the effectiveness of one- versus two-sided persuasion is the partisanship of the audience. As we might expect, if a member of the audience is already predisposed to believe the communicator's argument, a one-sided presentation has a greater impact on his or her opinion than a two-sided presentation. If, however, a member of the audience is leaning in the opposite direction, then a two-sided refutational argument is more persuasive. We should underscore that the research does not favor the effectiveness of a simple two-sided argument: It favors the effectiveness of presenting both sides and pointing out the weaknesses in your opponent's position.

Most politicians seem to be well aware of the partisanship phenomenon; they tend to present vastly different kinds of speeches, depending upon who constitutes the audience. When talking to the party faithful, they almost invariably deliver a hell-raising set of arguments favoring their own party platform and candidacy. If they do mention the opposition, it is in a derisive, mocking tone. On the other hand, when appearing on network television or when speaking to any audience of mixed loyalties, they tend to take a more diplomatic position, giving the opposing view a less emotional airing.

The evidence about the conditions under which a two-sided communication is more effective is a cause for concern for those who appreciate the ideal of Protagoras. The message-dense environment of the mass media is not conducive to thoughtful, intelligent processing of message content. The ease with which television channels can be switched means we can easily find the most agreeable and entertaining message. Competing in this environment, communicators may come to rely more and more on the one-sided, partisan communication, reducing further the audience's understanding of the issues of the day.

All is not lost for those who favor the Greek ideal of persuasion—after all, there are two sides to every issue. During the 1988 presidential campaign, the League of Women Voters refused to sponsor the presidential debates, as they traditionally had done. The reason: The political pundits had designed the rules of the debate so that true discussion could not occur; the candidates were thus free to deliver their one-sided stump speeches and were never placed in danger of being embarrassed by a careful comparison of their positions on the issues.

The success, albeit limited, of the FTC in the 1970s in increasing the number of comparative advertisements on television suggests that the League of Women Voters may be on the right track. John Chancellor, the NBC news commentator, would take it one step further. Given that American taxpayers, through funding laws, now pay for a major chunk of the campaign, taxpayers are entitled to determine the campaign rules and norms. Chancellor argues that the government should no longer provide money for thirty-second spots and sound-bites. In their place would be taxpayer supported debates, press conferences, and forums that would lead to in-depth discussions.

By paying attention to the form and style of the persuasive message, we can get the type of persuasion a democracy requires. Perhaps one attribute of a communicator's credibility should be the degree to which he or she considers and communicates fairly and intelligently both (or even multiple) sides of an important issue. The next time a presidential candidate tries to terminate debate and discussion by responding to an opponent's challenge with the words "There you go again," as Ronald Reagan did to Jimmy Carter in the 1980 presidential debates, perhaps the best response, regardless of our own position, would be to jeer and laugh as the early Greeks might have done. After all, whose intelligence is being insulted when debate is limited to a one-sided communication?

EMOTIONAL APPEALS: TOUCH THE HEART, PERSUADE THE MIND

THE FEAR APPEAL

In 1741, in the small New England town of Enfield, Jonathan Edwards delivered a sermon entitled "Sinners in the Hands of an Angry God." In this sermon, he preached:

> Thus it is that natural men are held in the hand of God, over the pit of hell; they have deserved the fiery pit, and are already sentenced to it...the devil is waiting for them, hell is gaping for them, the flames gather and flash about them, and would fain lay hold on them, and swallow them up....In short, they have no refuge, nothing to take hold of; all that preserves them every moment is the mere arbitrary will, and uncovenanted, unobliged forbearance of an incensed God.[1]

Eyewitness accounts indicate that the sermon left the congregation "breathing of distress and weeping." The records show that thousands gave over their lives to Christ as part of the Great Awakening of eighteenth-century America.

Two centuries later, in 1932, Adolf Hitler inspired his fellow countrymen and women with the words:

> The streets of our country are in turmoil. The universities are filled with students rebelling and rioting. Communists are seeking to destroy our country. Russia is threatening us with her might, and the Republic is in danger. Yes—danger from within and without. We need law and order! Without it our nation cannot survive.[2]

Millions of Germans gladly embraced Hitler's National Socialist party.

Although the goals of Edwards and Hitler were quite different, their method was the same—instilling fear. Both Edwards and Hitler threatened their audiences with dire consequences if, of course, a certain course of action was not followed.

Ministers and politicians are not the only ones who arouse fear in order to motivate and persuade. Life insurance agents use fear to induce purchase of their policies; parents use fear to persuade their children to come home early from a date; and physicians use fear to insure that patients adopt and maintain a prescribed medical regimen. Sometimes these fear appeals are based on legitimate concerns— smoking does cause cancer; "unsafe sex" increases one's chance of contracting AIDS; failure to brush and floss can led to painful tooth decay. But often fear appeals are based on dark, irrational fears—fears stemming from racial prejudice or the notion that there is a communist under every bed. At times a regime instills fear by terrorizing its own citizens, as in Hitler's Germany, Stalin's Soviet Union, Argentina of the junta, Hussein's Iraq, and at countless often times and places. Fear appeals are powerful because they channel our thoughts away from careful consideration of the issue at hand and toward plans for ridding ourselves of the fear. When illegitimate fears are used, the message promotes deception—not to mention the cruelty of the fear itself. It behooves us to look closely at just when and how fear appeals are effective.

Not all fear appeals are successful in obtaining their objectives. For the past few years, public service announcements have alerted viewers to the dangers of drug abuse and cigarette use and have frightened Americans about the possibility of contracting AIDS. Opponents of the nuclear arms race have often painted a graphic picture of nuclear winter. Yet drug abuse and cigarette smoking remain *high*, the practice of safe sex *low*, and the possibility of world annihilation through the use of nuclear weapons ever present. Just what are the factors that make a fear-arousing appeal more or less effective?

Let's begin with a seemingly simple question: Suppose you wish to arouse fear in the hearts of your audience as a way of inducing opinion change. Would it be more effective to arouse just a little fear, or should you try to scare the hell out of them?

For example, if your goal is to convince people to drive more carefully, would it be more effective to show them gory technicolor films of the broken and bloody bodies of highway accident victims, or would it be more effective if you soft-pedaled your communication— showing crumpled fenders, discussing increased insurance rates due to careless driving, and pointing out the possibility that people who drive carelessly may have their driver's licenses suspended?

Common sense argues on both sides of this street. On the one hand, it suggests that a good scare will motivate people to action; on the other hand, it argues that too much fear can be debilitating—that is, it might interfere with a person's ability to pay attention to the message, to comprehend it, and to act upon it. We have all believed, at one time or another, that it only happens to the other guy, it can't happen to me. Thus people continue to drive at very high speeds and to insist on driving after they've had a few drinks, even though they should know better. Perhaps this is because the possible negative consequences of these actions are so great that we try not to think about them. Thus, if a communication arouses extreme fear, we tend *not* to pay close attention to it.

What does the evidence tell us? Experimental data overwhelmingly suggest that all other things being equal, the more frightened a person is by a communication, the more likely he or she is to take positive preventive action.

The most prolific researchers in this area have been Howard Leventhal and his associates.[3] In one experiment, they tried to induce people to stop smoking and to obtain chest X-rays. Some subjects were exposed to a low-fear treatment: They were simply presented with a recommendation to stop smoking and get their chests X-rayed. Others were subjected to moderate fear: They were shown a film depicting a young man whose chest X-rays revealed he had lung cancer. The people subjected to the high-fear condition saw the same film the "moderate-fear" people saw—and, in addition, they were treated to a vivid, gory color film of a lung cancer operation. The results showed that those people who were most frightened were also most eager to stop smoking and most likely to sign up for chest X-rays.

Is this true for all people? It is not. There is good reason why common sense can lead us to believe that a great deal of fear leads to inaction: It does—for certain people, under certain conditions.

What Leventhal and his colleagues discovered is that the people who had a reasonably good opinion of themselves (high self-esteem) were the ones most likely to be moved by high degrees of fear arousal. People with low opinions of themselves were the least likely to take immediate action when confronted with a communication arousing a great deal of fear—but (and here is the interesting part) after a delay, they behaved very much like the subjects with high self-esteem. People who have a low opinion of themselves may have difficulty coping with threats to themselves. A high-fear communication overwhelms them and makes them feel like crawling into bed and pulling the covers up over their heads. Low or moderate fear is something they can more easily deal with at the moment they experience it. But, given time—that is, if it is not essential they act immediately—they will be more likely to act if the message truly scared the hell out of them.

Subsequent research by Leventhal and his colleagues lends support to this analysis. In one study, subjects were shown films of serious automobile accidents. Some subjects watched the films on a large screen from up close; others watched them from far away on a much smaller screen. Among those subjects with high or moderate self-esteem, those who saw the films on the large screen were much more likely to take subsequent protective action than were those who saw the films on the small screen. Subjects with low self-esteem were more likely to take action when they saw the films on a small screen; those who saw the films on a large screen reported a great deal of fatigue and stated they had great difficulty even thinking of themselves as victims of automobile accidents.

It should be relatively easy to make people with high self-esteem behave like people with low self-esteem. We can overwhelm them by making them feel there is nothing they can do to prevent or ameliorate a threatening situation. Much research has shown that if recipients of a fear appeal perceive that there is no way to cope effectively with the threat, they are not likely to respond to the appeal but will just bury their heads in the sand—even those who have high self-esteem.[4] Franklin D. Roosevelt knew the debilitating effect of extreme fear and sought to counteract it when he announced in his first inaugural address, "The only thing we have to fear is fear itself."

Conversely, suppose you wanted to reduce the automobile accident rate or to help people give up smoking, and you were faced with low self-esteem people. How would you proceed? If you were to construct a message containing clear, specific, and optimistic instructions, it might increase the feeling among the members of your audience that they could confront their fears and cope with the danger.

These speculations have been confirmed; experiments by Howard Leventhal and his colleagues show that fear-arousing messages containing specific instructions about how, when, and where to take action are much more effective than recommendations that omit such instructions. For example, a campaign conducted on a college campus urging students to get tetanus shots included specific instructions about where and when they were available. The campaign materials included a map showing the location of the student health service and a suggestion that each student set aside a convenient time to stop by.

The results showed high-fear appeals to be more effective than low-fear appeals in producing favorable *attitudes* toward tetanus shots among the students, and they also increased the students' stated intentions to get the shots. The highly specific instructions about how to get the shots did not affect these opinions and intentions, but the instructions did have a big effect on the *actual behavior*: Of those subjects who were instructed about how to proceed, 28% actually got the tetanus shots; but of those who received no specific instructions, only 3% got them. In a control group exposed only to the instructions, with no fear-arousing message, no one got the shots. Thus specific instructions alone were not enough to produce action—fear was a necessary component for action in such situations.

Very similar results were obtained in Leventhal's cigarette experiment. Leventhal found that a high-fear communication produced a much greater *intention* to stop smoking. Unless it was accompanied by recommendations for specific behavior, however, it produced little results. Similarly, specific instructions (buy a magazine instead of a pack of cigarettes, drink plenty of water when you have the urge to smoke, and so on) without a fear-arousing communication were relatively ineffective. The combination of fear arousal and specific instructions produced the best results; the students in this condition were smoking less four months after they were subjected to the experimental procedure.

In sum, a fear appeal is most effective when (1) it *scares* the hell out of people, (2) it offers a *specific recommendation* for overcoming the fear-arousing threat, (3) the recommended action is perceived as effective for reducing the threat, and (4) the message recipient believes that he or she *can* perform the recommended action.

This is exactly what Jonathan Edwards and Adolf Hitler offered their listeners. Both men described rising menaces—sin or communism—that, if allowed free rein, would devastate the soul or the national spirit. Each man offered a specific remedy for the crisis—commitment to Christ or joining the Nazi party. These courses of action were easy enough to perform—one needed only to answer the altar call or to vote for a Nazi candidate.

In contrast, fear appeals to increase nuclear disarmament or to decrease drug abuse rarely incorporate all four components of a successful fear appeal. We have all been alerted to the dread of nuclear winter and the personal and social destruction of drug abuse. However, there have been few specific recommendations for removing these threats that have been generally perceived as *effective* and *doable*.

Two counterexamples of effective anti-nuclear arms appeals will make our point. First, during the 1950s and early 1960s, many people purchased and installed "nuclear fallout shelters" in their homes. The reason: Fear of nuclear war was high and the installation of a home fallout shelter, at the time, appeared to be an effective, doable response.

Second, during the 1964 presidential campaign, Lyndon Johnson, in a series of television ads, was able to sway voters by portraying his opponent, Barry Goldwater, as a supporter of the use of nuclear weapons. One controversial ad featured a young girl counting to ten as she pulled petals from a daisy. A moment later, the television screen filled with the mushroom cloud of a nuclear bomb. Johnson's appeal was successful because it linked the fear of nuclear war to Goldwater and then proposed a vote for Johnson as a specific, doable way to avoid this threat.

Or consider the recent campaign to reduce the incidence of drug abuse by telling kids to "just say no." Although many children and teenagers are probably frightened by the drug scene, "just saying no" is not perceived as an effective and doable response. Imagine yourself as a teenager whose friends are pressuring you to try cocaine. Just saying no is likely to result in even more pressure—"Come on, just one try. What are you? A fraidy-cat?" Such pressure is not easy to resist.

The drug problem, given its scope and complexity, will require more than just a cleverly worded advertisement to solve. However, we can design our appeals so that they are more effective. For example, recently a teacher asked her elementary school class to come up with specific ways to say no when their friends pressure them to use drugs.

The students produced a book of "ways to say no"—for example, walking away, calling the dealer the fraidy-cat, offering the friend an alternative to doing drugs. Such an approach has the advantage of "self-selling" the class not to use drugs and also provides a list of specific ways that children will perceive as effective for dealing with peer pressure; such a list can then be illustrated on television or role-played in the schools. But in the final analysis, for our fear appeals to work, we need to offer our children a more effective and doable solution to life's problems than the advice to "just say no."

But there is a broader question: Should fear appeals be used at all? Given the power of fear to motivate and direct our thoughts, there is much potential for abuse. Illegitimate fears can always be invented for any given propaganda purpose. As persuaders, it is our responsibility, if we decide to use a fear appeal, to insure that the fear we instill is, at least, legitimate and that it serves to alert the target to potential dangers as opposed to obscuring the issue with emotion. As targets of such appeals, we owe it to ourselves to first ask, "How legitimate is this fear?" before taking the propagandist's bait.

24

THE GRANFALLOON TECHNIQUE

"My God," she said, "are you a Hoosier?"

I admitted I was.

"I'm a Hoosier, too," she crowed. "Nobody has to be ashamed of being a Hoosier."

"I'm not," I said. "I never knew anybody who was."

—Kurt Vonnegut, *Cat's Cradle*

One of the most interesting and often most unbelievable set of findings in social psychology is induced by what has come to be known as the *minimum group paradigm*, which forms the basis of an emotionally powerful persuasive technique. In this procedure, first identified by the British social psychologist Henri Tajfel, complete strangers are formed into groups using the most trivial, inconsequential criteria imaginable.[1] For example, in one study, subjects watched a coin toss that randomly assigned them to Group X or Group W. In another study, subjects were first asked to express their opinions about painters they had never heard of and were then randomly assigned either to a group that appreciates Klee or to one that enjoys Kandinsky, ostensibly due to their picture preferences. To use a term coined by the American novelist Kurt Vonnegut, Tajfel and his colleagues are creating *granfalloons*—proud and meaningless associations of human beings.[2]

What makes Tajfel's research so curious are the results that are often obtained. Despite the fact that the subjects were total strangers prior to the study, that they had never interacted with one another and never would, and that their actions were completely anonymous, they acted as if those who shared their meaningless label were their good friends or close kin. Subjects indicated that they liked those who shared their label. They rated others who shared their label as more likely to have a pleasant personality and to have produced better output than out-group members. Most strikingly, subjects allocated more money and rewards to those group members who shared their label and did so in a competitive manner—for example, subjects were more likely to prefer giving fellow group members $2 and the "other" group $1 rather than giving their group $3 and the other group $4.

What makes the granfalloon tick? Researchers have uncovered two basic psychological processes, one cognitive and one motivational. First, the knowledge that "I am in this group" is used to divide up and make sense of the world, much in the same way that words and labels can be used to pre-persuade (see Chapter 5). Differences *between* groups are exaggerated, whereas similarity among members of the granfalloon are emphasized in the secure knowledge that "this is what our type does." One serious consequence is that out-group members are dehumanized; they are represented in our mind by a simple, often derogatory label—gook, jap, backward southerner, kike, nigger—as opposed to unique individuals—Nguyen, Susumu, Anthony, Elliot, Doug. It is a lot easier to abuse an abstraction. Second, social groups are a source of self-esteem and pride, a form of reverse Groucho Marxism—"I'd be more than happy to join a club that would

GROUP PORTRAIT OF FIFTEEN TOTAL STRANGERS WHO JUST HAPPENED TO BE ON THE SAME BUS

have me as a member."* To obtain the self-esteem the group has to offer, members come to defend the group and adopt its symbols, rituals, and beliefs.

Herein lies the secret to the persuasiveness of the granfalloon. If the professional persuader, the advertiser, the politician, the televangelist can get us to accept his or her granfalloons, then we have a ready-made way to make sense of our lives—the propagandist's way—and as our self-esteem becomes increasingly linked to these groups, we have a strong motivation to defend the group and to go to great lengths proudly to adopt its customs. What the propagandist is really saying is: "You are on my side (never mind that I created the teams); now act like it and do what we say." Let's look at some specific examples of how granfalloons can be used to persuade.[3]

---

* Based on one of Groucho Marx's legendary statements. On learning that he was admitted to an exclusive club, he remarked, "I would not want to belong to a club that would have *me* as a member."

A study by Robert Cialdini and his colleagues[4] illustrates the attraction power of a granfalloon. Every autumn Saturday, many of America's universities and colleges battle it out on the gridiron— half win and the other half lose. Cialdini and his colleagues counted the number of college sweatshirts worn on the Monday following a football game at seven universities that take football seriously— Arizona State, Louisiana State, Notre Dame, Michigan, Ohio State, Pittsburgh, and Southern California. The results: more students wore their university insignias after a victory, and especially after a big win. Nothing succeeds like a winning granfalloon. Is it any wonder that advertisers pay dearly to link their products with winners, such as Michael Jordan for sneakers or Christy Brinkley for makeup, and to create merchandise-selling granfalloons based on a designer label, movies such as *Batman* or *Dick Tracy*, or the latest Saturday morning cartoon?

Sometimes granfalloons come ready-made. In recent decades, marketers have put forth extraordinary effort to classify America into groups and lifestyles, with the goal of designing communications and products to fit each group.[5] For example, one scheme advanced by the Claritas Corporation divides America into 40 neighborhood types based on values, lifestyles, income, and so on. You could be a member of the "Young Influentials," "Blue-collar Nursery," or "Blue-blood Estates." Each group is associated with a certain self-image and lifestyle. Advertising and products are then targeted to profitable markets. In other words, products are given a "personality" that fits the image of the target market; this advertising then goes on to create further the image of each granfalloon by specifying what needs to be done to maintain a certain image.

When ready-made groups don't exist, the skilled propagandist can create them by inventing new distinctions or by emphasizing old, forgotten ones, just as Tajfel and his colleagues have done in their laboratories.

A trip with a friend of ours to purchase a microwave oven illustrates the invention of a granfalloon in a sales situation. He loves to cook. In contrast, his wife, who accompanied him on this shopping trip, is of the mind that a woman's place (especially this one's) is not necessarily in the kitchen, but in the office. As is common, the salesman began by directing his pitch about the advantages of microwave cooking to the female. The salesman was abruptly informed by the wife, "He does the cooking; you should tell him about it." The salesman, without breaking stride, turned to our friend, positioning his body so that a two-person group was formed, and said: "That's great. I think it's wonderful that more men are cooking. There's nothing I like better than to get in the kitchen and do some cooking myself." The inherent persuasive message: "We share the same attitudes; we are of the same type; trust me!"

Shared emotion and feeling can also create a granfalloon. A sense of oneness with others can be produced by sharing a fun time, a sad situation, or a harrowing experience. Kathleen Hall Jamieson identifies this as one skill that made Ronald Reagan so persuasive a president—the ability to express the emotions we are currently feeling or would like to feel.[6] Reagan's speeches often described the emotional experiences of others—what it felt like to carry the Olympic torch; the feelings of a family as they watched their only son go off to war; the experience of a daughter who honored her promise to her father, a World War II veteran, to visit the beach at Normandy. By expressing our common feelings, Reagan provided the nation with a sense of unity and, not inconsequentially, made an attack on the teflon president seem tantamount to attacking ourselves.

Office politics provide yet another arena for the granfalloon technique. One common ploy used by organizational politicians is to create personal fiefdoms, complete with their own agenda and goals and, of course, enemies. For example, an office gamesplayer may rally the troops by declaring it is us against them—the marketing department versus production, the psychiatrists versus the psychologists, the city versus the college. Once the identities are fixed, the agenda is set.

Often workplace distinctions can be so trivial that they are not easily understood by an outside observer or a new group member. The cunning office politician may be so bold as to create temporary, fluctuating group identities. For example, today's Machiavellian may set one group against another by going to one person and saying "we women must stick together," to another and saying "we newcomers have to watch out for the old guard," and to a third and saying "those of us with an eye to the bottom line better pull together on this one"—all in an attempt to secure allegiance to a proposal.

Another office persuasion tactic is subtly to change a person's gran-falloon—a technique often known as *co-option*. This tactic is often used to squelch opposition. For example, consider a social activist who has been highly critical of a corporation's policies or a feminist who argues that his or her university's hiring practices are discriminatory. The cor-poration or university then gives the critic a new position, often highly visible, but without real power within the organization—for example, a place on the board of directors or appointment as head of a woman's affairs center. The position usually comes with a nice office, secretaries, letterhead, stationery, and maybe even a parking place. Gradually, the critic becomes increasingly isolated from old "activist" friends and in-creasingly dependent on the corporation or university for material resour-ces and a sense of identity. The opposition is defused.

Tragically, granfalloons are not limited to business offices but can appear at national and international political levels, where the stakes are much higher. Adolf Hitler was able to create a strong German identity by manufacturing a "Jewish" and a "communist" threat and by emphasizing a common "Aryan" heritage. During the Cold War, American and Soviet propagandists portrayed each other as im-perialistic warmongers with little regard for human rights and dig-nities. Once such identities form, the right and moral course of action becomes abundantly clear.

The modern masters of the granfalloon are televangelists—Chris-tian fundamentalist ministers such as Oral Roberts, Pat Robertson, Jimmy Swaggart, and Jim and Tammy Bakker, who use television to promote not only the gospel but, also, with rapid-fire frequency, their sales message.[7] For example, one study looking at the content of Christian programs found that a typical show makes requests for donations averaging $189.52 per hour, with the average Bible selling for a "pricey" $191.91. (Jerry Falwell wins the title of "God's biggest solicitor," offering Bibles, books, tapes, and other religious trinkets for sale at a rate of $1,671.00 per hour.) The results are quite profitable. In 1980, the top four religious programs took in over a quarter of a billion dollars, with the Jimmy Swaggart Ministry alone collecting more than $60 million in 1982. They succeed by defining the image of a "Christian" and then using the electronic media to create a "family of believers," based on this image.

Roughly 10 million Americans (or 4% of the U.S. population) regularly watch Christian programming. Although this is a large number of viewers (it is estimated that Jesus preached to no more than 30,000 souls in his entire lifetime), it is not exactly a moral majority, but more like, in marketing terms, a small but potentially profitable market segment. Who, then, are the members of the electronic church? Surveys and interviews reveal two broad categories of viewers: persons who are already converted to Christianity and those who are lonely and isolated or have recently suffered a loss, such as a personal disability or the death of a loved one. The success of Christian programming lies in directly matching the needs of both types of viewers.

The electronic church creates a "Christian identity" for its viewers. The identity, most clearly expressed by the minister-leader, comes complete with political attitudes (typically conservative ones, such as anti-abortion, anti-Soviet, pro-military intervention), religious beliefs (a literal interpretation of the Bible, the principle of "seed-faith"), shared feelings (the joy of a spontaneous, televised healing; the tears of Tammy Bakker), goals (the creation of a Christian nation, ridding the nation's schools of evolutionary teaching, returning prayer to the classroom), enemies (secular humanists; liberal politicians; at least until recently, the Supreme Court; homosexuals; intellectuals), and rituals and symbols (the 700 Club, PTL bumper stickers and buttons, "speaking in tongues").

For those who already believe, Christian broadcasting becomes a means for further expressing their identity. For those who are lonely or have suffered a loss, it is a way to replace, repair, or rationalize a self-conception that may be damaged by loss of job status or a close family member. A satisfying self-identity as one of "God's chosen people" can be obtained by watching, subscribing, donating, and adopting the behaviors suggested by religious programs. This image can then be used by the televangelist to sell and market products and ideas.

Given the booming buzz of modern reality, it is perfectly human to try to reduce the vast amounts of information we receive to a more manageable level by categorizing and labeling it. It is also perfectly human to want to belong to groups and to be proud of membership in these groups. Such feelings can have positive consequences: "We Are the World" and Jerry Lewis telethons have raised millions of dollars for worthy causes by tapping into our self-images as global, caring citizens. Many church and synagogue members find great meaning and religious identification in feeding the hungry, caring for the less fortunate, and taking the plank out of their own eye first.

At other times, however, granfalloons can be manipulated to get us to purchase unwanted products, to vote for less-than-qualified candidates, and to hate innocent people. What can be done to lessen the chances of falling prey to the granfalloon tactic?

Here are five simple rules of thumb that might help. First, be wary of those who attempt to create minimum groups and to define you as a member of a certain category. There are many ways to define and label a person. Ask yourself, "Why is this particular label being suggested?" Second, follow the old civil rights motto, "Keep your eye on the prize." Try linking your self-esteem to achieving an objective—be it a quality purchase at a reasonable price or a social good—rather than maintaining a self-image. Third, don't put all of your self-esteem eggs in one basket, one granfalloon—it might lead to fanaticism. Fourth, look for common ground—goals that might be acceptable to both the in- and the out-group—as a means of reducing the importance of group boundaries. And finally, try to think of an out-group member as an individual, someone who may share more in common with you than you might have previously thought.

25
GUILT SELLS

In a recent Girl Scout cookie sales drive, thirteen-year-old Elizabeth Brinton sold 11,200 boxes of cookies. When asked how she did it, Brinton replied, "You have to look people in the eye and make them feel guilty."

Guilt sells—a fact of persuasive life that seems to be intuitively grasped by parents, teachers, clergy, charities, and life insurance agents. But guilt, the feeling that we are responsible for some wrongdoing, can be used to sell more than cookies and life insurance. Guilt can cost you your freedom, as young Brad Page recently found out.

It was the morning of November 4, 1984, and Brad and his fiancée, Bibi Lee, both students at the University of California, had decided to go jogging with their friend Robin in Redwood Park in Oakland. Brad and Robin, both strong runners, lost sight of Bibi after a few miles and stopped to wait for her to catch up. After waiting for several minutes, they became concerned, doubled back, and began to search for her.

The park is a large one, with several trails that wind through the woods. Brad and Robin surmised that Bibi might mistakenly have wandered off the main trail. When they couldn't find her, they decided to head back to the parking lot and wait near the car, thinking that she would eventually head there. After a long wait, Brad decided that it would be more efficient if he searched for her by car, so he asked Robin to wait in the lot in case Bibi came looking for them, while he drove around the perimeter of the park.

After about fifteen minutes, he returned, reporting that he was still unable to find her. They waited for her for another half hour or so. Then Brad suggested that they drive back home. He felt that Bibi could easily hop a bus back to Berkeley; besides, he later admitted, he was feeling a little annoyed at Bibi because he suspected that she might have disappeared on purpose in order to punish him for a minor squabble they had had earlier that day.

Five weeks later, Bibi's body was found in a shallow grave in a wooded area of Redwood Park. Who killed Bibi Lee? It might have been a serial killer who had been active in the area. Indeed, an eyewitness reported seeing a burly, bearded man (fitting the description of the serial killer) dragging a young woman fitting Bibi's description into a van; at the time the witness wasn't certain whether it was a playful or an aggressive act, so she didn't bother to report the incident until after she read about Bibi's disappearance.

But as time progressed, and there were no hot suspects, the police asked Brad Page to come in for additional questioning. Their reasoning was that he might have found Bibi during the fifteen minutes that he left Robin waiting in the parking lot—and, in a fit of anger, might have killed her. After inducing Brad to waive his right to an attorney ("we're all friends, here, aren't we?"), the police interrogators had him go over his story several times. During the interrogation, they kept asking him how he could possibly have left his girlfriend alone in the park and driven back home.* Brad felt terribly guilty about it, saying several times, "It was the biggest mistake of my life!" Each time they asked the question, his guilt seemed to grow.

Finally, the interrogators told Brad that late on the night that Bibi had disappeared he had been seen near the site of the shallow grave and that his fingerprints had been found on a rock that had been used as the murder weapon. Neither of these statements was true. Brad said that he had no recollection of having left his apartment that night and had no idea how his fingerprints could have gotten on the murder weapon (he didn't even know what the weapon was). But he had no reason to distrust the interrogators, so, understandably, he became terribly confused and asked them if it is possible for a person to commit a horrible crime like this and "blank it out." The interrogators informed him that such things were common occurrences and that it might help him recall the circumstances and ultimately might help him relieve his *guilty* conscience if he closed his eyes and tried to imagine how he *might* have killed Bibi *if he had killed her*.** Brad proceeded to do as he was told, inventing what he later described as an imaginative scenario. Two hours after his alleged confession, when he was told that the police considered it to be a confession, he seemed genuinely astonished and immediately recanted.

The police continued to consider this to be a confession, even though a great many important details did not coincide with the actual physical evidence. Brad Page was indicted for first-degree murder. The jury was unable to decide whether or not the confession was real, and a mistrial was declared. In a second trial, the jury was similarly confused; they deliberated for six days before finally deciding that

---

* One of the authors (EA) subsequently testified at Brad Page's trial as an expert witness on noncoercive persuasion, and, accordingly, was given access to the audiotapes of the interrogation.

** It should be noted that this is the one aspect of the interrogation that was disputed; the interrogators deny that they stated these instructions in a hypothetical manner, whereas Brad Page insists that they did. Unfortunately, the police had turned off the tape recorder during this part of the interrogation, so it is impossible to obtain objective evidence on this disagreement.

while he was not guilty of murder, he *was* guilty of manslaughter! The verdict is currently under appeal.

We are in no position to state with certainty whether or not Brad Page killed Bibi Lee. But we do have a pretty good idea of why he complied with the police request to imagine how he might have killed Bibi. Guilt, whether real or imagined, often leads to compliance. During the interrogation, Brad Page was made to feel very guilty about how he had driven off and left Bibi alone. It is conceivable that the feelings of guilt helped to make him susceptible to the influence of his interrogators.

The effects of guilt on compliance have been isolated in a very clever set of experiments performed by Merrill Carlsmith and Alan Gross.[1] In their studies, subjects were induced to deliver a series of painful electric shocks to another individual as part of an experment on teaching. (In actuality no shocks were received, but the subjects were led to believe that the shocks were real.) Such an experience would undoubtedly lead the participants to feel guilty about their behavior. Other "not-guilty" subjects were merely instructed to ring a buzzer to indicate a wrong answer. All subjects were then asked by the shock "victim" to make phone calls on behalf of a "Save the Redwood Forest" committee. The results showed that subjects who were induced to feel guilt were three times as likely to comply with the request than were the not-guilty subjects. Guilt sells!

Why is guilt so effective in motivating human behavior? Carlsmith and Gross reasoned that there are at least three possible explanations for why guilt sells: (1) *sympathy*, or feeling sorry for the victim; (2) *restitution*, or feeling the need to compensate for the wrongdoing; and (3) *generalized guilt*, or the desire to repair a self-image tarnished by a transgression.

A second study by Carlsmith and Gross teased apart these three explanations by varying who was transgressing against whom. To induce sympathy for the victim, some subjects first watched someone else supposedly shocking a third person and then were asked by the shock "victim" to help save the redwoods. To induce a need for restitution, other subjects were first led to believe they were shocking a person and later were asked by this "victim" to help save the redwoods. To induce generalized guilt, a third group of subjects were also led to believe that they were shocking a person, but this time the request to save the redwoods came from another individual who was unrelated to the administering of shocks. The results showed little compliance by those subjects who felt only sympathy for the victim. However, those subjects who either felt a need for restitution or who were experiencing generalized guilt were significantly more likely to volunteer to make more phone calls in an attempt to save the redwood forests.

The power of guilt to convict and to persuade stems, as with most emotional appeals, from its power to direct our thoughts and to channel our energies. When we feel guilty we typically pay little attention to the cogency of an argument, to the merits of a suggested course of action. Instead, our thoughts and actions are directed to removing the feeling of guilt—to somehow making things right or doing the right thing. We fall into the rationalization trap.

Guilt can have its pro-social uses. Imagine a society in which no one felt remorse for any transgression that he or she performed. Many social commentators have noted that the success of Martin Luther King, Jr.'s campaign to desegregate the South was due, in part, to the guilt feelings induced in many white Southerners when his nonviolent actions were met with billy clubs, fire hoses, and attack dogs.

Nevertheless, many effects of guilt are, of course, not positive; many guilty feelings are undeserved. Guilt can be induced by reminding the target of past sins that have long since been atoned for, by making small transgressions loom large, or by making it appear that the target is responsible for a crime that he or she did not commit. Once we are filled with guilt, our thoughts and behavior are directed toward ridding ourselves of this feeling. The end result is, at best, the manipulation of our behavior and, perhaps at worst, long-term damage to our self-esteem.

26

WHAT IS THE INFLUENCE OF ONE FLOWER GIVEN?

A. C. Bhaktivedanta spent much of his life in India as a manager of a successful pharmaceutical company. In the early 1960s, after leaving his wife and family and accepting the name of Swami Prabhupada, he came to America and founded the International Society for Krishna Consciousness, a movement devoted to improving the world's spiritual health by chants and love for Lord Krishna. Starting from a storefront mission on Manhattan's Lower East Side, the swami, in less than a decade, was able to gather the resources to establish a worldwide network of more than a hundred Hare Krishna temples and communes, including forty located in the United States.

Swami Prabhupada's primary source of income during this period of rapid expansion came from public donations and sales of religious merchandise, including his two most popular items, *Back to Godhead* magazine and a designer edition of the *Bhagavad Gita*. What makes the Hare Krishna's success so remarkable was the sales force the swami recruited to sell the society's merchandise. The swami selected young people—often teenagers, many of them with psychological problems—dressed them in saffron robes, holy beads, and B. F. Goodrich sandals, shaved the heads of the males, fed them a diet consisting primarily of vegetables (most notably dahl and chickpeas), and then sent them into the marketplace singing, dancing, and chanting the Hare Krishna. Would you buy a copy of the *Bhagavad Gita* (or anything else, for that matter) from a chanting, orange-clad, stubble-headed sales agent? Not likely. The Hare Krishna sales force breaks just about every persuasion rule (save one) found in this book—they were low in source credibility, low in interpersonal attraction and liking, and high in vested self-interest.

How did the swami get thousands of people to part with their hard-earned cash to finance his spiritual kingdom? Robert Cialdini, one of the world's leading authorities on influence tactics, wondered how he did it, too.[1] At first, Cialdini notes, the Hare Krishnas were quite unsuccessful in their solicitations. Indeed, many towns enacted laws and ordinances prohibiting Krishna begging and even banned them from certain parts of town, especially airports. Occasionally violence would erupt between Krishnas and townspeople. All of this turned around, according to Cialdini, when the Krishnas discovered one of society's most effective persuasion devices, one capable both of overcoming the Krishnas' negative image and of placing of an overpriced copy of the *Bhagavad Gita* into the hands of many a weary traveler. Their technique made use of what is called the *norm of reciprocity*.

A norm is a specific guide to conduct—for example, tip 15% of the dinner bill; don't cut in front of people standing in line at the movies; don't urinate in public; don't read other people's mail. If we break a norm, we most likely receive some form of social sanction and disapproval—a glaring look, gossip and ridicule, shunning and ostracism, and sometimes even physical punishment, jail, banishment, or death. (Note the reaction of some people to the Krishnas because they broke society's dress and social interaction norms.) As a consequence of these sanctions, even a young child begins to learn not to break the norms. Indeed, when put in a position of transgressing a norm, we often feel highly anxious—a feeling that we would like to avoid. We may end up obeying the norm almost automatically without much thought as to why.

Often norms can be associated with a specific role (cooking is women's work; businessmen are competitive) or a specific culture (eat with a fork [as opposed to chopsticks]; don't goldbrick [overproduce] in this workshop). Other norms are widely shared and appear in many cultures and societies (incest is taboo; honor your commitments). The norm of reciprocity is one such norm. It states: "If I do something for you, then you are obligated to return the favor and do something for me." Perhaps one reason why this norm is found in so many cultures is its value to a society. The norm of reciprocity regulates exchange in a culture; it insures that the person who makes the first exchange will not be cheated.

A study by Dennis Regan illustrates the persuasive power of the norm of reciprocity—a tactic so powerful that it can overcome the effects of being disliked.[2] In his experiment, two male students reported for a study that supposedly was investigating "aesthetic judgments." One of the men was really an accomplice who, at the beginning of the study, attempted to make himself unlikable (by being rude and inconsiderate to another person) or likable (by being kind and considerate to another). After both "subjects" rated art slides for about five minutes, the accomplice slipped out of the room for a couple of minutes and returned either empty-handed or carrying two Cokes and said, "I asked him [the experimenter] if I could get myself a Coke, and he said it was OK, so I bought one for you, too." At the end of the study, the accomplice asked the real subject if he would like to buy some raffle tickets. The results showed that when the accomplice gave the other student a Coke and thus invoked the norm of reciprocity, he sold nearly twice as many raffle tickets, compared to when no Coke was given and regardless of how socially attractive he was perceived to be!

How did the Krishnas use the norm of reciprocity to solicit money? Quite simply, they gave the influence target a gift of a flower. As Cialdini, who spent hours at the airport observing the Krishnas in action, tells it, the sect member would spy a "victim," who would suddenly find a flower pressed into his or her hand or pinned to a jacket. If the target attempted to give it back, the Krishna would refuse by saying, "It is our gift to you." Only then was the request made for a donation. The gift of a flower established a feeling of obligation and indebtedness. How could this favor be repaid? Quite obviously by providing the Society with a donation or with the purchase of an attractive edition of the *Bhagavad Gita*.

Hare Krishnas are not the only ones to employ the norm of reciprocity for persuasive purposes. This may have started on a mass scale with the well-known "Fuller-brushman," a fixture of the 1930s who went from door to door selling brushes. He always began by giving the home owner a small inexpensive brush as a way to establish the reciprocity norm. A phenomenon of the 1950s, Tupperware parties, began with a gift from the company (typically a small Tupperware item) and a gift from the party host (refreshments), thereby obligating the party goer to both company and host (who receives a gift from the company if you and your friends buy enough). A recent television ad for an antacid began with an authoritative looking man stating, "We believe in our product so much, that, after watching this ad, if you would like to try our product just call us toll-free and we will send you a pack." Marketers know that a free sample—a taste of sausage or orange juice at the supermarket or a trial packet of cold medicine or shampoo in the mail—can greatly increase product sales. Sales presentations for such things as vacuum cleaners, automobiles, encyclopedias, and beachfront property in Florida often begin with a free prize, such as a road atlas, a transistor radio, or a trial magazine subscription. Charities and political parties frequently mail free gifts of buttons and bumper stickers with catchy slogans when they ask for a contribution. Many university professors will receive a free copy of this book in the hopes that they will assign it to their classes.

One ingenious variation in the use of the norm of reciprocity occurs in negotiations and has been dubbed the door-in-the-face technique. Here's how it works. Imagine that you worked for a local blood bank and you wanted to increase blood donations. Using the *door-in-the-face* technique, you would begin by asking for a very extreme favor—say, donate blood once every two months for at least three years. Such a request would surely be rejected (hence the name "door-in-the-face") but might lead to more acceptances of a compromise—say, donating one unit of blood—than would otherwise be the case. This is exactly what Robert Cialdini and Karen Ascani found.[3] In one study, they asked passersby on a University of Arizona walkway to either (1) donate a unit of blood sometime tomorrow or (2) donate a unit of blood once every two months for a period of three years and, when this request was rejected by the passerby, to merely donate a unit of blood sometime tomorrow. The results showed that more people agreed to give blood and actually gave more blood when they received the extreme request first.

The door-in-the-face technique makes use of two basic psychological processes. First, the large request sets up a contrast effect, similar to the one that occurs with decoys (see Chapter 9)—giving a pint of blood doesn't seem nearly so bad when compared to donating at regular intervals for the next three years. Second, the immediate concession by the requester invokes the norm of reciprocity. The requester is implicitly saying, "I just reduced my request from three years of blood donations to just once; now it is your turn to reciprocate my concession." And many an influence target does just that!

Car dealers have learned the value of the door-in-the-face technique. Dealers often pad the asking price for an automobile by adding an extra price sticker that raises the price of a car by as much as a few thousand dollars. Early in the negotiations, the dealer will graciously concede this extra charge. Now it is *your turn* to reciprocate and to pay *more* for that car.

In general, the norm of reciprocity is successful as a persuasion device because it directs our thoughts and carries its own motivation to act on those thoughts. We are directed to think *"How can I repay my obligation?"* as opposed to *"Is this a good deal?"* Our primary motivation is to avoid the uneasy feeling that comes from transgressing the norm. Other norms can similarly motivate our thinking. Next, we will look at just one of these norms to see how the rule "honor you commitments" can be exploited.

27

THE COMMITTED HEART

A visit from the encyclopedia salesman can illustrate many persuasion tactics. The "free" road atlas given for listening to the sales representative invokes the norm of reciprocity. The features of the volumes are described in glowing, influential words. The salesman encourages you to generate dozens of good reasons (at least you think so) for owning a set of encyclopedias. The fact that your children and other loved ones don't already have access to a world of knowledge makes you feel a little guilty.

But perhaps one of the most powerful inducers to buy occurs "after" the sales presentation. The salesman continues:

"Well, if there are no more questions about the books, that will conclude the presentation. Oh yes, one more thing. My boss would really like it if I could get your opinion about our encyclopedias. Would you mind completing a form with me?"

You respond, "OK."

"Its a series of questions about what *you* would like in an encyclopedia. It would really help if you would respond *as if you were buying a set today*."

The salesman goes on to ask a series of questions. "Which color binding do you like—white, maroon, or black? With or without gold leaf? With or without double-strength binding?" and so on. You answer each question mindlessly as the salesman checks off your responses on a preprinted official form.

At the end of the inquiry he asks, "Would you mind initialing this sheet as a way of authorizing your answers?" Again, you do so in a half-mindless state.

From that point on, that formal-looking paper is treated as *your* order for a set of encyclopedias. The salesman suggests, "Let's see how much it would cost to buy *your* set of encyclopedias today; hmmmmm, with a 5% discount, that would be_____," as he hands you a slip of paper with a handwritten number on it. As you read it, the salesman asks, "Shall I order *your* set today?" You stammer, half-confused, "Well, 'em, I'd...well."

We don't know if you will buy that set of encyclopedias today or not. Many of us will undoubtedly see through his ploys. But we bet this procedure of "taking your order" will increase encyclopedia sales and will do so because of the feelings it engenders. In general, it is important to all of us to be "persons of our word," that is, to be self-consistent and to honor our commitments. Granted, we did not say we would buy an encyclopedia, but the salesman seems to think so—perhaps we *did* indicate we would like one. When we go back on our word, we often feel uneasy, even when it is a seemingly flimsy commitment like the one given to the encyclopedia sales-man. To maintain a positive view of ourselves, we act on our commitments. The rationalization trap has captured another un-suspecting victim.

Preying on our sense of commitment as a way of to induce per-suasion is often accomplished in small doses. Suppose you would like to enlist someone's aid in a massive undertaking, but you know the job you have in mind for the person is so difficult, and will require so much time and effort, the person surely will decline. What should you do? One possibility is to get the person involved in a much smaller aspect of the job, one so easy that he or she wouldn't dream of refusing to do it. This action serves to commit the individual to "the cause." Once people are thus committed, the likelihood of their complying with the larger request increases.

This phenomenon was demonstrated by Jonathan Freedman and Scott Fraser.[1] They attempted to induce several home owners to put up a huge, unattractive sign in their front yards reading "Drive Careful-ly." Because of the ugliness and obtrusiveness of the sign, most residents refused to put it up; only 17% complied. A different group of residents, however, were first "softened up" by an experimenter who "put his foot in the door" by getting them to sign a petition favoring safe driving. Because signing a petition is an easy thing to do, virtually all who were asked agreed to sign. A few weeks later, a different experimenter went to each resident with the ugly "Drive Carefully" sign. More than 55% of these residents allowed the sign to be put up on their property.

Thus, when individuals commit themselves in a small way, the likelihood they will commit themselves further in that direction is increased. This process of using small favors to encourage people to accede to larger requests had been dubbed the *foot-in-the-door* tech-nique (a technique opposite in form to the door-in-the-face tactic described in Chapter 26). It is effective because having done the smaller favor sets up pressures toward agreeing to do the larger favor; in effect, we comply with the large request to be consistent with our earlier commitment.

Similar results using this technique have been found in studies of charitable donations and voting. For example, people induced to wear a lapel pin publicizing an American Cancer Society fund-raising drive were approximately twice as likely to give a donation the next day as were those who were simply approached for a contribution.[2] Other investigators have found that the chances of getting people to vote on election day could be increased just by asking them if they planned to go to the polls.[3] In this study, the researchers contacted potential voters and asked them to predict if they would vote in an election to be held on the upcoming Tuesday. All of those contacted, perhaps out of a desire to appear civic-minded, said "yes," they would be voting. The respondents then acted on this commitment, with 86.7% of them voting in the election compared to 61.5% of those not asked to make self-predictions.

Car dealers also know how to use commitment to sell automobiles. Indeed, when Robert Cialdini temporarily joined the sales force of an automobile dealer, he discovered a common and successful ploy called *lowballing* or "throwing the customer a lowball."[4]

The technique works this way. Suppose you enter an automobile showroom intent on buying a new car. You've already priced the car you want at several dealers—you know you can purchase it for about $9,300. Lo and behold, the salesman tells you he can sell you one for $8,942. Excited by the bargain, you agree to the deal and write out a check for the downpayment. While the salesman takes your check to the sales manager to consummate the deal, you rub your hands in glee as you imagine yourself driving home in your shiny new car. But alas, ten minutes later, the salesman returns with a forlorn look on his face—it seems he made a calculation error and the sales manager caught it. The price of the car is actually $9,384. You can get it cheaper elsewhere; moreover, the decision to buy is not irrevocable. And yet, far more people in this situation will go ahead with the deal than if the original asking price had been $9,384—even though the reason for purchasing the car from this dealer (the bargain price) no longer exists.

What is going on in this situation? There are at least three important things to notice. First, while the customer's decision to buy is certainly reversible, a commitment was emphasized by the act of signing a check for the downpayment and handing it over to the salesman. Second, this commitment triggered the anticipation of a pleasant or interesting experience: driving out with a new car. To have the anticipated event thwarted (by not going ahead with the deal) would have produced disappointment. Third, although the final price is substantially higher than the customer thought it would be, it is only slightly higher than the price somewhere else. Under these circumstances, the customer in effect says, "Oh, what the hell. I'm already here, I've already filled out the forms—why wait?

Commitment can be self-perpetuating, resulting in an escalating commitment to an often failing course of action. Once a small commitment is made, it sets the stage for ever increasing commitments. The original behavior needs to be justified, so attitudes are changed; this change in attitudes influences future decisions and behavior. The result is a seemingly irrational commitment to a poor business plan, a purchase that makes no sense, a war that has no realistic objectives, or an arms race gone out of control.

The processes of escalating commitment may have been an important factor in the deepening U.S. involvement in the war in Vietnam. As an analysis of the *Pentagon Papers* by the news magazine *Time* stated:

> Yet the bureaucracy, the Pentagon Papers indicate, always demanded new options; each option was to apply more force. Each tightening of the screw created a position that must be defended; once committed, the military pressure must be maintained.[5]

In a thought-provoking analysis of the *Pentagon Papers*, Ralph White suggested that previous commitments blinded our leaders to information incompatible with the decisions they had already made.[6] As White put it, "There was a tendency, when actions were out of line with ideas, for decision-makers to align their ideas with their actions." To take just one of many examples, the decision by the Joint Chiefs of Staff to continue to escalate the bombing of North Vietnam was made at the price of ignoring crucial evidence from the CIA and other sources that made it clear that bombing would not break the will of the North Vietnamese people but, quite the contrary, would only strengthen their resolve. White surmises the reason the Joint Chiefs prevailed in their efforts to escalate the bombing was that their advice was consonant with decisions already made and with certain key assumptions that later proved to be erroneous. In other words, the Joint Chiefs' escalation of the war was in part an attempt to reduce their own dissonance about their previous war efforts, a process reminscient of what happened after Mrs. Keech's end-of-the world prophecy failed and after the city of Santa Cruz was informed about an impending, destructive earthquake (see Chapter 4).

As with other self-motives and emotions, commitment and consistency have their purpose and value. No one wants to live in a society of inconsistent, two-faced liars! However, commitments can form a persuasion trap—we commit ourselves, sometimes inadvertently, sometimes inappropriately, and then live out our commitments in all honesty. The clever propagandist will know how to secure our commitment and set a rationalization trap.

In such cases, it may be useful to ask, "How did I get myself into this situation?" Fortunately, many states require that consumers be given a period of time to "change their minds" about a particular purchase—a time to rethink mistaken commitments. It may also help us if we remember that the most *honorable* action is *always* that of *not* honoring *dishonorable* commitments.

28

THE PSYCHOLOGY OF SCARCITY AND THE MYSTIQUE OF PHANTOMS

Potatoes have not always enjoyed the popularity that they do today. In the late eighteenth century, the French believed that potatoes caused leprosy; the Germans grew spuds only for cattle and for prisoners; the Russian peasant considered them to be poisonous. All that changed when Catherine the Great, ruler of Russia, cleverly ordered that fences be built around potato fields. Large notices were posted warning the populace not to steal potatoes.[1] The potato became a staple of the Russian diet, and the rest is potato history.

Catherine the Great's campaign to introduce the potato into the Russian diet made use of a common, but nonetheless effective, principle of persuasion—*scarcity sells*. The attractiveness of an object can be increased by making it appear scarce and unavailable, by erecting barriers that make the object difficult to obtain. To paraphrase an old saw, "Scarcity makes the heart grow fonder."

Advertisers and sales agents are well aware that scarcity sells. Their ads announce: "not available in any store," "get 'em while supplies last," "limited edition," "available for a limited time only." Sometimes they deliberately limit supplies. For example, the Franklin Mint, a direct marketer of such "collector items" as commemorative dinner plates, keepsake figurines, and souvenir coins, regularly claims: "Only a limited number of items were produced. No more will be made. The molds will be destroyed." Another gold coin merchant restricts sales to "only five coins per order." Car dealers often make such remarks as, "We only received two models like this one, and we sold the other one yesterday." The local salesclerk will gladly tell you, "That's all we have in stock; we can't keep 'em on the shelf—sorry."

A few years ago one of the most successful toys on the market was the Cabbage Patch doll manufactured by Coleco. The doll had features that many found appealing—each doll was unique, they carried their own adoption papers, and the dolls had a distinctive "homely" look. However, the Cabbage Patch dolls had one feature that especially made the cash registers ring—they were frequently out of stock. Parents would line up for hours in the hope of getting a doll for their children. Battles would break out in toy departments over who would get that last doll. Stores would conduct lotteries to see who would win an opportunity to buy a Cabbage Patch doll. Some owners auctioned off their dolls at upwards of $250. Sales for the doll skyrocketed. In 1985 alone, sales for Cabbage Patch dolls topped $600 million. In subsequent years, as they became more readily available, the public's interest began to wane.

What is the lure of scarcity? What happens when an object is made unavailable and thus becomes a *phantom* choice? Consider what the typical Russian peasant must have thought and felt upon seeing a newly restricted potato field: *"Hey, why are they roping off these potatoes? They must be valuable. I wonder if they will post a guard? Sure they will; they'll see to it that only the rich get to eat potatoes. Not if I can help it. I'm sick of beet soup day in and day out. I want potatoes."*

As indicated by our hypothetical peasant, phantoms can capture the imagination. The unavailable becomes exotic. When we discover that a commodity is scarce or may be unavailable, one of our first inferences is that it must also be desirable. Why else would it be so rare? We tend to use a simple rule or heuristic: If it is rare, if it is unavailable, it must be valuable. This is what lies behind research findings showing that female college students believed that a scarce pair of nylon hosiery should cost more than a readily available pair, that children rated cookies in scarce supply as more desirable than similar cookies in abundant supply, and that, in response to news of an upcoming shortage of imported beef, orders by supermarkets and other food stores increased to between two and six times the normally ordered quantities.[2] Given the ease with which information about scarcity and availability can be manipulated, the propaganda potential of this technique is nearly unlimited and is available to all.

Scarcity and unavailability can do more than just make an object appear more desirable. When a phantom alternative is present, it can also result in a change in the perception, evaluation, and ultimate choice of the available options. We along with Peter Farquhar have conducted a series of experiments in which college students were asked to choose among brands of products.[3] On some sets of the choices, a very attractive alternative was included, but the students were told that the item was unavailable and that they could not select it. In other words, a phantom alternative was presented.

What do the results show? First, the presence of an attractive phantom made the other brands look less attractive—a contrast effect similar in nature, but opposite in direction, to that found with decoys (see Chapter 9). Second, the phantom changed the relative importance given to the criteria for making a decision. Specifically, the attribute on which the phantom was superior was rated as most important for making the decision. For example, if the phantom was a new computer with lots of memory or a new car that gets great gas mileage, then the attributes of computer memory and gas mileage became the focus of decision making. This change in decision criteria also resulted in a change in choice; the students were much more likely to indicate that they would purchase an available brand that rated high on the attribute on which the phantom was best.

Thus the presence of a phantom may subtly affect our perceptions. For example, hearing about the possibilities of a defense shield in the sky, commonly referred to as the Strategic Defense Initiative, or Star Wars, may cause us to view our present defense capabilities as inadequate. It can also cause us to shift the focus of our attention toward strategic high-tech weapons systems and away from conventional military hardware, even though sophisticated conventional hardware may be more useful in fighting a limited war in places such as the Persian Gulf.

Phantoms, like scarce but available alternatives, can also arouse our emotions, emotions that can be played upon by the skilled propagandist.[4] As with most consumer goods, owning an object that is scarce or unavailable for everyone else is a means of defining one's self: "I am unique and special because I own something that no one else (or at least not many) has been able to obtain." Just hearing about a phantom may induce worry and concern: "If they bring out a better product, I'll be stuck with this thing. Maybe I should wait." This experience is so common in the computer industry that computer experts have a special term for preannounced but unavailable products—vaporware. Not obtaining a hoped-for phantom can be a frustrating experience leading to aggression (one explanation for why riots and revolutions occur) and sour grapes (devaluing the once hoped-for phantom as a way to reconcile not getting it). Being the only child on the block without that new toy can often arouse feelings of inadequacy and incompetence. Finally, taking away an object or choice can result in what has been termed psychological reactance— the individual, upset at having his or her freedom denied, attempts at all costs to restore a sense of autonomy and control.

Given the power of scarce and unavailable items to alter our perceptions and to arouse our emotions, it is not surprising that propagandists often use a phantom as a persuasion device. We call this the *phantom trap*.

One important aspect of the phantom trap is *phantom fixation*: our tendency to focus our attention and resources on obtaining scarce and unavailable items. By concentrating on the unavailable, we may forget and overlook the possible. A program of research by Walter Mischel illustrates the point.[5] Mischel was investigating the ability of children to delay gratification. In his studies, children were given a choice: They could get a small candy bar right away or they could wait and receive a much more attractive prize later (a big candy bar). Which children were most likely to wait for the currently unavailable prize? Mischel found that children who could distract themselves from focusing their attention on *either* prize—for example, by thinking of other things—would wait the longest and therefore fared better. Children who became fixated on receiving the prizes experienced considerable conflict that was hard to resist and thus were more likely to take the immediate but lesser prize.

The Mischel experiments demonstrate how phantoms can direct thought. The presence of an attractive but currently unavailable object focuses our attention and resources on obtaining the

"This car is not for everyone, sir.
Would you care to take our aptitude test?"

desired prize. Settling for less than the phantom becomes a conflict that can only be resolved by "strength of willpower," a test that many of us often fail.

Such a fixation can have positive consequences; it may be helpful in mobilizing energies to obtain an elusive goal of perhaps great personal or societal benefit. It can also be exploited for propaganda purposes. For example, early promoters of the New World recruited settlers with promises of fountains of youth, gold, and riches beyond belief, and lands (as one pamphlet put it) "so marvelous as to seem incredible." Many signed on, having become increasingly dissatisfied with their own lives (as a result of the propaganda) and went in search of the phantom, *El Dorado*. In other cases, phantom fixation can be a waste of time and energy, especially when the phantom is really a "red herring"—a truly unavailable option. In such cases, an individual or organization may expend great amounts of resources to obtain a desired new employee or access to new markets, only to find that the effort is wasted and the phantom never existed.

An experiment we conducted with Ken Freeman and Peter Farquhar demonstrates another side of the phantom trap—how emotions aroused by a phantom can serve to persuade.[6] In our study, students first earned money by completing a manual labor task of turning screws and refilling a box of spools. The money was used to purchase common office supplies such as erasers and paperclips. However, when some of the students went to purchase the paperclips, they encountered a surprise phantom—after selecting the most attractive option, they were told that they had not earned enough money to purchase it. Although, the students probably didn't care much about the paperclips, the news that they couldn't get want they wanted (even for something as as trivial as a paperclip) was in many ways personally threatening—just as many people feel threatened when told that they are too late for a sale or that they don't qualify for financing of that new car.

Because the students felt vulnerable, their emotions could be easily aroused and their choices were susceptible to manipulation. For example, half of the subjects encountering the surprise phantom were told, "Given that you are short of money for the paperclip you want, I'll give you the next most similar clip. *It's your only choice.*" Such a communication was designed to arouse reactance, and it did: All but a few subjects pointedly refused to select the brand the experimenter recommended, instead opting for another, quite different alternative. In a different condition, subjects, after finding out that they could not have their first choice, were manipulated much more subtly; they were told, "You might want to consider the next most similar clip." This communication was designed so as *not* to arouse reactance. Consequently, almost all of the subjects chose the paperclips subtly recommended by the experimenter. The astute reader will recognize this subtle strategy as being almost identical to the "lowballing" tactic (commit the customer, then switch 'em) used by many unscrupulous sales agents and described in Chapter 27.

What is particularly interesting in both conditions is that, whether subjects resisted direct pressure or succumbed to subtle pressure, their decisions were based not on the merits of the products but on the emotions aroused by a phantom.

Another version of the phantom trap has been termed the "consumer catch-22 carousel" by C. R. Snyder.[7] As we mentioned earlier, obtaining a scarce and rare product adds to one's self-image as a unique and special person. Manufacturers know this and design and market their products accordingly. If the marketer does a good job of creating a perception of the product as unique, then you desire and acquire it. But the catch is, *so does everyone else*; suddenly you are no longer an original. Instead of acquiring a product that makes you unique, you have obtained one that makes you just like everyone else. This further heightens the need for uniqueness, and off we go in an endless pursuit of the next faddish phantom. As Erich Fromm points out, once we begin using material goods to define ourselves, we are doomed to be on an endless treadmill of dissatisfaction.[8]

The phantom trap also points up some of the possible pitfalls in using censorship to regulate human behavior. By trying to make something "unavailable" through censorship, the perceived value of the forbidden item may increase. For example, *The Satanic Verses* was an interesting novel by Salman Rushdie, but it certainly was not blockbuster material. It might have sold several thousand copies except for one thing: The Ayatollah Khomeini declared it was sacrilegious and urged Muslims to assassinate the author. The book immediately rocketed to the top of the best-seller list.

Further, by limiting commodities such as X-rated movies and "nudie" magazines to adults only, we provide children a ready-made method of proving their adulthood and defining themselves as "grown-up"—in a sense, we encourage them to go out and get the fruit forbidden to all but adults. The point is nicely illustrated in an experiment conducted by David Zellinger and his colleagues.[9] In this study, college students received a description of a book much like the descriptions that appear on dust jackets. Half of the students were told that the book had a "21-year-old age restriction." When such a message was given, the book was rated as more desirable—the students indicated they would like to read it to a far greater extent than did the students in the control condition.

How can the phantom trap be avoided? We have three suggestions.[10] First, consider that phantoms may exist where you might not expect them—either through devious design or simply through unintentional unavailability. In such cases, it is wise to develop contingency plans in advance. For example, if the car you want proves to be unavailable, you could walk off the car lot rather than sliding to the "most" similar alternative. Second, when dealing with phantoms it may be a good idea to imagine other scenarios—for example, attempting to obtain other phantoms or receiving a readily available option. This will lessen the likelihood that you will become fixated on the unavailable. It can also make clear the relative costs and benefits of pursuing a phantom or perhaps suggest new, viable alternatives. Finally, use the emotions that often accompany phantoms as a cue that something is awry. Try to react not to the emotions, but to the circumstances of the situation. Again, this may mean that the best strategy is to simply walk away and gain the time and composure to look more carefully before you leap. Whether one is talking about a defense system costing billions, a multimillion-dollar introduction of a new computer product, or merely a few hundred dollars extra for the family car, avoiding the potential pitfalls of phantom traps may be no small potatoes.

—

COUNTERACTING THE TACTICS OF PERSUASION

—

SUBLIMINAL SORCERY:
WHO IS SEDUCING WHOM?

Imagine that it is the 1950s and you are off to see *Picnic*, one of the more popular films of the day. However, the movie theater, located somewhere in New Jersey, is unlike any you have been in before. Unbeknownst to you, the projectors have been equipped with a special device capable of flashing short phrases onto the movie screen at such a rapid speed that you are unaware that any messages have been presented. During the film, you lean over to your companion and whisper, "Gee, I'd love a tub of buttered popcorn and a Coke right now." To which he replies, "You're always hungry and thirsty at movies, shhhhhh." But after a few moments he says, "You know, some Coke and popcorn might not be a bad idea."

A short time later you find out that you and your friend weren't the only ones desiring popcorn and Coke in the theater that day. Far from it. According to reports in newspapers and magazines, James Vicary, an advertising expert, had secretly flashed at 1/3,000 of a second the words, EAT POPCORN and DRINK COKE onto the movie screen. He claimed that this had increased Coke sales by 18.1% and popcorn sales by 57.7%. Upon reading their newspapers, most people were outraged and frightened. It is a scary world indeed if advertisers can use such a devilish technique to bypass our conscious intellect and beam subliminal commands directly to our subconscious. By *subliminal* we mean a message so faint or fast that it is presented below the threshold of awareness.

In a 1957 article for the *Saturday Review* entitled "Smudging the Subconscious," Norman Cousins captured such feelings as he pondered the true meaning of such a device.[1] As he put it, "If the device is successful for putting over popcorn, why not politicians or anything else?" He wondered about the character of those who would dream up such a machine to "break into the deepest and most private parts of the human mind and leave all sorts of scratchmarks." Cousins concluded that the best course of action would be "to take this invention and everything connected to it and attach it to the center of the next nuclear explosive scheduled for testing."

Cousins was not alone in his concern over the use of subliminal techniques. In a series of four bestselling books, Wilson Bryan Key has brought to national attention the possibility of widespread use of subliminal tactics.[2] Key argues that such techniques are not limited to television and movies. Cleverly hidden messages aimed at inducing sexual arousal are often embedded in the pictures and photographs of print advertisements. His concern over the use of subliminal persuasion is clear: "Every person reading this book has been victimized and manipulated by the use of subliminal stimuli directed into his unconscious mind by the mass merchandisers of media. The techniques are in widespread use by media, advertising and public relations agencies, industrial and commercial corporations, and by the Federal government itself."[3]

Governments have responded to the outcries of the critics. Subliminal advertising has been banned in Australia and Britain. In the United States, the Federal Communications Commission has ruled that the use of subliminal messages could result in the loss of a broadcast license. The National Association of Broadcasters has prohibited the use of subliminal advertising by its members. A Nevada judge has ruled that subliminal messages are not covered by the First Amendment protection of freedom of speech. In many ways, the furor over subliminal influence captures what many of us fear most about persuasion in general: Persuasion is a mysterious force that cannot be resisted.

Nevertheless, widespread media coverage and governmental rulings have not put an end to subliminal influence practices. In fact, such practices have spread to self-help products. Today a consumer needs only to visit the local bookstore to find a vast array of subliminal audio- and videotapes designed to accomplish such worthwhile goals as increasing self-esteem, improving memory, reducing weight, controlling anger and temper, and enhancing sexual responsiveness. In their search for better self and health, American consumers spent over $50 million dollars in 1987 alone on subliminal tapes designed for therapeutic purposes—a 10% increase over 1986 sales.[4] The tapes work, according to one manufacturer, because subliminal messages bypass the conscious mind and imprint directly on the subconscious mind, where they create the basis for the kind of life the consumer wants.

Accusations concerning the sinister use of subliminal persuasion continue as well. In the summer of 1990, the rock band Judas Priest was placed on trial for allegedly recording, in one of their songs, the subliminal implant *"do it."* This message supposedly caused the suicide deaths of two young, avid listeners of the group's music, Ray Belknap and James Vance.

Given all the media coverage, the governmental involvement, and the dollars spent, surprisingly little public attention has been paid to a most basic question: Does subliminal influence really work?

During the last few years, we have been collecting published articles on subliminal processes, gathering more than 150 articles from the mass media and more than 200 academic papers on the topic (a stack nearly 2 feet tall).[5] In none of these papers is there clear evidence in support of the proposition that subliminal messages influence behavior.* Many of the studies fail to find an effect, and those that do are either fatally flawed on methodological grounds or cannot be reproduced. Other reviewers of this literature have reached the same conclusion. As cognitive psychologist Timothy Moore puts it, "There is no empirical documentation for stronger subliminal effects, such as inducing particular behaviors or changing motivation. Moreover, such a notion is contradicted by a substantial amount of research and is incompatible with experimentally based conceptions of information processing, learning, and motivation."[6]

If subliminal messages don't change behavior, then why do people continue to buy self-help tapes? It seems that many people, touchingly, *want* to believe they work. For example, in one study conducted by the Canadian Broadcast Corporation in 1958, the message PHONE NOW

---

* There is some evidence for subliminal perception—minimal processing of information outside of awareness. One of the best examples of this is the cocktail party phenomenon. Suppose you are at a party and you are paying attention to what your friend is saying and ignoring all the other background noise. Someone in the background says your name. Your ears perk up and you start to pay attention to whoever said your name even though a few minutes earlier you may not have known the person to be in the room. Such an effect indicates that you are doing some processing outside of awareness. Exactly how much processing takes place is still a matter of scientific inquiry. However, no study has demonstrated motivational and behavioral effects similar to those claimed by the advocates of subliminal seduction.

was subliminally flashed 352 times during a popular Sunday night television show called "Close-Up."[7] Telephone use did not go up during the period. When asked to guess the message, viewers sent in close to 500 letters, not one of which contained the correct answer. But almost half of the respondents claimed to be hungry or thirsty during the show. Apparently, they guessed (incorrectly) that the message was aimed at getting them to eat or drink. This not only shows that people *want* to believe the phenomenon works; it also demonstrates the power of expectations created by Vicary's theater study.

Interestingly enough, when confronted with this and other negative findings on subliminal persuasion, James Vicary reportedly told the trade newspaper *Advertising Age* that his original "eat popcorn/drink Coke" study was a fabrication intended to increase customers for his failing marketing business![8]

And what of Key's evidence for the effectiveness of subliminal seduction? Most of the studies he reports lack a control or comparison group. Finding that 62% of all subjects feel sexual, romantic, or satisfied when they see a gin ad with the word *sex* embedded in the ice cubes tells us nothing about the effectiveness of the "sex" implant. What would happen if the word *sex* was removed from the cubes? Perhaps 62% of the subjects would still feel sexy, romantic, or satisfied. Perhaps more, perhaps less would feel this way. Without such a comparison, we just do not know.

To illustrate the *in*effectiveness of subliminal audiotapes and to demonstrate the power of expectations, we, along with Jay Eskenazi and Anthony Greenwald, conducted a study of mass market audiotapes with subliminal messages designed to improve either self-esteem or memory abilities.[9] Both types of tapes contained the same supraliminal content—various pieces of classical music. However, they differed in their subliminal content. According to the manufacturer, the self-esteem tapes contained such subliminal messages as "I have high self-worth and high self-esteem." The memory tape contained such subliminal messages as "My ability to remember and recall is increasing daily."

Using public posters and ads placed in local newspapers, we recruited volunteers who were interested in the value and potential of subliminal self-help therapies (and who would probably be similar to those people most likely to buy such tapes). On the first day of the study, we asked our volunteers to complete various self-esteem and memory measures. Next, they received their subliminal tape, but with an interesting twist. Half of the tapes were mislabeled so that some of the subjects received a memory tape but thought it was intended to improve self-esteem, whereas other subjects received a self-esteem tape but thought it was intended to improve memory. (Of course, half the subjects received correctly labeled tapes.)

The volunteers took their tapes home and listened to them every day for five weeks (the period suggested by the manufacturer for maximum effectiveness). After five weeks, they returned to the laboratory and completed, once again, self-esteem and memory tests; they were also asked to indicate whether they believed the tapes were effective. The results: The subliminal tapes had *no* effect (improvement or decrement) on either self-esteem or memory. But our volunteers had a different impression. Subjects who thought they had listened to a self-esteem tape (regardless of whether they actually did or not) were more likely to be convinced that their self-esteem had improved, and those who thought they had listened to a memory tape were more likely to believe that their memory had improved. In sum, the subliminal tapes did nothing to improve self-esteem or memory abilities, but, to our subjects, they appeared to have had an effect. As we put it in the title of the article, "What you expect is what you believe, but not necessarily what you get." Our results are not a fluke. We have repeated our original study twice more using different tapes and have yet to find an effect of subliminal messages upon behavior as claimed by the manufacturer. In addition, we are aware of eight additional independent tests of subliminal self-help tapes. In none of these studies were the manufacturer's claims for the efficacy of subliminal therapy substantiated.[10]

The history of the subliminal controversy teaches us much about persuasion—but not of the subliminal kind. Despite the claims in books and newspapers and on the backs of subliminal self-help tapes, subliminal influence tactics have not been demonstrated to be effective. Of course, as with anything scientific, it may be that someday, somehow, someone will develop a subliminal technique that may work, just as some day a chemist may find a way to transmute lead into gold. In the meantime, there are many other types of effective persuasion tactics (such as the ones described throughout this book) that warrant more attention than subliminal persuasion.

If subliminal messages are so ineffective, why is the belief in their power so widespread? One poll taken around 1970 found that almost 81% of the respondents who had heard of subliminal advertising believed it to be a current practice and over 68% believed it to be successful in selling products.[11] Most strikingly, surveys also reveal that many people learn about subliminal influence through the mass media and through courses in high school and college—a further indication of the need for science education in American schools.

A partial reason for the appeal of the concept of subliminal influence lies in the coverage that the mass media have given subliminal persuasion. Many of the news stories about subliminal persuasion fail to mention negative evidence. When disconfirming evidence is presented, it is usually near the end of the article, giving the reader the impression that, at worst, the claims for subliminal effectiveness are somewhat controversial.

A second reason lies in our expectations, hopes, and fears. The issue of subliminal influence first emerged as a national concern soon after the Korean War—a time when other apparently mysterious mind-altering practices such as "brainwashing" and hypnotic suggestion captured the nation's imagination in films such as *The Manchurian Candidate*. Interest in subliminal seduction rose again in the post-Watergate years, when many Americans felt that their leaders were involved in devious conspiracies and massive cover-ups of the type dramatized in the movie *Network*. W. B. Key rejuvenated the issue of subliminal influence by portraying it as yet another example that big business and big government were conspiring to get us. Today, there appears to be a growing tendency to turn to quick-fix, *Rambo*-like solutions to complex problems, whether these solutions be trillion-dollar defense systems in the sky or $14.95 subliminal cassette tapes designed to improve painlessly our self-esteem. Our theories of what should be may have caused us to be too uncritical of claims for the power of subliminal influence.

Belief in subliminal persuasion serves a need for many individuals. In our age of propaganda, citizens are provided with very little education concerning the nature of persuasion. The result is that many feel confused and bewildered by basic social processes. Subliminal persuasion is presented as an irrational force outside the control of the message recipient. As such, it takes on a supernatural "devil made me do it" quality capable of justifying and explaining why Americans are often persuaded to engage in seemingly irrational behavior. Why did I buy this worthless product at such a high price? Subliminal sorcery.

But belief in subliminal persuasion is not without its cost. Perhaps the saddest aspect of the subliminal affair is that it distracts our attention from more substantive issues. By looking for subliminal influences, we may ignore more powerful, blatant influence tactics employed by advertisers and sales agents. Consider the tragic suicides of Ray Belknap and James Vance brought to light in the recent trial of Judas Priest.* They lived troubled lives—lives of drug and alcohol abuse, run-ins with the law, learning disabilities, family violence, and chronic unemployment. What issues did the trial and the subsequent mass media coverage emphasize? There was no spotlight on the need for drug treatment centers, no evaluation of the pros and cons of America's juvenile justice system, no investigation of the schools, no inquiry into how to prevent family violence, no discussion of the effects of unemployment on a family. Instead, we were mesmerized by an attempt to count the number of subliminal demons that can dance on the end of a record needle.

In this trial, Judge Jerry Carr Whitehead ruled in favor of Judas Priest, stating: "The scientific research presented does not establish that subliminal stimuli, even if perceived, may precipitate conduct of this magnitude. There exist other factors which explain the conduct of the deceased independent of the subliminal stimuli."[12] Perhaps now is the time to lay the myth of subliminal sorcery to rest and direct our attention to other, more scientifically documented, causes of human behavior.

---

* One of us [ARP] testified in this trial. His testimony consisted of much of the evidence presented in this chapter.

30

IS FOREWARNED FOREARMED?
OR HOW TO REALLY RESIST PROPAGANDA

Throughout this volume we have attempted to explore the question: How credible and effective are obvious attempts to package and sell products and ideas (toothpaste, aspirin, presidential candidates) through clever influence tactics? On a personal level, many people claim that such blatant attempts at persuasion are so pitifully obvious that they are not much affected by them.

Yet, the prima facie evidence suggests they are extremely effective. Success stories abound. The sales of Benson & Hedges 100s cigarettes increased sevenfold during a four-year period of heavy advertising. The Mattel Toy Company increased company size twenty-four-fold after they began to extensively advertise on television. Grape-Nuts, a venerable but nearly forgotten cereal, experienced a sudden 30% increase in sales when a well-known natural foods enthusiast began plugging this rather bland cereal. It appears that tremendous numbers of consumers set aside their skepticism even though they know the message is an obvious attempt to sell a product.

Moreover, as parents, most of us have seen our children being seduced by toy commercials that artfully depict the most drab toys in an irresistible way. Similarly, children watching cartoons on any Saturday morning are deluged by fast-paced ads for sugar-coated cereal, carryout food, and candy bars, and they in turn deluge their parents with requests for the products.

Much research confirms what every parent knows.[1] Over 90% of preschool-age children ask for toys or food they see advertised on television, according to a survey of their mothers. In fact, almost two-thirds of the mothers reported hearing their children sing commercial jingles they learned from television, most by the age of three. Another survey found that children who were frequent viewers of children's programs are more likely to like, request, and consume advertised snacks, cereals, and fast foods. In general, children below the age of eight demonstrate very good recognition of advertised brand names, poor recall of the specifics of the advertised claims, and are highly persuaded by advertising. Perhaps one of the saddest demonstrations of the influence of advertising comes from an experiment which found that four- and five-year-old children, after watching an ad for a toy, were twice as likely to say that they would rather play with a "not so nice boy" *with* the toy than a "nice boy" *without* the toy.

That children are highly susceptible to persuasive appeals has not gone unrecognized by U.S. government agencies and officials. In 1934, in the case of *FTC v. R. F. Keppel & Brothers, Inc.*, the Supreme Court ruled that children were a special class of consumers "unable to protect themselves." How the government goes about protecting children depends on the political and economic circumstances of the era. For example, during the 1970s, pressure groups such as Action for Children's Television (ACT) lobbied the Federal Trade Commission (FTC) and the Federal Communications Commission (FCC) for greater regulation of television advertising directed at children. As a result of their support, the FTC negotiated an agreement with the National Association of Broadcasters (NAB) to establish guidelines for children's advertising. Members of the NAB, which included the three major networks and approximately two-thirds of the local stations, agreed to reduce the amount of advertising to nine and a half minutes per hour for children's weekend programs and twelve minutes for weekday shows, require a clear separation between programming and advertising, and regulate advertising content to be consistent with values most parents endorse. In addition, the FTC and NAB also adjudicated consumer complaints about specific ads, often removing ads that violated the NAB standards.

However, in the early 1980s, as a result of Ronald Reagan's deregulation policies, the FTC and FCC abandoned their roles as watchdogs of the children's airwaves. The NAB also ceased to enforce its broadcast code of ethics, including those portions dealing with children and television. Regulation of children's advertising and programming is now left to each individual television network and station—a case of the foxes becoming the guardians of the henhouse.

Nevertheless, most children do catch on after a time. We have all seen children, after several disappointments, develop a healthy skepticism (even a certain degree of cynicism) about the truthfulness of these commercials. Indeed, a survey found that only 12% of sixth-graders believed television commercials told the truth all or most ᵒᶠ the time; by the tenth grade, only 4% felt they were truthful even most of the time. In general, research shows that many children before the age of eight find it difficult to detect a false utterance. However, after this age, children show a growing distrust of advertisers and come to realize that the intention of advertising is not to inform, but to persuade.

This kind of skepticism is common among adults as well. A public opinion poll showed that the overwhelming majority of the adult respondents believe television commercials contain untruthful arguments. Moreover, the results indicate that the more educated the person, the more skeptical, and that people who are skeptical believe their skepticism makes them immune to persuasion.

This might lead us to conclude that the mere fact of knowing a communicator is biased protects us from being influenced by the

"Kids, here I am, all hooked up to this lie detector, ready to tell you all about Zapples, the exciting new breakfast cereal...."

message. But as indicated earlier, this is not always the case. Simply because we *think* we are immune to persuasion does not necessarily mean we *are* immune. For example, attempts to teach children about advertising and its purposes have been shown to lead to more skepticism about advertising, but this skepticism seldom translates into *less* desire for advertised brands. Similarly, many adults tend to buy a specific brand for no other reason than the fact that it is heavily advertised. It behooves us, then, to look at just how being forewarned of persuasive intent influences persuasion.[2]

Research commonly shows that, indeed, to be forewarned is to be forearmed. In other words, members of an audience can be made less receptive to a message if explicitly forewarned that an attempt is going to be made to persuade them. This phenomenon was demonstrated in an experiment by Jonathan Freedman and David Sears.[3] Teenagers were told they would be hearing a talk entitled "Why Teenagers Should Not Be Allowed to Drive." Ten minutes later, the speaker presented them with a prepared communication. In a control condition, the same talk was given without the ten-minute forewarning. The subjects in the control condition were more thoroughly convinced by the communication than were those who had been forewarned.

Why were the forewarned teenagers less persuaded? We would argue that phrases such as "And now, a message from our sponsor" have the potential to render the message that follows less persuasive than it would have been if the communicator had simply glided into it without prologue. The forewarning seems to say "Watch out, I'm going to try to persuade you," and people tend to respond by marshaling defenses against the message. They tend to marshal their defenses in two ways—by playing attitudinal politics and by preparing a possible rebuttal to the anticipated communication.

By "attitudinal politics" we mean holding and expressing an opinion not because it is what is believed but in order to secure some strategic purpose. For example, many people dislike having their perceived freedom threatened by a communication and thus seek to appear independent, but consistent. When these motives are invoked, the goal is to appear unpersuaded—regardless of the merits of the communication. One may claim, "I knew he was out to persuade me. But I make up my own mind. See—my opinion is unchanged." On the other hand, there are times when one seeks to appear informed, reasonable, and open for discussion. In such cases, a forewarning may result in *more* persuasion, or at least becoming more moderate in one's opinion.[4]

As a result of attitudinal politics, forewarning effects may be short-lived. As the audience or the strategic purpose changes, so does the opinion. For example, one study found that the effects of forewarning wore off in about a week, resulting in little *immediate* persuasion, but considerable *delayed* impact of a message.[5] Because of its often short-lived effects, forewarning does not always provide full protection from the tactics of persuasion. We may think skeptically about the advertisement as we view it comfortably in our homes. However, once at the supermarket, our skepticism may go out the window when the only information for making a decision is that which is recalled from the ad.

The second line of defense that may be engaged by forewarning—rebuttal—affords more protection, but, alas, is not always used. By "rebuttal" we mean preparing oneself to scrutinize and counterargue an upcoming message. Much research indicates that a forewarning increases message scrutiny. Delivering a forewarning of persuasive intent five minutes before delivering the message as opposed to immediately before usually results in more resistance to persuasion, precisely because the target has more time to think of counterarguments. On the other hand, a forewarning has little effect when an individual is distracted from fully thinking about the message.

A forewarning does not *always* lead to an attempt to refute the message. Forewarnings have been shown to have little effect in inducing resistance to persuasion when the recipient believes the message or topic is unimportant. For example, Richard Petty and John Cacioppo[6] warned college students that they would be receiving a persuasive message designed to change their beliefs about academic regulations. They then heard a message arguing for the institution of an onerous senior comprehensive exam. Some of the students were told that the change would take place almost immediately (i.e., they would have to take the exam). Others were told that it would happen in the distant future or at another university. Forewarning did reduce persuasion and increase counterarguing but only among those students who thought they would be taking the senior exam in the very near future. The other students, who did not believe the exam would affect them soon, if at all, found the argument quite convincing. Forewarning alone was not enough to induce these students to make the effort to scrutinize and counterargue the message.

Such results present a problem to those who believe that they are immune to persuasion just because they "know all about the advertiser's tricks." We often watch the mass media in a mindless state. The communications are typically just not that involving or interesting. But, ironically, that often makes them all the more persuasive. In such cases, despite knowing that the advertiser is "out to get us," we still do not make much of an attempt to refute the message and, as a consequence, are often persuaded.

What, then, are the best ways to reduce susceptibility to the tactics of persuasion—recognized and otherwise? We can suggest three strategies.

One strategy, attempted by the FTC and FCC along with various consumer and industry groups, is to *regulate* and *legislate* persuasion practices so that they are fair and honest—for example, to forbid tactics that take advantage of special populations, such as children, or that deviously play on our emotions, such as lowballing. The idea is that, just as in a court of law some evidence is inadmissible and some legal maneuvers are not permitted, so, too, certain mass media persuasion tactics are unfair and not in society's best interest to allow.

Regulation of persuasion has potential pitfalls. One such problem is that rules regulating persuasion may violate First Amendment protections of free speech. Violations are especially likely to occur when content (e.g., prohibiting the teaching of evolution or the news coverage of a controversial event such as a Nazi rally in the U.S. or an anti-apartheid rally in South Africa) is regulated, as opposed to process (e.g., outlawing lowballing or particularly deceptive advertising). Another problem is that the idea of regulating mass persuasion is a relatively new one in American history. As such, the codes governing persuasion are limited in nature and can be easily overturned, thus affording the consumer minimal protection. Nevertheless, we would argue that it is beneficial for citizens of a society such as ours, which depends heavily on persuasion, to engage in discussions of what forms of persuasion are moral and what, if any, types of persuasion should be declared illegal—a charge we take up later in the book.

A second defense against the tactics of propaganda is to play devil's advocate—to adopt for yourself, at least for the moment, the role of champion of the opposite cause. The research on forewarning and persuasion suggests that knowing that you are about to be persuaded, in and of itself, is of little consolation in preventing persuasion. What matters is what you do with that forewarning—how it leads you to react toward the message and to evaluate its content. Just because you know there will be an earthquake tomorrow doesn't mean you will be safe unless that forewarning leads you to take appropriate safeguards. What are the necessary safeguards to prevent persuasion? How does one play a devil's advocate? Here are some questions that can be asked to help diagnose a persuasive communication. The questions can be used when the intention to persuade is clearly recognized and, perhaps most importantly, when it is not, but yet decisions must be made.

What does the source of information have to gain?

Why are these choices being presented to me in this manner? Are there other options and other ways of presenting those options?

What would happen if I chose something other than the recommended option? What are the arguments for the other side?

Asking such questions should be a good first step in generating the types of cognitive responses that are likely to limit our susceptibility to propaganda.

A third strategy for resisting persuasion is based on what has been termed the *inoculation effect*. We have already seen that a two-sided (refutational) presentation is more effective for convincing certain audiences than a one-sided presentation (see Chapter 22). Expanding on this phenomenon, William McGuire and his colleagues have suggested that, if people receive prior exposure to a brief communication that they are able to refute, they then tend to become "immunized" against a subsequent full-blown presentation of the same argument, in much the same way that a small amount of an attenuated virus immunizes people against a full-blown attack by that virus.

In an experiment by William McGuire and Dimitri Papageorgis, a group of people stated their opinions; these opinions were then subjected to a mild attack—and the attack was refuted.[7] These people were subsequently subjected to a powerful argument against their initial opinions. Members of this group showed a much smaller tendency to change their opinions than did the members of a control group whose opinions had not been previously subjected to mild attack. In effect, they had been inoculated against opinion change and made relatively immune. Thus not only is it sometimes more effective to use a two-sided refutational presentation, but, if it is used skillfully, such a presentation tends to increase the audience's resistance to subsequent counterpropaganda. Similarly, to protect ourselves from persuasion, we can begin to question our own beliefs, thereby discovering the strengths and weaknesses of the position we hold.

In an exciting field experiment, Alfred McAlister and his colleagues inoculated seventh-grade students against existing peer pressures to smoke cigarettes.[8] For example, the students were shown advertisements implying that truly liberated women are smokers—"You've come a long way, baby!" They were then inoculated by being taught that a woman couldn't possibly be liberated if she was hooked on tobacco. Similarly, since teenagers tend to smoke because it seems cool or "tough" (like the Marlboro man), McAlister felt that peer pressure might take the form of being called "chicken" if one didn't smoke. Accordingly, the seventh-graders were asked to role-play a situation in which they practiced countering that argument by saying something like "I'd be a real chicken if I smoked just to impress you." This inoculation against peer pressure proved to be very effective. By the time the students were in the ninth grade, they were half as likely to smoke as those in a control group from a similar junior high school.

In the war of persuasion, cigarette advertisers have also discovered the value of inoculation. In recent years the percentage of Americans who have quit smoking or are trying to quit smoking has dramatically increased. If tobacco companies are to maintain their sales, they must prevent the additional conversion of smokers to nonsmokers. To this end, the R. J. Reynolds Tobacco Company ran a series of two-sided magazine ads appealing for tolerance between smokers and nonsmokers. Half of the ad was titled "For those who don't" and contained a series of arguments in support of allowing smoking in public places. The other half of the ad was titled "For those who do" and consisted of a gentle presentation of the anti-smoking position. The ad thus contained the information needed by smokers, who would probably be most interested in the topic, on how to counterargue and resist an anti-smoking campaign.

Research has found that, in producing resistance, inoculation is most effective when the belief under attack is a cultural truism—a belief accepted as unquestionably true by most members of a society, such as, "The United States is the best country in the world to live in" or "If people are willing to work hard, they can succeed." Cultural truisms are rarely called into question; when they are not, it is relatively easy for us to lose sight of why we hold them. Thus, if subjected to a severe attack, such beliefs may crumble.[9]

To motivate us to bolster our beliefs, we must be made aware of their vulnerability, and the best way to do this is to attack those beliefs mildly. Prior exposure, in the form of a watered-down attack on our beliefs, produces resistance to later persuasion because (a) we become motivated to defend our beliefs and (b) we gain some practice in doing so. We are then better equipped to resist a more serious attack.

This is an important point frequently ignored or misunderstood by policy makers. For example, in the aftermath of the Korean War, when several American prisoners of war were supposedly "brainwashed" by the Chinese Communists, a Senate committee recommended that, in order to build resistance among the people to brainwashing and other forms of Communist propaganda, courses on "patriotism and Americanism" should be instituted in our public school system. But the above research demonstrated that the best way to help our soldiers resist anti-American propaganda would be to challenge their belief in the American way of life, and the best way to build resistance to pro-Communist propaganda would be to teach courses on Communism, presenting both sides of the argument.

If such an idea had been proposed in the 1950s, when the Cold War was in full swing and Senator Joseph McCarthy was conducting his witch hunt, this idea would probably have been considered to be part of the Communist conspiracy. It is hoped the day of the ostrich is over: We cannot resist propaganda by burying our heads in the sand. The person who is easiest to persuade is the person whose beliefs are based on slogans that have never been seriously challenged.

31
EDUCATION OR PROPAGANDA?

Legend has it that the Greek philosopher Protagoras was the first person in history to have his books burned in public. Protagoras, who lived in the fifth century B.C., was a Sophist—an individual who made his livelihood by *teaching* others the ways of *persuasion*. His incinerated volume, lost now to antiquity, was similar in many respects to the one you are currently reading; it, too, described various persuasion devices that could be used on any occasion. It appears that, almost from the beginnings of Western civilization, people have found the idea that one individual can influence another, using persuasion, to be distasteful if not downright despicable. Propaganda is often viewed as the work of an evil manipulator.

On the other hand, Protagoras' other profession, that of educator, is often held in high esteem. We eagerly send our children to schools and universities hoping that they will learn a useful trade, develop an appreciation for the finer things of life, become productive citizens. But what really is the difference between propaganda and education?

Some would argue that breakfast cereal and aspirin commercials are obvious attempts to sell something at a high price by intentionally misleading the audience. They can be considered propaganda. "Selling" a presidential candidate, however, is more complicated. The devices used by political pundits and campaign staff to display a candidate in a favorable manner could conceivably be considered education—an attempt to educate the public on the policies and virtues of the candidate by allowing her to present her views as clearly, efficiently, and articulately as possible.

The American Heritage Dictionary of the English Language defines *propaganda* as "the systematic propagation of a given doctrine" and *education* as "the act of imparting knowledge or skill." Again, we could all agree that breakfast cereal and aspirin ads are propaganda designed to promote the sale of certain brands. But what about American television programs, which still tend to depict women and minorities in stereotyped roles? Or, more subtly, what about the vast majority of high school textbooks in American history that virtually ignore the contributions of blacks and other minorities? Is this merely imparting knowledge?

The problem of distinguishing between education and propaganda can be more subtle still. Let us look at arithmetic as taught in the public schools. What could be more educational? By that we mean, what could be more pure, objective, factual, untainted by doctrine? The issue, though, isn't as clear-cut as it may appear. Remember the examples used in your elementary school arithmetic text? Most of the examples dealt with buying, selling, renting, working for wages, and computing interest. As Phillip Zimbardo and his colleagues have pointed out, these examples do more than simply reflect the capitalistic system in which the education is occurring: They systematically endorse the system, legitimize it, and, by implication, suggest it is the natural and normal way.[1]

As a way of illustrating multiplication and percentages, the textbook might have Mr. Jones borrowing $8,000 at 14% interest from a bank in order to purchase a new car. Would this example be used in a society that felt it was sinful to charge interest, as early Christian societies believed? Would this example be used in a society that believed people shouldn't seek possessions they can't afford? We are not suggesting it is wrong or evil to use these kinds of illustrations in arithmetic books; we are merely pointing out that they are a form of propaganda and it might be useful to recognize them as such.

In practice, whether a person regards a particular course of instruction as educational or propagandistic depends, to a large extent, on his or her values. Reflect, for a moment, on the typical film about drug abuse that children are often required to see in high school. Such films typically mention that many hardcore narcotics addicts began by sampling marijuana. Most school officials would probably regard the presentation of this piece of factual knowledge as a case of "imparting knowledge," and most marijuana users would probably regard it as "the systematic propagation of a given doctrine"—because it implies that smoking marijuana leads to the use of hardcore addictive drugs without mentioning that most marijuana users do not become hardcore drug users.

By the same token, consider the topic of sex education in the schools as viewed by a member of the Moral Majority on the one hand and by the editor of *Playboy* magazine on the other hand. For one individual it is propaganda; for the other, education. Similarly, advertisers are often known to argue that, far from serving a propaganda purpose, their advertising seeks to inform the consumer about brands of products and the benefits that may be obtain from them.

This is not to say all communications are drastically slanted and one-sided. Rather, when we are dealing with an emotionally charged issue about which people's opinions differ greatly, it is probably impossible to construct a communication that people on both sides of the issue would agree was fair and impartial. Not surprisingly, researchers have found that pro-Israeli and pro-Arab partisans rated identical samples of major network television coverage of the Beirut massacre as being biased against their sides.[2] Other research shows that many Americans agree that the evening news is biased, but disagree, however, as to the nature of this bias.[3] Those who view the evening news as biased are evenly split, claiming that it is too liberal or too conservative, too Republican or too Democratic, too supportive of the status quo or too change-oriented. The point is that the bias of a communication is often in "the eye of the beholder." What is labeled as propaganda and what is labeled as education depend on one's own propaganda purposes. Protagoras' book was considered heretical in his day. Today, a similar volume may be called a "textbook." Undoubtedly some readers may choose to question our educational purpose, preferring instead to see this volume as propaganda for the use of persuasion.

In many ways, it is dangerous to apply the labels "education" and "propaganda" to a communication merely on the basis of whether it agrees or disagrees with one's values. Consider the case of war propaganda, with its goal of convincing a nation to commit acts of aggression against an evil enemy. If the appeal is successful, the act of war becomes consistent with our values and the most blatant propaganda is labeled "news" and "information needed to pull the nation together." In such cases, we may let our guard down just at the moment when we need it the most. Consider the opposite case, in which we learn about a disagreeable fact—for example, that the policies of the president we elected are in many ways responsible for increased racism and poverty. To reduce our dissonance, we label the disconcerting information "propaganda" and deny the validity of the claim. Thus discredited, the fact no longer needs to be considered in our decision making. In such cases, we miss the opportunity to educate ourselves about important issues of the day and to discover perhaps more successful courses of action.

As our discussion indicates, the issue of whether a given piece of information is education or propaganda is quite complex and goes well beyond whether we just like or dislike the fact. It behooves us, then, to look closely at how the tactics that we have presented throughout this volume are used in propaganda campaigns with an eye toward asking, "What forms of education and persuasion will serve our society and ourselves best?"

WHEN
INFORMATION FAILS:
THE CHALLENGE
OF PROPAGANDA
TO SOCIETY

32

ON THE INEFFECTIVENESS
OF INFORMATION CAMPAIGNS

Suppose you inherited controlling interest in a television network. Here is a golden opportunity to influence people's opinions on important issues. Let's say you are an enthusiastic proponent of national health insurance, and you would like to persuade others to agree with you. Having nearly finished reading this book, you know how to do it, and you are in control of a very powerful medium of communication. How do you set about doing it?

That's simple: You choose a time slot following a highly intellectual program (in order to be certain that well-informed people are watching) and, accordingly, you present a two-sided argument (because two-sided arguments work best on well-informed people). You arrange your arguments in such a manner that the argument in favor of national health insurance is stronger and appears first (in order to be fresh in the viewer's mind). You describe the plight of the poor, how they get sick more frequently and die earlier for lack of affordable medical care. You use vivid personal examples of people you know. You discuss these events in a manner that inspires great fear; at the same time, you offer a specific plan of action, because this combination produces the most opinion change and the most action in the most people. You present some of the arguments against your position and offer strong refutation of these arguments. You arrange for the speaker to be expert, trustworthy, and extremely likable. You make your argument as strongly as you can, in order to maximize the discrepancy between the argument presented and the initial attitude of the audience. And then you sit back, relax, and wait for those opinions to start changing.

It's not that simple, however. Imagine a typical viewer: Let's say she is a 45-year-old, middle-class real estate broker who believes the government interferes too much in private life. She feels any form of social legislation undermines the spirit of individuality, which, she believes is the essence of democracy. She tunes in your program while looking for an evening's entertainment. She begins to hear your arguments in favor of free health care. As she listens, she becomes slightly less confident in her original convictions. She is not quite as certain as she had been that the government shouldn't intervene in matters of health. What does she do?

If she is anything like the subjects in Lance Canon's experiment, she would reach over, turn the dial on her television set, and begin to watch "Wheel of Fortune."[1] Canon found that, as one's confidence is weakened, a person becomes less prone to listen to arguments against his or her beliefs. Thus the very people you most want to convince and whose opinions might be the most susceptible to being changed are the ones least likely to continue to expose themselves to a communication designed for that purpose.

Information campaigns frequently fail to change attitudes, a fact of persuasive life that was observed by Herbert Hyman and Paul Sheatsley back in 1947.[2] In explaining the frequent failure of information campaigns, Hyman and Sheatsley noted that people tend to acquire information mostly about things that they find of interest and tend to avoid information that does not agree with their beliefs. Should someone find that they have been unavoidably exposed to uninteresting and disagreeable information, a common response is to distort and reinterpret that information, thus ignoring its implications for updating beliefs and attitudes.

Despite these apparent psychological barriers, attempts to influence attitudes and change behavior by providing reasonable information—whether it be a mass mailing on the AIDS epidemic from the U.S. Surgeon General, crisis information in the front of the phone book, or our health insurance documentary—are as common as ever. To the extent that such campaigns fail to consider our tendency to expose ourselves selectively to information and systematically to distort discrepant communications, they are likely to fail.

Must you resign yourself to broadcasting your message to an audience composed of viewers who already support national health insurance? That may be the case—if you insist on airing a serious documentary devoted to the issue. After considering your alternatives, however, you might decide to take another approach.

You call a meeting of your network executives. The programming director is instructed to commission several scripts dramatizing the plight of families facing financial ruin because of high medial costs associated with serious illness. You order the news department to do some feature segments on the success of national health insurance in other countries. Finally, you provide the late-night talk show host with a couple of jokes he might tell about his inept but affluent doctor.

Although none of these communications would match the documentary in terms of the information provided, their cumulative impact could be more significant. Embedded in dramas or news segments, they would not necessarily come labeled as arguments supporting national health insurance; they seem innocuous, but their message is clear. Not appearing to be explicit attempts at persuasion, they should arouse little resistance, avoiding an inoculation effect and inhibiting the formation of counterarguments by distracting the audience. Most importantly, people will probably watch them without switching channels.

We are not the only ones to realize that our informative national health insurance documentary is doomed to failure whereas our highly dramatic, highly personalized, and very entertaining coverage of health care in America is likely to succeed. Robert Entman argues that, although the opportunity to gain more information about political affairs has increased dramatically in the last twenty years, Americans' interest in and knowledge of such affairs have not increased and may well have declined during this period.[3] The public, the press, and political leaders are caught in a spiral. Sophisticated news coverage requires an interested and informed public. Without an educated audience, journalists and leaders must simplify their message and package it as "entertainment," thus reducing further the sophistication of the public at large. The result may be, as Entman puts it in the title of his book, *a democracy without citizens*.

33

WHAT IS NEWS?

Imelda Marcos's shoes. There are few people living in an information-dense society like our own who won't know what we are talking about when we use this simple phrase. Most of us will immediately see, in our mind's eye, a closet containing hundreds of pairs of shoes, of various colors, styles, and uses. This image has served as the symbol of the incredible degree of corruption that characterized Ferdinand Marcos's long reign as president of the Philippines. As a symbol, the picture of Imelda Marcos's shoes is vivid and effective, but also simplistic. And very, very useful. It is characteristic of the type of news we are most likely to get, particularly on television, and contributes to the creation of a democracy without citizens.

Every day television, radio, magazine, and newspaper editors hear about a lot of events and interesting stories. It has been estimated that, for the typical daily newspaper, over 75% of the potential news items of the day are rejected and never see print. For national media such as network television news, the percentage of rejected news is probably much higher. For example, on any given day, there are hundreds of wars and armed conflicts occurring throughout the world. The viewer of the nightly news or the reader of the daily paper typically learns of approximately two or three of these conflicts and, after years of watching and reading, could probably name fewer than a dozen current wars.

Selectivity of news is the beginning of propaganda. As Walter Lippmann once put it:

> Without some form of censorship, propaganda in the strict sense of the word is impossible. In order to conduct a propaganda there must be some barrier between the public and the event. Access to the real environment must be limited, before anyone can create a pseudo-environment that he thinks wise or desirable. For while people who have direct access can misconceive what they see, no one else can decide how they shall misconceive it, unless he can decide where they shall look, and at what.[1]

Any revolutionary or would-be leader worth his or her salt knows that a primary objective is to secure the public's source of news. Very early in its existence, the Nazi party established its own publishing company, the Eher Verlag, which in its heyday controlled more than 150 publishing houses, employed an estimated 35,000 persons, and had profits exceeding over 100 million marks a year. During his reign as Führer, Hitler was successful in holding the press captive by systematically rewarding agreeable journalists (with choice interviews, promotions, and party favors) and punishing those that disagreed with Nazi policy (by limiting their access to news, subjecting them to government investigations, and suspending their operating licenses).[2]

Five years before coming to power in the 1917 October revolution, the Soviets established the newspaper *Pravda*. For more than seven decades, *Pravda*, which means "truth," has served the Soviet Communist party by censoring and filtering the news presented to Russian and Eastern Europeans.[3]

Closer to home, President Franklin D. Roosevelt, much like other U.S. presidents, attempted to influence the news, albeit more subtly than his European counterparts, by flooding the news media with pro-administration information. For example, during a typical three-month period in 1936, the Roosevelt administration employed 146 full-time and 124 part-time publicity agents who issued 7 million copies of about 4,800 public news releases. The Works Progress Administration alone spent over $1 million in one year on printing—all in an effort to encourage the news media to convince the American people of the necessity of New Deal policies.[4]

In present-day Western democracies, what factors determine which news items are selected for television and radio newscasts and for publication in magazines and newspapers? In totalitarian regimes, news is routinely censored by ruling elites. Such blatant control is rare in Western democracies and when it does occur, often results in immediate public outcries—witness, for example, reactions to censorship of the rap group 2-Live Crew or the popularity of "network censor" jokes by Johnny Carson and other comedians. The jokes tap into a wellspring of animosity to such censorship in spite of the fact that studies of network practices find that, by the time a script reaches the network censor, only minor changes, if any, are needed to make the show "air-worthy."

However, there are certain circumstances in which direct censorship is not only accepted but appears to be encouraged by American citizens. Such was the case during the Persian Gulf war when the Pentagon established rules designed to regulated information flow concerning the war effort.[5] Journalists were permitted to cover the war scene only if they were in organized pools escorted by a military leader, a situation that kept them far from the real action. Any journalist operating independently was subject to arrest by military police. If reporters did happen to stumble onto newsworthy items, officials were assigned to guide them quickly away from the action. With few opportunities to gain firsthand information, reporters became dependent on official statements and government-issued videotapes. Few Americans complained. One "Saturday Night Live" skit poked fun at the coverage of the war by depicting reporters as comically self-absorbed, with little understanding of national security. John Sununu, the White House chief of staff, ordered a videotape copy of the show for viewing at the White House as further evidence that the public support the military's press policy.

Clearly, however, in Western democracies, the selection of *everyday* news involves more than traditional censorship. With the mass of information that comes over the news wires, how do journalists select what to print in the papers and to show on TV?[6] The typical news reporter faces many pressures—stories must be prepared on a deadline, needed information may not be available, the opinions of advertisers and political groups may need to be considered, it may be a slow or fast news day, a balanced airing of the issue must be maintained. As difficult as these pressures may seem, the journalist faces one more pressure that may mean his or her livelihood—the ability of the news story to hold the audience's attention. All television programming, including the evening news, must strive for ratings and viewers. A study of why people watch the news concludes that most viewers want to be amused and diverted, and being informed is only a secondary motive for watching. As the director of the British Broadcasting Corporation has noted, television news is a form of entertainment.[7]

Accordingly, when those in charge of news programming make decisions about which events to cover and which fraction of the miles of daily videotape to present to the public, they make their decisions, at least in part, on the basis of the entertainment value of their material. Film footage of a flooded metropolis has much more entertainment value than footage devoted to a dam built to prevent such a flooding: It is simply not very exciting to see a dam holding back a flood. And yet, construction of the dam may be more important news.

Just as such action events as football games are more entertaining on television than such quiet events as chess matches, so it is more likely that riots, bombings, earthquakes, massacres, and other violent acts will get more air time than stories about people helping one another or people working to prevent violence. Indeed, news agencies station reporters at "action centers," such as courts and police stations as opposed to schools, churches, and research laboratories where more important events may be occurring. Thus news telecasts tend to focus on the violent behavior of individuals—terrorists, protesters, strikers, or police—because violent action makes for more exciting

"Does anyone __really__ want to hear about a fire in a shoe factory out in the boondocks?"

viewing than does a portrayal of people behaving in a peaceful, orderly manner.

Such coverage does not present a balanced picture of what is happening in the nation, not because the people who run the news media are evil and trying to manipulate us but simply because they are trying to entertain us. And, in trying to entertain us, they may unwittingly influence our opinions about the world we live in. For example, as we noted before, people who watch a lot of TV tend to see the world as a far more violent place than those who watch very little TV.

Such biased coverage was dramatically illustrated by the manner in which the media handled the nonriot that occurred in Austin, Texas, during the first week of May 1970. Tensions had been running high between University of Texas students and local police following a confrontation at an impromptu student demonstration against the invasion of Cambodia by U.S. troops. During the demonstration, some 6,000 students marched on the state capitol, broke a few windows, and skirmished with police; the students were tear-gassed and several police officers and students were injured.

But this was a mere preface—a minor event compared to what seemed to be coming. A few days later, students at the University of Texas were outraged at the wanton slaying of four students by members of the Ohio National Guard during a peaceful demonstration at Kent State University. To protest this event, the Texas students planned a gigantic march into downtown Austin—20,000 students were expected to turn out. The Austin City Council, fearing trouble, refused to issue a parade permit. In frustration and anger, the students decided to march anyway. Rumors spread that hundreds of armed rednecks and hooligans were descending on Austin with the intention of assaulting the students. Other rumors abounded to the effect that state troopers and Texas Rangers had been called in and were determined to take strong and violent action against anyone disobeying the law.

In retrospect, it appears these rumors were almost certainly untrue, but the important point is that they were widely believed. The situation seemed certain to be a prelude to extreme violence. Sniffing an exciting story, news teams affiliated with the major television networks were alerted. As it turned out, however, the explosive situation was defused at the eleventh hour: A team of university psychologists, law professors, and law students succeeded, at the last moment, in convincing a federal judge to issue a temporary restraining order to prevent the city from enforcing the antiparade ordinance. Moreover, it quickly became known that the testimony of several members of the police force, in favor of allowing the students to march, was instrumental in the judge's decision.

This event—especially because of the role played by the police—resulted not only in the total absence of violence but in a genuine explosion of goodwill and solidarity among diverse elements of the community. Twenty thousand students did march, but they marched in a spirit of harmony. Some of them offered cold drinks to the police officers who were diverting traffic away from the parade route; students and police exchanged friendly greetings, shook hands warmly, and so on. This was an important event, coming as it did in an atmosphere of apparently universal distrust between students and police.

Interestingly enough, the national television networks completely ignored this encouraging turn of events. Given that teams of nationally prominent reporters from a variety of news organizations had descended on the city during the week, the lack of coverage seemed puzzling indeed. An unsettling explanation was provided by community psychologists Phillip Mann and Ira Iscoe: "Since there was no violence, news media teams left town and there was no national publicity, a commentary whose implications are by now sadly self-evident."[8]

It is interesting to note that thirteen years later in the same city, a great deal of coverage was given to an event of higher drama but far less importance. On February 19, 1983, some fifty members of the Ku Klux Klan staged a march to the Capitol building in Austin. They were greeted by about 1,000 hecklers. Some rocks and bottles were thrown, and a few people received minor cuts and bruises. The skirmish was featured in network television news reports, and major stories as well as photographs appeared in newspapers from coast to coast. Clearly, a minor Klan-and-town conflict was deemed more entertaining than a peaceful expression of goodwill.

The moral of the Austin, Texas, story is simple: If you want access to the mass media, be entertaining. Jerry Rubin, a leader of the Yippie movement, which captured much media attention in the late 1960s, observed that:

> Every revolutionary needs a color TV. Walter Cronkite is SDS's*
> best organizer. Uncle Walter brings out the map of the U.S. with
> circles around campuses that blew up today. The battle reports.
> Every kid out there is thinking, "Wow! I wanna see *my* campus on
> that map!"[9]

He also said, "It's gotta be more fun to be in the revolution than out of it."[10] Rubin and the Yippies provided that fun by appearing before Congress in costumes, supposedly burning money on Wall Street, and running a pig for president—all the while gaining media attention.

Terrorists have also learned the lesson of news as drama. Consider the Beirut hostage crisis of 1985, in which some forty innocent American passengers on a TWA jet were held captive by Shiite terrorists. TV cameras offered viewers back home around-the-clock coverage of all aspects of the crisis, important and trivial alike. There were press conferences held by the terrorists, press conferences held by the hostages, intimate shots of anguished families, demands, counterdemands, pistol-wavings, outrageous statements, luncheon menus. The TV cameras did everything but follow the hostages into the restrooms. The drama was spellbinding.

The result is sound-bite news—a montage of brief visual images that play to the crowds. Each event and every idea must be part of a dramatic story amply illustrated with visual displays. Stories that are easily dramatized and visualized, such as a child trapped in an abandoned well, are readily covered. More complex issues, such as the economy or regulatory policy, receive little attention unless they can be made concrete and visual.

Would-be leaders, whether they be Yippies, terrorists, or the nominee for president, must compete for attention in this entertain-

---

* Students for a Democratic Society—a relatively radical student organization that gained prominence in the 1960s and early 1970s.

ment environment. They do so by staging canned nominating conventions; using catchphrases guaranteed to make the evening news, such as "Make my day" or "Read my lips"; and engaging in endless photo sessions involving, for example, the Vietnam war memorial, a child with AIDS, a visiting dignitary, or a visit to a flag factory.

Television coverage of a political campaign comes to look more like an episode of the popular television show "Dallas" than a discussion of democracy and leadership. Just as we heard about JR's sex life, his competition for deals with Cliff Barnes, his squabbles with family members, so too we are likely to find out about the political candidate's sexual escapades, the competition in the opinion polls with his or her rival, and the intricacies of intraparty squabbles. A discussion of the oil regulatory practices that underlay JR's deals would be boring. So, too, would be an analysis of the Savings and Loan regulatory procedures. The only difference: JR used "play money" for his deals. Each U.S. taxpayer owes roughly $30 a month for the next thirty years to cover the savings-and-loan bailout—slightly more than a lifetime cable television subscription.

Advertisers and direct marketers constantly rediscover the observation that "News is entertainment." With the advent of interactive cable and computer bulletin boards, some marketers, sincerely proud of their products, thought that these new technologies would afford an opportunity to go beyond the usual 30-second spot and provide some real information to the consumer. They dutifully prepared large databases containing information on product attributes, new usage ideas, what to do about typical problems, and so on, only to find that no one looked at the information. Now marketers realize that if they are to use this new technology, then their presentations must be entertaining; therefore they have replaced the information displays with product-oriented video games, contests, and bake clubs.

One wonders whether anyone would watch if television advertisers replaced all the slick thirty-second spots with ads that only contained useful information. Advertisers, politicians, and journalists have come to rely on entertaining images and sound-bites to convey their messages—a practice that distorts and simplifies reality by editing out all but the most entertaining information. In the long run, our seemingly insatiable desire for entertainment may succeed where Hitler and *Pravda* ultimately failed.

PERSUASION DIRECT

Every month the average American receives eighteen pieces of direct mail—a total of seventeen pounds of junk mail each year. Indeed, 37% of all mail consists of unsolicited sales pitches. These appeals are designed to sell everything from books to clothes to furniture to kitchen cutlery. They collect money for every conceivable political cause and needy charity. Over a million persons are employed in consumer mail-order selling.

Let's look at two pieces of such mail that we received recently to see how they work. One item came from Greenpeace, the liberal political organization that describes its purpose as environmental protection. The other came from Publishers Clearing House, which conducts a sweepstakes with the goal of selling magazine subscriptions.

Before investigating this mail further, we should note that direct marketers—people who sell directly to the consumer via the mail or telephone—take great pride in identifying effective selling strategies. Typically, direct marketers will receive most of their replies within a matter of weeks after posting the appeal. As such, they are very sensitive to what works and what does not. Often, simple split-mail experiments are conducted in which two versions of an appeal are sent out to see which yields a higher response rate. If you want to learn about persuasion tactics, watch what direct marketers do.[1]

One of the first things to notice about a direct mail appeal is the envelope. It has the task of breaking through the message-dense environment to attract your attention and get you to open the piece and read on. The first line of persuasive attack is the name and address. To cut costs and increase response, the pieces are mailed primarily to those who would be most interested in the message. One source of Greenpeace's mailing list is the lists of contributors to other, similar causes. Publishers Clearing House has a larger target audience and is most interested in directing mail to those who are likely to respond to direct-mail appeals in general (i.e., people who have purchased other direct-response items, have credit cards, own their own homes, and so on). It is unlikely that former Secretary of the Interior James Watt will receive an appeal from Greenpeace or that a homeless person will receive an entry blank for the Publishers Clearing House sweepstakes.

The Greenpeace envelope is large (9 by 12 inches), brown, and official-looking. The return address features the distinctive Greenpeace whale. In bold print across the middle of the package is the message: "Enclosed: Community Toxic Report. Please return to Greenpeace within 10 days."

The Greenpeace envelope makes use of a number of fundamental persuasion tactics to encourage you to open it. First, the large envelope stands out among the smaller 4-by-9-inch envelopes that typically appear in the mailbox. Second, the brown envelope resembles government and other official mail. The half-mindful recipient may open it up, thinking it is something important. The technique of packaging the appeal as something official is quite common; many times the elderly will receive sales appeals in envelopes that look like government checks or inquiries. (A variant of this technique is to make the appeal look personal by using a "real" postage stamp and inscribing a handwritten note in blue ink on the envelope.) Third, the symbol of a whale serves as a heuristic for the environmentally conscious. Finally, the message concerning community toxins further piques interest with a mixture of fear and urgency.

The envelope from Publishers Clearing House takes a less subtle approach. The 4½-by-11-inch envelope (still larger than most) is covered, front and back, with more than fifteen short messages and symbols. The messages are designed to create excitement and interest: "Twelve million dollars up for grabs in our new millionaire-a-month giveaways!" "Introducing E-X-P-R-E-S-S entry. Details inside."

"Your 12 entry tickets are enclosed." Seemingly pasted on the envelope is a yellow note with blue lines. This fifty-six-word message (rather long for an envelope) congratulates the recipient on being eligible for a "SuperPrize"—implying either that you are special or that you've already won something. The return address features the distinctive Publishers Clearing House logo to alert the recipient that this is the "sweepstakes you've been hearing about on TV." Also displayed is the symbol of the Special Olympics to serve as a heuristic for the socially conscious. Needless to say, we've guessed what's inside this envelope: a chance of a lifetime to win millions. Let's open it immediately.

Once inside the envelopes, the most striking feature is the amount of material. Greenpeace sent one and a half ounces of paper, a total of eight pages of information plus one reply envelope. Publishers Clearing House sent thirteen pages (plus a reply envelope and cents-off coupons), weighing in at two and a half ounces. Recall that message length equals message strength.

The first item of note in the Greenpeace package is a "gift" of twelve colorful stickers featuring the Greenpeace logo and cute but threatened animals such as kangaroos, dolphins, and penguins. The stickers are yours to use free of charge. As a persuasion tactic, they kill two not-so-rare birds with one stone. First, the stickers invoke the norm of reciprocity: "We've given you these nice stickers. Now it is your turn to return the favor." Second, by using the stickers, you adopt a "social identity" as a Greenpeacer and thus become more agreeable to the cause.

The next item of note from Greenpeace is a four-page appeal addressed, "Dear Friend" (a granfalloon technique). The letter begins with a request to complete an enclosed survey. It is doubtful that a survey with such a nonrandom sample could serve a legitimate "information-gathering" purpose. However, by completing the survey and thinking about toxic waste issues, the target begins the process of self-generated persuasion.

The survey is structured to produce cognitive responses sympathetic to Greenpeace's cause. Who would disagree with the thrust of these questions (and by default would not support the Greenpeace initiative)?

Each year, more than 300 million tons of hazardous waste are produced in the U.S. alone. Do you believe your state, local, and federal authorities are doing all they can to protect you and your community from these wastes?

[Are you opposed] to locating Toxic Waste Incinerators or Storage Facilities in or near your community?

Such questions elicit knee-jerk responses; note that such appeals never include difficult questions that might cause recipients to think twice about their answers. For example, they wouldn't dream of asking: "How much more would you be willing to pay for groceries that didn't use pesticides?" or "Would you be willing to sell your family car and use mass transit to decrease the need for off-shore drilling?"

The bulk of the letter, however, uses a classic fear appeal. Recall from Chapter 23 that fear appeals are most effective when they raise high levels of fear and suggest a doable, effective response. The Greenpeace appeal does just that. First, it states the problem in no uncertain terms: "Millions of our fellow citizens now agree that toxic waste is *the* most serious threat to public health today." Graphic examples of toxic pollution are included in the letter. What's the solution to this menace?

Many people believe that the problem of toxic wastes is just too big to do anything about. Well, we at Greenpeace don't. *Greenpeace is one organization that is taking direct action* against the polluters of our water, our air, and our land—fighting to cut off toxics at their source. And with your help, we're going to do a whole lot more.

The letter goes on to list vivid examples of Greenpeace success stories and future action plans. It asks you, not necessarily to become a "front-line" activist confronting major polluters directly, but to send in your Community Toxic Survey along with a contribution. Note that the mention of front-line activists serves as a decoy to make the "act of a contribution" seem less difficult and more doable. To further underscore the threat of toxic waste and what you can do about it, Greenpeace offers, on a separate insert, a guide to home toxins. It's free with your contribution of $15 or more to Greenpeace.

One potential pitfall with fund raising is that requests for money can often appear simply self-serving. Greenpeace minimizes this possible cognitive response by noting that its activists are putting their health and safety on the line for your environment.

The last item on the survey is a request for money. The target is asked to check the dollar amount—$15, $25, $35, $50, $100—of the contribution. Note how puny $15 or $25 appears next to a suggested contribution of $100—an example of contrast effects similar to those produced by decoys. A stamped, self-addressed reply envelope is included; the fact that these good, selfless people have already spent the money for a stamp puts additional pressure on the recipient not to "waste it" by pitching the appeal in the trash.

Publishers Clearing House uses some of the same persuasion tactics as Greenpeace, along with some additional ones. The goal of the communication is to induce you to subscribe to one or more magazines. Their reply card consists of space for ordering magazine subscriptions plus "12 lucky prize numbers" that could win you a million dollars. To order a subscription, you must find a stamp (from a 10½-by-22-inch sheet) corresponding to the magazine you want and paste it on your sweepstakes entry blank. Although you may enter the sweepstakes without ordering magazines (or else it would be illegal), placing a subscription is encouraged with such phrases as "Express entry! Place at least one [magazine] coupon at left for automatic entry in all giveaways" and "If you haven't ordered lately, this may be the last bulletin we can send to you."

In the packet, Publishers Clearing House offers a free "gift" of coupons redeemable for more than $10 on Procter & Gamble products. As with the Greenpeace stickers, the gift of coupons can invoke the norm of reciprocity. Further, by using the coupons one can adopt a self-image of "helpful and concerned" because Procter & Gamble will donate 10¢ to the Special Olympics for each coupon redeemed.

One insert states: "Don't throw away the number that can win you one million dollars." Recall that earlier we noted that it is more painful to lose money than it is pleasurable to gain the same amount. By framing the proposition as avoiding the loss of a million dollars, Publishers Clearing House provides extra motivation for returning an entry.

Other inserts describe possible sweepstakes prizes and past winners and, in a use of the self-sell technique, ask you to imagine "what it would be like to win a million dollars." Many of the inserts are personalized with the name of the recipient to attract attention and aid in self-persuasion. Other inserts describe magazines that can only be obtained through Publishers Clearing House or free gifts that cannot be obtained by purchasing the magazines at the newsstand (see the discussion of phantoms in Chapter 28.) One flier even notes that you can win an American flag by returning your order (see the discussion of heuristics and symbols in Chapter 16).

One interesting feature of the Publishers Clearing House packet is what can be called the "sticker-hunt game." Customers are eligible for special prizes and bonuses if they find the right stickers and paste them in the right spots. The version we received offered double prize money for finding ten special stamps. How does this sticker-hunt game increase the likelihood that you will send in an order? One way to figure this out is to keep track of your cognitive responses as you hunt down the stickers and compare them to what might have been your thoughts if the sticker-hunt game were not there.

We once played the sticker-hunt game. The first few stamps were easy to find. After that, it was much tougher and we began to think:

> *"Where's that double prize sticker? Hmmmm. It's not over here by the Business Week sticker or over there by the Consumer Reports stamp. Oh, here it is taped to the entry form. Clever. Now, where's the bonus-prize-sticker?"*

After twenty minutes of such thoughts we were able to locate all ten stickers. Notice, however, what we weren't thinking during this time: *"Gee, do I really need a subscription to yet another magazine?"* In other words, the sticker-hunt game was distracting us from counterarguing the true persuasive message. If you don't have anything to say, sing it!

(A similar analysis can be made of the sweepstakes itself. By concentrating attention on the long shot of winning big prizes, thoughts are directed away from counterarguing the sales appeal).

The sticker-hunt game offers another persuasive advantage—it invokes the need to reduce cognitive dissonance. The ease with which the first few stickers are found sucks you into the game and elicits a commitment to finding all ten. After twenty minutes of effort, you are not likely to say, "Gee, that was stupid; I'll throw it all in the trash." On the contrary, to justify your efforts, you are more likely to post the entry immediately.

Our description of direct marketing techniques presents a rather cynical picture of this form of persuasion. Whenever techniques are carefully scrutinized, one can be left with a feeling of betrayal and manipulation. This might occur even if you are dissecting a work of art, such as Dali's *Last Supper* or Shakespeare's *The Tempest*, each of which has their own point of view. Our goal is not to cast aspersion on the products being peddled or condemn direct marketers for using these techniques. Indeed, the astute reader can doubtless pick out, from our own essays, numerous examples of the use of granfalloons, decoys, vivid images, and so on to illustrate the points of this book and, we hope, command your attention.

We are not opposed to the use of attention-getting devices per se. We *are* opposed to their use in a deceptive manner that obfuscates rather than clarifies the issues at hand. For example, a sticker hunt game obscures legitimate reasons for purchasing a magazine and biased wording of question can cloud important environmental issues by falsely arousing emotions. Persuasion does not always need to result in deception and a confusion of the issues at hand.

In this context, we should mention that direct marketing is often the object of consumer complaints. The two most common objections to direct marketing are the existence of flim-flam (fly-by-night operations that offer goods and service but either do not deliver or deliver a product far inferior to the one advertised) and the obtrusiveness of the appeal (the mailbox is cluttered with junk mail). Reputable direct marketers are probably more concerned about these issues than the average consumer—after all, it cuts into their sales. For that reason, they have set up an association with a members' code of ethics and a procedure for having your name removed from members' mailing lists.*

Despite these complaints, the use of direct marketing techniques is on the increase. More catalogs, mailers, and 800 numbers appear every day. Direct marketing does offer the consumer a number of advantages: a wide variety of goods that cannot be profitably stocked at the local store, the ability to provide a high degree of customer service, and a quick and convenient means of shopping for today's time-pressed consumer. It also has the ability to offer the consumer a "superior" form of persuasion—one based not on irrelevant brand images and misleading "packages" but on useful information.

Consider a typical ad for a pair of sport shorts appearing in a Lands' End catalog. The ad shows a picture of the shorts, along with available colors and sizes plus an extensive list of features describing every detail of the shorts from fabric quality to waist design to the construction of the pockets. Admittedly this information is not unbiased. No ad is. We all seek to put our best foot forward. However, the ad provides more information about the product than can typically be gained from a televised "image" ad featuring beautiful men and women actively wearing a pair of shorts. (Sadly, we probably know more about the qualities of Lands' End sport shorts than we do about most political candidates.) A consumer equipped with catalogs from other merchants (and there were more than 12 million catalogs produced in 1990) could conveniently engage in comparison shopping and thus make selections with some sense of rationality.

Recall that we said earlier that direct marketers are very concerned with insuring high rates of customer response. This affords customers the opportunity to influence the marketer's selection of persuasion tactics. If the merchant uses tactics that you do not find acceptable—for example, an inappropriate use of a fear appeal,

---

* To have your name removed from mailing lists, write Direct Marketing Association, 6 East 43 Street, New York, NY 10017.

devious use of distraction—you can throw the mail in the trash or recycle bin. Or better yet, call the free 800 number and explain why you will not be buying the goods. Reputable merchants will learn from such complaints, and we should see more and more persuasive messages containing arguments that stand up to thoughtful scrutiny.

35

HOW TO BECOME A CULT LEADER

On November 18, 1978, not many people knew much about the small South American country of Guyana. Even fewer outside of the San Francisco Bay area knew that a group of followers of the Reverend Jim Jones had set up a "model" community of believers in the jungles of Guyana. However, on that day 914 members of Jones's People's Temple committed mass suicide. A tub of fruit punch laced with cyanide and sedatives was brought out. Jones ordered his people to drink, informing them that they would soon be attacked by the CIA and that it would be better to die a revolutionary's death. Adult members induced their children to drink first and then drank the mixture themselves.

The behavior of cult members is as mysterious as it is frightening. Members of Sun Myung Moon's Unification Church periodically engage in a mass marriage, being randomly assigned by Moon and his associates to mates whom they have never previously met. Members of David Berg's Children of God willingly give all they own to the church. The backyard of one Children of God commune was filled with automobiles, buses, jeeps, and motorcycles that members, mostly teenagers and young adults, had donated to Berg. The followers of Swami Rajneesh turned over all of their worldly posessions to their leader and smiled benignly as he accumulated eighteen Rolls Royces for his personal use. One member of the Church of Armageddon jumped from a tree to his death believing that, because he had purified himself, he could fly. Other members of the cult sit hand in hand in a circle and connect themselves to electrical devices to see how much electricity their bodies can stand because "all substances are from God."

Many claim that cult members are "brainwashed." This rather frightening term was originally used to describe the persuasion tactics used on American prisoners in Communist Chinese prison camps during the Korean War. These camps were totalitarian environments in which the captors came to control the thoughts of the POWs by controlling all sources of information and by systematically rewarding and punishing appropriate and inappropriate thought. Since then, the term *brainwashing* has been used rather loosely and has taken on a meaning surrounded by mystery. It has come to refer to exotic (and often undescribed) persuasion tactics that are practically irresistible. Victims of brainwashing are depicted on television and in the movies as if they are in a hypnotic trance. This representation is extremely misleading.

Although they may seem mysterious, the persuasion tactics of cults are nothing more or less than the same basic propaganda tactics that we have seen throughout this book. Cults simply use these techniques in a much more systematic and complete manner than we are accustomed to. Simply because the end result is dramatic and bizarre does not require that the means to get there be mystifying. Indeed, in case any of you would like to be a cult leader, we can list seven mundane but nonetheless "proven-effective" tactics for creating and maintaining a cult.[1]

1. *Create your own social reality.* The first step in creating a cult is to consturct your own social reality by eliminating all sources of information other than that provided by the cult. Cult headquarters should be isolated from the rest of the world—a farm in Oregon, a secluded house on the outskirts of town, a jungle in Guyana. Members' mail should be censored. Family should be prevented from visiting members. Strict boundaries between "believers" and the "un-redeemed" must be maintained. Such censorship can be physical, that is, forcibly excluding outsiders and physically restraining wayward members. However, it is much more practical to teach members self-censorship by labeling everything that is not "of the cult" as "of the devil."

The second step in constructing a social reality is to provide a cult's-eye view of the world. This picture of the world is then used by members to interpret all events and happenings. For example, Jim Jones taught that there is a constant threat of nuclear war and that the world is full of racism. To be prepared to live in this evil world, one must be ready to die. Suicide practice drills were conducted to prepare members for the inevitable attack on the Temple by this evil world. The Unification Church teaches the Divine Principle, a doctrine claiming that humanity must be restored to God's grace through payment of indemnity (penance) and the advent of a new messiah (the Reverend Moon). The believer is thus prepared to atone for sins through service to the church and to accept the leader's word as truth. David Berg, known as Moses to his followers, creates social reality for his Children of God through a series of "Mo Letters." These letters purport to be revelations from God and describe the cult's theology as well as providing guidance on how to interpret world events. For example, his letters advise cult members that they are special and thus above the law, that the world is rotten and thus it is acceptable to lie and steal for the church, and that sex with Berg is a good idea.

To get a real feel for the full power of a cult, imagine adopting their beliefs for just a moment. Try seeing the world as if you were a cult member. In a bizarre way, the world makes sense, perhaps for the first time in a cult member's life.

One useful technique for constructing social reality is to create your own language and jargon. For example, Divine Light Mission members call their services "satsang" and "darshan." The Unification Church refers to lying to the unredeemed as "heavenly deception." Scientology teaches that the "thetan" (soul) is impeded in its many lives by "engrams" (aberrations) that result from wrongdoing. A good vocabulary is useful for putting the "right" spin on things. By teaching a battery of clichés such as "bourgeois mentality," "Krishna consciousness," "of the world," and "in the Lord" any event is quickly defined as good or evil and critical thinking is abruptly terminated.

When it comes to teaching your social reality, here is one additional point to keep in mind: Repeat your message over and over and over again. Repetition makes the heart grow fonder, and fiction, if heard frequently enough, can come to sound like fact.

2. *Create a granfalloon.* The granfalloon technique requires the creation of an in-group of followers and an out-group of the un-redeemed. The technique allows you to control members by constantly reminding them: "If you want to be a *chosen*, then you must *act* like a chosen one. If you are not chosen, then you are wicked and un-redeemed. To be saved, you must act like you are supposed to act."

Love Israel, head of the Church of Armageddon, teaches his followers that he is the "king" and "Christ's go-between connecting the members with heaven." He tells his followers, "Don't use your little mind inside. Use your big mind, the collective family's mind. We're your mind." Love Israel understands the granfalloon technique.

The essential ingredient in establishing an in-group of believers is the creation of a social identity—an image of who "we" are. Joining a cult represents a break from the "other" world and the acceptance of this new identity. Many cults require a "baptism" or other initiation to indicate acceptance of the new identity. A new name can be given; all the members of the Philadelphia-based group MOVE took as their last name "Africa;" the members of the Church of Armageddon use the last name "Israel." Hare Krishnas adopt distinctive orange robes and eat a special vegetarian diet. Moonies do not possess their own clothes, but share among themselves; when their clothes get dirty, they turn them in to be washed and take another set from the commune's supply. Thus a simple indicator of one' personal identity—what one wears—belongs to the group. The Divine Light Mission "satsang," or religious sermon, is designed to encourage new members to start answering the question: "What is a premie [the term for a member]?" Church of God followers adopt new biblical names. To further increase the cohesion of the group, all new recruits must learn three Bible verses in the morning before any of the new recruits can eat breakfast.

The outward trappings of the believer—the new name, distinctive garb, a special diet—all confirm that the member is indeed a chosen one. To retain this valued membership, all one needs to do is continue to grow in this newfound life and, of course, continue to obey.

The reverse side of the granfalloon tactic is the creation of an out-group to hate. The Children of God teach members to hate their parents. One Mo letter states that parents are evil; they are not your *true* family; we are your family now. Chinese prison wardens taught

Americans POWs that the capitalist system is corrupt. The Unification Church teaches that only believers will be resurrected at the final coming. The Church of Armageddon teaches that the "world" is bad. The creation of an evil out-group serves the dual purpose of making members feel good about belonging to the group ("I'm glad I'm not like them") and increasing their fears about leaving the group ("I don't want to be like them").

If granfalloon techniques are correctly applied, then you should be successful in creating fear of the "outside" world and the belief that the cult is the only solution to a happy life. Life is thus impossible outside the cult—the only solution to life's problems.

3. *Create commitment through dissonance reduction.* Cults can insure members' obedience by establishing a spiral of escalating commitment; the cult member, at first, agrees to simple requests that becoming increasingly more demanding. Jim Jones used such a technique, extracting great trust from his followers one step at a time. Some light can be shed on what led to the final mass suicide if we look at it as part of a chain of events.

Let's start at the beginning. Jim Jones was a dynamic speaker and preacher. It is easy to understand how a charismatic leader like Jones might extract money from the members of the church. Once they had committed themselves to donating a small amount of money in response to his message of peace and universal brotherhood, he was able to request and receive a great deal more. Next he induced people to increase their tithes to support the church. Jones would often ask his members to perform loyalty tests, such as signing a blank confession of "sins" and admitting to feelings of homosexuality or the commission of aberrant sexual acts. Jones would tell members that "if you were really committed you would be willing to do anything for the church."

Next, Jones induced members to sell their homes and turn over the proceeds to the church. Soon, at his request, several of his followers pulled up stakes, leaving family and friends, to start life anew in Guyana. There, not only did they work hard (thus increasing their commitment), but they also were cut off from potential dissenting opinion; they were surrounded by true believers. The chain of events continued. Jones took sexual liberties with several married women among his followers, who acquiesced, if reluctantly; Jones claimed to be the father of their children. Finally, as a prelude to the climactic event, Jones induced his followers to perform a series of mock ritual suicides as a test of loyalty and obedience. Thus, in a step-by-step fashion, the commitment to Jim Jones increased. Each step *in and of itself* was not a huge and ludicrous leap from the one preceding it.

After making an initial commitment one does not feel comfortable reneging on the deal. To justify the sensibility of the initial commitment, the member is often willing to do more and then still more—to make increasingly demanding commitments. In this way, the resolution of dissonance and maintenance of one's self-image as honoring commitments form a powerful rationalization trap.

Cults employ other rationalization traps as well. The guilt of a sinner can be reduced by a gift of everything one owns to the cult; embarrassment over forced sex with a leader can be relieved by thinking that one needed such self-sacrificing "discipline;" cruelty to outsiders such as parents can be justified by seeing the need for even more cruelty; a feeling of stupidity for giving all to the cult can be overcome by rationalizing it as devotion to a noble cause. Note also that the member, after having done all these things, is faced with a dilemma: "How can I explain all that I have done to those outside the group?" This requires the creation of a sensible, coherent justification that is not easily forthcoming. The rationalization trap is sprung.

4. *Establish the leader's credibility and attractiveness.* Most cults have leader myths—stories and legends passed from member to member concerning the life and times of the cult leader. Unification Church biographers compare Moon's birth in Pyung-buk, North Korea, with Jesus' birth in Bethlehem—both were at night, both were in small unknown villages, and both marked the dawn of a cosmic transition. When Moon was 16 years old, Jesus appeared and told him, "You will be the completer of man's salvation by being the second coming of Christ." According to Divine Light legend, Maharaj Ji, as a young child, was already a great spiritual leader and teacher and was thus appointed to head a holy family in India. In answer to the question, "Just who is the Guru Maharaj Ji?" premies will often answer, "The Guru Maharaj Ji is God." After an initial period of indoctrination, wardens in Communist Chinese prison camps strove to maintain an

image as wise and caring teachers whose job it was to instruct the wayward prisoner in the ways of the truth. Children of God leader David Berg, blessed in his mother's womb so he would be like Moses, Jeremiah, Ezekiel, Daniel, and his namesake David, is the fulfillment of many biblical prophesies. David Berg's powers, described in his pamphlet "The True Story of Moses and the Children of God," are so great that, "You can even rebuke the devil in the name of David and he will flee. No power in the world can stand against the power of David."

What is the purpose of such myths? It is hard to disobey a person believed to be "the son of God" or, at least, blessed by a divine purpose. Anybody in their right mind should seek to identify and be like a holy person.

5. *Send members out to proselytize the unredeemed.* Witnessing to the unconverted has the obvious advantage of bringing in new members. Perhaps just as important, proselytizing can ensure that members are constantly engaged in self-sell, or self-generated persuasion. The act of witnessing requires the member to state anew to many different people the positive advantages of being in a cult. In arguing to convince others, members convince themselves. Evangelical activity also strengthens resolve. Each witness is likely to elicit many negative responses or an attack on the cult. In defending their beliefs, cult members learn to refute a wide range of attacks, thus inoculating themselves against counterarguments and thereby maintaining belief in the cult.

6. *Distract members from thinking "undesirable" thoughts.* Most cult doctrines are hard to take seriously, much less accept. The cult member, especially a new recruit, is likely to question and counterargue such basic points as the value of giving all one owns, especially a new sports car, to the cult and the merits of working sixteen-hour shifts and turning over all proceeds to the cult leadership. The old advertising saw "If you don't have anything to say, sing it," probably never applied more. How, then, does a cult leader distract a member from carefully scrutinizing and questioning the cult's doctrine?

The Children of God use a combination of techniques. First, they never leave new recruits alone to think for themselves. Bible verses are played continually on a loudspeaker, and a trainer follows the new recruit around preaching Bible verses and Mo letters—even as the new recruit goes to the bathroom. The new recruit is deprived of food, water, and sleep. It is difficult to think when you are hungry and thirsty and fatigued. Famed deprogrammer Ted Patrick went through this indoctrination; having been deprived of sleep for forty-four hours, he describes his feelings:

> At first you are frantic for silence—just five minutes of peace and privacy. Then your senses begin to get numb—you grow accustomed to the constant noise. You also, as you get tired, stop really registering what they tell you. You don't hear individual words anymore, just a stream of babbling and shrieking. I guess that's when the programming starts becoming effective—when the conscious mind stops functioning out of weariness and all that propaganda begins to seep into your unconscious.[2]

There are other ways to disrupt counterarguing in a cult. Chanting and singing prevent thinking about anything else but the chant and the song. Meditations such as those performed by the Divine Light Mission, in which the premie spends hours trying to visualize light, hear music, taste nectar, and speak the primordial vibration of existence, prevent the meditator from focusing on other, more worldly concerns. Nonstop activities such as proselytizing, working, and cooking and cleaning for other members further limit the opportunity for careful thought and personal reflection.

Once the recruit has accepted the cult, the task becomes one of preventing further close scrutiny and thought about the merits of membership. This can be done by teaching that any "disagreeable thought" is evil and from the devil. For example, if a member doubts a leader's command or starts to wonder about the merits of a particular theological point, he or she is counseled that this is "out of the Lord" or "from Satan" and should be rebuked. Hare Krishnas are required to take frequent cold showers to eliminate thoughts about sex. Members thus become their own mind police. Should this fail, more overt tactics may be necessary. For example, Jim Jones required a female member of Jonestown to have sex in public with someone she disliked as punishment for wrong thoughts. Observers get the message too: Control your own thoughts, or at least the expression of those thoughts.

7. *Fixate members' vision on a phantom.* The successful cult leader is always dangling a notion of the promised land and a vision of a better world before the faithful. Unification Church members follow and attend to the teachings of the "Lord of the Second Advent" so that they can be resurrected to the perfection state during the third and final testament stage. Jim Jones offered Jonestown to poor residents of San Francisco as a place that would, of course, require hard work, but would afford members the opportunity to "live comfortably—you'll have your own home, get a good school, college, swim, fish." Similarly, the nineteenth-century Oneida commune was working to build "heaven on earth." Divine Light Mission faithful are striving to see a light during their meditation and thus become a premie. It can be accomplished by service and devotion to Guru Maharaj Ji. Hare Krishnas believe that their chanting and dancing is a way to stave off the inevitable decline and downfall of humanity. In L. Ron Hubbard's Church of Scientology, members are working for a state of "clear." To become a "clear," members pay a high tuition to attend Scientology classes; devoted members may spend $10,000 to $15,000 in a matter of months.

By fixating a member's gaze on a future phantom, you provide a powerful incentive to maintain service to the group. Believers will be afraid to stop working, fearful that they or the world may lose the desired prize if they take even just one break. The average Moonie puts in an estimated sixty-seven hours a week working for the cause. It is also likely that most new recruits will be in a state of despair. Phantoms can establish hope—a powerful motivator of human be- havior—by providing a sense of purpose and mission.

Our purpose in presenting these seven tactics is, quite obviously, not to have readers of this book go out and start their own cults. Because "brainwashing" can be viewed as "hocus-pocus," some people are apt to deny the very real power of cult tactics. Others are likely to attribute all sorts of magical powers to the cults, standing in awe and fear of their abilities to control minds. By discussing the persuasion tactics utilized by cults, we are attempting to remove some of the mystery and ultimately reduce the danger of cults.

But there is another reason for understanding the persuasion tactics of cults. Cults use the same persuasion tactics often used by other propagandists; cults just use them in a more thorough and complete manner. It may be useful to reread this discussion and, instead of thinking of cults, consider your everyday social groups such as family, church, country, or place of work. We bet you'll find that there is a touch of cult-like behavior in much of our social lives.

36

PROPAGANDA IN THE THIRD REICH: A CASE FOR UNCERTAINTY

The year was 1924 and a young aspiring artist named Adolf Hitler sat thinking in his jail cell. Like many of his generation, he had found it painful to accept Germany's defeat in the World War, a war in which he had served in vain as a combat soldier. He shared his country's humiliation over the punishments dictated by the Treaty of Versailles. Adolf Hitler considered just how it all came about.

Hitler believed that one of the key factors in Germany's defeat was the skillful use of propaganda by British and American governments. As Hitler put it:

> But it was not until the War that it became evident what immense results could be obtained by a correct application of propaganda. Here again, unfortunately, all our studying had to be done on the enemy side, for the activity on our side was modest, to say the least...For what we failed to do, the enemy did, with amazing skill and really brilliant calculation. I, myself, learned enormously from this enemy war propaganda.[1]

What did Hitler learn from Allied war propaganda? Both the British and Americans established steering committees and organizations to develop and disseminate propaganda. For example, in the United States the Committee on Public Information (CPI), dubbed the Creel Committee after its chair, newspaper editor George Creel, assisted in training "Four-Minute Men," volunteers who would speak at local gatherings on behalf of the war effort. The CPI encouraged the film industry to make pro-war films and saw to it that "facts" about the war were disseminated widely to the press.

The most striking aspect of British and American propaganda, however, was the "atrocity story"—reports of alleged cruelty performed by the enemy on innocent civilians or captured soldiers. The purpose of such tales was to stiffen the resolve to fight (we can't let this cruel monster win) and to convince citizens of the morality of the war. For example, rumors circulated that the Germans boiled the corpses of enemy soldiers to make soap and that they mistreated the citizens of occupied Belgium. Much was made of the execution of an English nurse serving in Brussels for helping Allied soldiers return to the war and the German sinking of the luxury liner *Lusitania*, which, incidentially, happened to be carrying arms and war supplies. Although some of these atrocity stories contained a grain of truth, some were greatly exaggerated and others were pure fiction.[2]

Hitler realized that if Germany was ever to regain its dignity and win the next war, it would have to go the Allies one better in the war called persuasion.[3] He outlined his plan of attack in two chapters of the book he wrote in jail, *Mein Kampf* (*My Struggle*). For Hitler, propaganda was a means to an end—in this case, the promotion of the German state and the establishment and maintenance of the rule of the Nazi party. As such, there were no ethics that governed persuasion; there was only the rule of success or failure. As Hitler put it when talking about propaganda, "the most cruel weapons were humane if they brought about a quicker victory."[4]

Hitler was contemptuous of the ability of the masses to understand events. If he were alive today, he might remark that the people can operate only in the peripheral route to persuasion and that they use simple heuristics to guide their thinking. Effective propaganda relies on heuristics and appeals to the emotions. Hitler wrote in *Mein Kampf*:

> Its [propaganda's] effect for the most part must be aimed at the emotions and only to a very limited degree at the so-called intellect. We must avoid excessive intellectual demands on our public. The receptivity of the great masses is very limited, their intelligence is small, but their power of forgetting is enormous. In consequence of

these facts, all effective propaganda must be limited to a very few points and must harp on these slogans until the last member of the public understands what you want him to understand by your slogan.[5]

Having learned from the Allied efforts in World War I the value of an organization capable of coordinating and delivering effective propaganda, Hitler established an apparatus of his own. This organization was privy to all the dealings of the Reich and had the responsibility of selling the government's actions to the masses. To head up this organization, Hitler selected as his Minister of Popular Enlightenment and Propaganda Joseph Goebbels, the son of a lower-middle-class Catholic family from a small town in the Rhineland. Goebbels served as minister of propaganda from the time the Nazis came to power in 1933 until he committed suicide (after first poisoning his six children) near the end of the war. To get a flavor of what Nazi propaganda was really like, let's look at a few of the persuasion tactics used.

One of the first, and most important, tasks of the Ministry of Popular Enlightenment and Propaganda was to gain control of the mass media and to attract the attention of the masses. Hitler and Goebbels controlled journalists and filmmakers through a mixture of punishments and rewards. The Nazi regime made certain that it was the primary source of news and easily accessible to certain journalists. Most importantly, the Nazis gained the attention of the masses by making their propaganda entertaining. For example, the 1936 Olympics, which were held in Berlin, were used as a vehicle to promote the image of a strong "Aryan" nation and to build the self-esteem of the German people. Nazi posters used eye-catching graphics such as bold print and slashing, violent lines as well as attention-getting headlines. Radio news programs were often packaged as entertainment, featuring famous singers and celebrities. With such complete control of the press, radio, theater, cinema, music, and the arts, the essential themes of the Nazi party were repeated and repeated. It was nearly impossible in Germany during the 1930s to read a book or newspaper, listen to a radio broadcast, or see a film without coming into contact with the Nazi picture of the world.

Goebbels masterfully spread the agenda of the German nation by labeling events with easily learned slogans or terms that captured Germans' attention and directed their thinking. For example, he insisted that the word *Führer* (leader) be used only to refer to Hitler. To link the Russians and British as enemies of Germany, he labeled an aborted British raid as the "Maisky Offensive," after the Russian envoy to London, thereby creating the impression that the raid was conducted to appease the Soviets. To provide hope in 1942, Goebbels coined the phrase *schleichende Krise* (creeping crisis) to suggest economic, social, and political unrest in England. Although in hindsight these phrases may seem contrived, they did create a "picture in the head" of world reality: "The Russians and the British are in cahoots to get us; fortunately, there is unrest in England and we have our leader."

Goebbels also established "pictures in the head" through the use of innuendo and rumor. In the years of the Nazi party's rise to power, Goebbels would denigrate the character of members of the "opposition" by circulating rumors of scandals involving them. Toward the end of the war, as Germany suffered defeats on the battlefield, rumors were circulated that German scientists were nearing the completion of two new weapons—a U-boat capable of traveling underwater at high speeds and an anti-aircraft gun whose missiles were magnetically drawn to aircraft in the sky. The purpose of such rumors was to instill the belief that Germany could still win the war and should continue the struggle, despite a rash of defeats.

Nazi propaganda used heuristics extensively to secure agreement with its message. For example, rallies and propaganda films always showed masses of cheering, applauding, saluting Nazi supporters. We know this as the social consensus heuristic—if everyone else agrees, so should I.

Nazi slogans expressed an air of confidence: "Join Our Struggle;" "Fight With Us;" "Adolf Hitler Is Victory." Whenever Hitler spoke, he spoke with confidence and certainty of the Nazi purpose and the ability of the German people to accomplish this purpose. As we saw earlier, a speaker's confidence serves to increase the likelihood that a message will be accepted.

Hitler and Goebbels used historical symbols and monuments

extensively to package the regime. As Hitler was coming to power, he announced his "25 Theses," reminiscent of the 95 Theses that German religious leader Martin Luther had tacked to a church door in Wittenberg. Nazi artwork and posters often employed the style of Albrecht Dürer to suggest the historical roots of the regime. A popular genre of Nazi film was the historical biography. In such films, the life of a national historic hero such as Friedrich Schiller or Otto von Bismark was described with an emphasis on parallels (often irrelevant) to the life and times of Adolf Hitler.

Architecture was also used to package the Third Reich. Under the direction of Albert Speer, the Nazis planned an extensive effort to erect public buildings of a special nature. Due to the war effort, few were built. Those that were served Nazi purposes. For example, priority was given to erecting sports arenas, gigantic assembly halls, cinemas, and theaters—all of which could be used for political purposes. The Nazi style, which might best be termed "Nordic Hellenism," was classical in design, but on a gigantic scale. Public buildings were designed to look like enlarged Greek temples with towering steps and row upon row of columns. The design reinforced the image of the Nazis as heir to the great cultures of the past. An individual who entered such an edifice would feel his or her own stature dwarfed by the power of the state as represented by the building. In contrast, the original Greek temples were always built to human proportions, leaving the visitor with the feeling that, as Protagoras said, "humans are the measure of all things."

Another concern of Nazi propaganda was the creation of a band of supporters loyal to the Nazi party. As he was gaining power, Hitler dressed his supporters in brown shirts. Wearing the Nazi brown shirt in public became an act of commitment to the cause. The response of other Germans, at first, was one of ridicule. For many supporters, such a response likely produced even more commitment to the cause. As a means of reducing cognitive dissonance, the young brown-shirted Nazi would likely think *"This ridicule is just a small price to pay for the noble Nazi cause,"* rather than admit that brown shirts and Nazi fanaticism were rather silly. He would undoubtedly turn to fellow brown-shirters for social support, and Hitler would have added another loyal member to his band of cohesive followers.

Goebbels also employed the inoculation technique. One problem faced by any war propagandist is what to do when your side suffers a defeat in a major battle. Such a defeat could lower morale and the credibility of the regime. Goebbels anticipated this possibility by frequently issuing warnings about false hopes and illusions and by portraying the enemy as formidable, but defeatable. Thus, when the Allied forces achieved a victory, Germans were prepared to think *"This is a difficult struggle; we must try harder,"* not *"What has Hitler gotten us into?"*

Perhaps the most demonic and effective Nazi propaganda ploy combined the fear appeal with the granfalloon tactic. After World War I, Germany's economy was in ruins, partly as a result of the demands of the Treaty of Versailles. The result was devastating for German citizens. A high rate of inflation coupled with high rates of unemployment disrupted families and left many in poverty. Many men felt humiliated because they could not support their families.

Hitler and Goebbels were able to take advantage of the nation's fears by proposing a granfalloon solution. A single theme was echoed in most if not all Nazi propaganda: The Jews were to blame for all the nation's problems. Couched as a documentary about the role of Jews in history, the 1940 film *The Eternal Jew*, for example, portrayed the Jew as a money-grabbing villain who not only is a drain on society but also carries diseases and lacks proper values. Scenes from the film showed "kosher-style" ritual animal slaughter embellished to create the illusion of sadistic practices in the Jewish religion. In a similar vein, the film *The Jew Süss* vividly tells the story of a Jewish man raping a German maiden. The image of the Jew as despicable, inferior, and menacing was repeated over and over again in speeches, posters, films, newspapers, and even academic treatises.

What was the solution to this Jewish menace? The German people were once a proud nation; under the leadership of Adolf Hitler Germany can put an end to the Jewish threat and once again return to its past grandeur. To get this message across, Nazi propaganda first demonstrated that the party supported traditional German values. Nazi posters often featured scenes of traditional family life—a woman breastfeeding her child, children happily staring off into a distant future with the Nazi banner waving in the background, a father proudly standing next to his family.

Next, Nazi propaganda showed that a united Germany could achieve its goals. This theme was powerfully expressed in the 1934 film *The Triumph of Will*. The film opens with scenes of handsome young men in preparation to become soldiers. Hitler oversees their training. By the film's end, these young men have been turned into a powerful Nazi war machine. The message: By working together we can be strong again.

Finally, Nazi propaganda located the source of this newfound achievement in one man—Adolf Hitler. As one campaign poster put it—"Hitler, our last hope." Goebbels's goal was to portray Hitler as a kind father whose nation had called him to serve in its time of greatest need. Propaganda thus needed to present two sides of Hitler. On the one hand, posters showed Hitler smiling and shaking the hands of children; newsreels showed him awkwardly accepting the praises of his nation. As Goebbels once wrote in a magazine article, "The simplest people approach him with confidence because they feel he is their friend and protector."[6] The other side of Hitler was that of Führer. To capture this side of the image, posters portrayed Hitler in military garb standing erect and confident in purpose; newsreels presented endless scenes of Hitler reviewing the nation's troops.

The success of the Nazi propaganda machine, however, was based on more than just the use of some clever persuasion tactics. It was also due to a nearly wholesale acceptance of the idea that persuasion was to start at the top of society and be directed downward toward the masses. It was the responsibility of the ruling elite to make the decisions and then inform the masses of the wisdom of those decisions through propaganda; the responsibility of the masses was to follow. And what better role for the masses?—since, by and large, they are ignorant and cannot think. We have seen this model of the role of persuasion in society before. Aristotle argued that persuasion was needed to instruct those who could not reason fully. Propaganda is a means to communicate the "truth" to the ignorant.

Although such a model of persuasion may more or less describe any society at a given time, it is not an inevitable outcome. The Greek sophist Protagoras saw a different role for persuasion—through argument, the advantages and disadvantages of any course of action can be made clearer. The early founders of the U.S. government recognized that no party could be privy to the total truth; a society consists of competing interests. The U.S. Constitution, with its system of checks and balances, was one attempt to prevent any given group from gaining absolute control and to provide a forum for resolving differences of opinion.

The most dangerous aspect of Nazi propaganda, however, is its assumption that there is an absolute truth and the ruling elite alone are privileged to know this truth. In his film series *The Ascent of Man*, the eminent scholar and humanist Jacob Bronowski catalogs the dangers of believing in this myth of absolute truth.[7] In one of the films, Bronowski looks at the culture and thought of Germany just before World War II and finds that there were two radically different philosophies, two fundamentally different ways of looking at the world—one represented by some of the scientists of the time and the other by the Nazi party.

These scientists were coming to the realization that human knowledge could never be absolute. There was no "God's-eye view." Based on their scientific findings, physicists such as Albert Einstein, Werner Heisenberg, and Max Born were proposing such ideas as the theory of relativity and the uncertainty principle, which led to the recognition that there is no absolute fixed point of reference and that human knowledge is limited. In the social sciences, the exploration of other cultures and other peoples was fast leading to the conclusion that habits and beliefs differed widely and that it was becoming increasingly difficult to say which is "best."

In the infancy of social psychology, Kurt Lewin was developing his theory of the psychological field. His theory emphasized how an individual's psychological needs and tasks influence his or her perception of the world. According to Lewin, different individuals with differing needs and tasks would come to perceive the same event differently. Ironically, the inspiration for Lewin's theory came from his experiences as a soldier in World War I, where Lewin noticed that, as he approached the battlefield, his perception of the environment changed: No longer did he see beautiful gullies and interesting rock formations, but rather places to hide and things that could kill. Just before World War II, Lewin, who was Jewish, was forced to flee Nazi Germany. He came to America, where he trained many of the first generation of American social psychologists. The irony is that Kurt Lewin and Adolf Hitler fought on the same side in World War I. Both men experienced the same event; each reached a different conclusion.

The alternative position was one of dogma. The Nazi party embodied the truth; there was no needed to tolerate other points of view. Hitler expressed this alternative philosophy succinctly:

> The function of propaganda is, for example, not to weigh and ponder the rights of different people, but exclusively to emphasize the one right which it has set out to argue for. Its task is not to make an objective study of the truth, in so far as it favors the enemy, and then set it before the masses with academic fairness; it's task is to serve our own right, always and unflinchingly...As soon as our own propaganda admits so much as a glimmer of right on the other side, the foundation of doubt in our own right has been laid.[8]

What are the fruits of the myth of absolute dogma? Six million of the 9.5 million Jews living in Europe were killed. The Allied forces lost more than 11 million soldiers in battle, including 7.5 million Russian, 2.2 million Chinese, and a quarter of a million American soldiers. The Axis powers lost more than 5 million soldiers in battle, including 3.5 million German and 1.2 million Japanese soldiers. Civilian casualties are harder to estimate. Direct civilian casualties as a result of the war include 2.5 million Russian, 860,000 Japanese, 300,000 German, and 60,595 British citizens. Another estimated 10 million Russians lost their lives through indirect causes, such as famine and disease. In all, over 36.5 million persons lost their lives. And for what reason?

At the end of his film, Bronowski offers an antidote to this "itch for absolute knowledge and power." There is a shallow pond just outside the concentration camp and crematorium at Auschwitz. The ashes of some 2 million people were flushed into this pond—an act caused by arrogance, by ignorance, by dogma. In one of the most dramatic moments on film, Jacob Bronowski walked out into this pond, bent down and scooped up a handful of the ashes of some of these 2 million people. He made a simple request taken from Oliver Cromwell, "I beseech you, in the bowels of Christ, think it possible you may be mistaken."

If there is one thing to be learned from our study of persuasion, it is that we can be mistaken and misled. We have seen how information about our world can be selectively edited by news and entertainment organizations or managed by experienced political consultants. The picture of the world that emerges, mistaken as it may be, serves to guide our thinking and our actions. We have also seen that it is possible for a propagandist to play on our emotions and to take advantage of our decision-making processes by invoking simple heuristics. All of this leads to a single conclusion: *As human beings, we can be wrong.* Let us keep this fact in mind whenever we make decisions—especially those that cause damage to others.

One cannot study Nazi propaganda without passion and emotion. Both of the authors of this book lost friends and relatives during World War II, either in combat or in the Holocaust. We are sure that most readers of this book have suffered similar losses or have felt pain and anguish when watching footage of Nazi concentration or death camps. Joseph Goebbels once boasted, "Nothing is easier than leading the people on a leash. I just hold up a dazzling campaign poster and they jump through it."[9] We owe it to the memory of his victims and to ourselves to learn as much as we can about the ways of propaganda so that we may prove Herr Goebbels false.

37

PEITHO'S CHILDREN

Novelists have often portrayed the dark and devious side of persuasion. In the American classic *Elmer Gantry*, Sinclair Lewis tells the story of a hypocritical preacher who delivers spellbinding sermons capable of mesmerizing the faithful and, not inconsequentially, maintaining a tidy income for the Reverend Gantry. In *1984*, the British author George Orwell describes a totalitarian state that successfully employs propaganda techniques to maintain its control over the people. In *A Man of the People*, the African novelist Chinua Achebe chronicles the rise to power of the Honourable M. A. Nanga through rhetoric and policy designed to deceive and fool the masses.

Throughout this book we have seen this dark side of persuasion, whether it be trickery on the used car lot, misinformation in the mass media, "mind control" in cults, or the propaganda of hate in the Third Reich. In the hands of a demagogue, persuasion can be full of treachery and trickery, appealing primarily to our irrational impulses.

The ancient Greeks present another side of persuasion. During the heyday of democracy in Athens, the Greeks worshiped Peitho, the goddess of persuasion. According to Aeschylus' play *Oresteia*, Peitho succeeded in calming the Furies, three avenging spirits of retributive justice whose task it was to punish those who commit crimes. Orestes is on trial for the murder of his mother and her lover, a crime he freely admits he committed. But there is a twist. It is also known that his mother and her lover have killed Orestes' father in order to assume the throne of Mycenae. An Athenian jury must decide if young Orestes is a common murderer or if the homicide is justified. After hearing the arguments, the jury is split and the deciding vote must be cast by Athena, the goddess of wisdom. She votes that Orestes should go free.

The Furies who prosecuted the case are outraged. For them, murder is murder and blood must be atoned by blood. To appease the Furies, Athena offers them a new shrine on the Acropolis and a new name—the Eumenides, or the gracious ones. In return, the Furies must recognize the majesty of Peitho. The message to the Greek audience is clear: Wisdom dictates that persuasion must be used to overcome the baser nature of humankind.

This dual nature of persuasion, as a source of both human destruction and human wisdom, raises a final but crucial question: What should be the nature and role of persuasion in society?[1] For we are not only the recipients of persuasive communications, we are also the sources of such messages. Like it or not, we are all Peitho's children. Sometimes we play the role innocently, recommending a particular restaurant or a certain brand of stereo equipment to a friend. Sometimes it's not so innocuous. Many professions demand a high degree of persuasive skill—not just sales, law, and politics, but such professions as medicine, science, and teaching as well. Likewise, people who work

"*Remember, kids, these political debaters are experienced professionals. Do not try this kind of trickery and lying at home.*"

for political candidates or in support of social causes or charitable organizations depend on their persuasive abilities to attract votes, to garner signatures for petitions, to raise funds, or to spread information. In fact, we can be said to be engaging in attempts at persuasion any time we praise or criticize an object, defend or attack an idea, advocate or oppose a position.

Now that we have discussed how to deliver persuasive messages *effectively*, it would be worthwhile to consider explicitly how to decide *whether or not or how* to do so. The ethical question is a complex one with many gray areas. While this is not the place for an elaborate discussion of moral philosophy, we feel obliged to point out the existence and importance of ethical issues and to suggest a few ways to consider them.

Before doing so, we should note that the "morality" of a persuasive tactic is often based, rightly or wrongly, on its success in accomplishing a goal. For example, an oppressed minority that achieves its goal through a tactic such as a bus boycott is often criticized by the losing majority for its choice of tactics—"I agree with the goal, but not the means" is a common response. Further, history looks kindly on winners and often ignores their excesses. "Successful" traitors, for example, are a rarity: They either fail and are labeled "treacherous" or succeed and are called "patriot."

One approach is to judge the ethics of a persuasive attempt by assessing its goals; the extreme statement of this viewpoint would be that the ends justify the means. Suppose you are living in Poland in 1942. The Nazis are rounding up Jews and sending them to the death camps; you are safeguarding a Jewish family, hiding them in your cellar. When the Nazis knock at your door asking if there are any Jews inside, you answer that there are not. Few would argue that to lie persuasively in this instance is immoral or unethical; lying is necessary to save the lives of innocent people, and the more convincing you are the more likely you are to save their lives as well as your own.

When the goals of a persuasive attempt are not so easily defensible, the ethical issues become more problematic. Imagine you are employed as a salesperson at a clothing store selling bluejeans. Your boss suggests you tell your customers "no jeans have been shown to wear longer than ours." This is technically correct, though it is also true that the jeans you are selling have not been shown to wear longer than any *other* brand of jeans. Furthermore, suppose you are paid a sizable commission for every pair of jeans you sell. Would you feel any hesitation in using the sales pitch? Would this change if you really *believed* the jeans were extraordinarily durable and inexpensive? What if you believed they *weren't*? Finally, if you are reluctant to use this sales pitch, what message *would* you feel comfortable with? With this last question, we have broadened our focus from the goals of the communication to include explicitly a consideration of the content of the message.

Another perspective on ethics is to judge the actions according to the means employed by the source of the communication. Generally, it can be agreed that one should avoid knowingly dispensing false information, hiding facts, using specious reasoning, or falsely playing on the emotions. But problems arise from this approach too: What about a white lie, for example, where a person might use deception in order to avoid hurting someone's feelings unnecessarily?

Evaluating the ethics of a persuasive attempt requires consideration of both the goals and the content of the message. Let's say you are a staunch opponent of nuclear power, convinced that all nuclear power plants should be shut down immediately. You are on your way to visit a friend, and you feel it is important to convince him to join you in your opposition. In past conversations, you have told him that the waste generated by nuclear plants, which is highly radioactive and currently impossible to dispose of safely, creates a serious and ever increasing threat; he responded that "good old American know-how" will solve the problem in time. You have argued that it is wrong for energy to be controlled and distributed for profit by the centralized, big-business interests necessary to finance nuclear power plants; your friend merely scoffed, chuckling about "the Marxist stuff they keep putting on the tube these days."

So when thinking about your upcoming visit, you admit to yourself that he will probably remain unpersuaded by your two major reasons for opposing nuclear power. Since you believe the threat is such that convincing him of the danger of nuclear power is crucial, you begin to search for additional arguments to present. Recalling that your friend is quite afraid of cancer—his father died of the disease after a long, painful illness—you consider emphasizing the potential effects of radiation emanating from the plants, though you are aware the risks are undocumented. Knowing his business relies on a dependable energy supply and that he is concerned about costs, you plan to avoid mentioning the reduction in electricity and increase in costs a shutdown of the nuclear plant in your area would entail.

Just before arriving, you think about whether your attempt to convince him is ethical. You tell yourself your cause is a vital one, you aren't telling any direct falsehoods, and you are merely presenting your arguments in their best possible light. On the other hand, you feel uneasy that you are not sharing all the information as you know it.

The judgment is not an easy one. You may believe strongly enough in an issue to have no qualms about presenting the information in the best way to further your cause, or you might feel uncomfortable giving anything but as complete and neutral an account as you can. Your decision will depend in part on the situation. For example, a trial lawyer, who is expected (and compelled) to advocate a position, might be less constrained by some ethical considerations than a speaker who is thought to be nonpartisan. Someone whose message is preceded or followed by counterarguments might feel free to take more liberties than someone who will speak uncontested. Some people would assert that important causes justify the use of strong persuasion tactics; others would argue the converse, that the more important the topic, the greater the necessity for objectivity.

The issues are complex; there are no simple ethical solutions. This is especially true when we are the ones making the decisions and are not just passive observers and Monday-morning quarterbacks. As Goethe once noted, "Conscience is the virtue of observers and not of agents of action."[2]

At the risk of making the issues even more complex, we would like to suggest another way of evaluating the ethics of persuasion: *The means often determine the ends*. In other words, the choice of persuasion tactics often ends up determining the nature of our beliefs and actions. As the Chinese philosopher Mencius put it, immediate goals may be accomplished with devices that produce long-term evil. Suppose, for example, your friend is convinced by your cancer argument but later finds out that it may not be wholly accurate. For example, suppose he reads a rather emotional article in a magazine written by a nuclear power enthusiast asserting that (1) the evidence linking radiation leaks to cancer is unsubstantiated and (2) the continued use of fossil fuels and other petrochemicals might destroy the atmosphere and result in greater penetration of harmful, cancer-causing ultraviolet rays from the sun. The article concludes by suggesting that the risk of cancer might actually *increase* if nuclear power is eliminated.

What is your friend likely to think and feel? Your persuasive message, at best, is for naught; your friend, confronted by two seemingly valid but emotional appeals, does not know who or what to believe. At worst, your friend may feel that you betrayed his emotions; his anger causes him to reject your message and to henceforth consider you to be a discredited source of information. Perhaps the results would have been different if another type of appeal—one that did not manipulate the emotions—had been used.

The reliance on simplistic persuasion tactics such as invoking heuristic devices or setting the rationalization trap carries an implicit danger: If you can successfully use the technique, so can anyone else. The handicraft of one demagogue can be easily undone by the next. The result is a great mass of people who appear fickle and confused. Further, when we realize that we have been cheated and manipulated we often respond by becoming skeptical and cynical. Historians argue that the widespread knowledge of the misuse of atrocity propaganda by British and Americans during World War I was one reason, along with pro-isolation sentiments and anti-Semitism, that much of the world did not at first believe the truth about Hitler's atrocities. Similarly, contemporary analysts feel that large numbers of Americans do not vote because they believe that all campaign rhetoric is meaningless puffery. To paraphrase an old saw, "Live by the persuasion heuristic, die by the persuasion heuristic."

What about the consequences of withholding vital information from your friend, such as the possible negative economic consequences of closing nuclear power plants? Obviously, leaving your friend uninformed about this aspect of nuclear power might backfire as well. The pro-nuclear advocate could score big points merely by stating these possibilities. Moreover, the decision not to discuss the economics of energy has another, perhaps more serious consequence: It leaves your friend ignorant.

If using emotional appeals or oversimplified arguments can produce such negative outcomes, why do people use them? Recall that our age of propaganda is message-dense; few citizens have the time, the opportunity, or the capacity to process the vast array of information they receive. Further, as we have seen, news is frequently watched not so much for its information value as for its ability to entertain. This increases the temptation of communicators to manipulate beliefs and opinions not by reason but by appeals to emotions and simplistic thought. Communicators seem to be relying more and more on persuasion devices that make use of heuristics and emotions over fully informed discussion, vivid images over thoughtful discourse, meaningless association over reasoned causal analysis, the propaganda of the demagogue over the persuasion of Peitho.

The consequences for democracy can be dire. As more and more propagandists use simplistic persuasion, the competitive urge to use simpler and simpler persuasion devices increases. As simpler and simpler persuasion devices are used, people become increasingly less informed and sophisticated about civic matters. As the populace becomes less informed, the propagandist must use even more simplistic persuasion devices. The result is an ignorance spiral—a cynical populace bombarded with more and more thoughtless propaganda that they have less and less skill and inclination to process and ability to understand. Adolf Hitler's belief that the masses are ignorant thus becomes a self-fulfilling prophecy.

We believe that it is possible to avoid these dire consequences. That is why we wrote this book. It is our hope that knowledge about the process of persuasion will allow all of us to detect and resist some of the more obvious forms of trickery and demagoguery. Perhaps, more importantly, it should encourage us to be aware of the consequences of our selection of persuasion devices. After all, an individual's choice of persuasion tactics reveals much about his or her character and ability to think about the issues at hand. By giving close scrutiny to the ways of persuasion we can promote those techniques that lead to a full and open discussion of the issues at hand while rebuking the antics of the demagogue. In large measure, the responsibility for raising Peitho's children is ours.

REFERENCES

1 OUR AGE OF PROPAGANDA

1. Colford, S. W. (1990, March 19). Athlete endorsers fouled by slayings. *Advertising Age*, p. 64.
2. Barrett, L. T. (1990, November 19). Race-baiting wins again. *Time*, p. 43.
3. Statistics obtained from recent issues of *American Demographics*; Ries, A., & Trout, J. (1981). *Positioning: The battle for your mind*. New York: Warner Books; Aaker, D. A., & Myers, J. G. (1987). *Advertising management*. Englewood Cliffs, NJ: Prentice-Hall.
4. Holifield, E. B. (1989). *Era of persuasion: American thought and culture, 1521–1680*. Boston: Twayne.
5. Bahne, C. (1990). *The complete guide to Boston's Freedom Trail*. Cambridge, MA: Newtowne.
6. For an excellent history of advertising, see Fox, S. (1984). *The mirror makers*. New York: Morrow.
7. See Adams, H. F. (1916). *Advertising and its mental laws*. New York: Macmillan; Poffenberger, A. T. (1932). *Psychology in advertising*. New York: McGraw-Hill; Scott, W. D. (1917). *The psychology of advertising*; Boston: Small, Maynard, & Co; Starch, D. (1923). *Principles of advertising*. New York: McGraw-Hill.
8. Creel, G. (1920). *How we advertised America*. New York: Harper and Brothers.
9. For excellent discussions of persuasion in the Greek and Roman eras, see Billig, M. (1987). *Arguing and thinking*. New York: Cambridge University Press; Kennedy, G. A. (1963). *The art of persuasion in Greece*. Princeton, NJ: Princeton University Press; Kennedy, G. A. (1972). *The art of rhetoric in the Roman world*. Princeton, NJ: Princeton University Press; Kennedy, G. A. (1980). *Classical rhetoric*. Chapel Hill, NC: University of North Carolina Press; Maccoby, N. (1963). The new science of rhetoric. In W. Schramm (Ed.), *The science of human communication*. New York: Basic Books.
10. Cicero. (1949). *De inventione*. Cambridge, MA: Loeb Classics, p. 3.
11. Ries, A., & Trout, J. (1981). See note 3.
12. See also Cialdini, R. B. (1984). *Influence*. New York: William Morrow.

2 MYSTERIOUS INFLUENCE

1. For excellent histories of Mesmer's influence on American thought, see Fuller, R. C. (1982). *Mesmerism and the American cure of souls*. Philadel-

phia: University of Pennsylvania Press; Fuller, R. C. (1986). *Americans and the unconscious.* New York: Oxford Press.

2. See Darnton, R. (1986). *Mesmerism and the end of the Enlightenment in France.* Cambridge, MA: Harvard University Press; Gould, S. J. (1991). *Bully for Brontosaurus.* New York: Norton.

3. For a discussion of the facts concerning hypnosis, see Baker, R. A. (1990). *They call it hypnosis.* Buffalo, NY: Prometheus.

4. Aristotle. (1954). *Rhetoric.* In. W. Roberts (Trans.), *Aristotle, rhetoric and poetics.* New York: Modern Library.

5. Packard, V. (1957). *The hidden persuaders.* New York: MacKay.

6. Dichter, E. (1964). *Handbook of consumer motivations.* New York: Mc-Graw-Hill.

7. Scott, W. D. (1917). *The psychology of advertising.* Boston: Small, Maynard, & Co.

8. Hovland, C. I., Lumsdaine, A. A., & Sheffield, F. D. (1949). *Experiments on mass communication.* Princeton, NJ: Princeton University Press; Hovland, C. I., Janis, I. L., & Kelley, H. H. (1953). *Communication and persuasion.* New Haven, CN: Yale University Press; Hovland, C. I. (1957). *The order of presentation in persuasion.* New Haven, CN: Yale University Press; Hovland, C. I., & Janis, I. L. (1959). *Personality and persuasibility.* New Haven, CN: Yale University Press; Hovland, C. I., & Rosenberg, M. J. (1960). *Attitude organization and change.* New Haven, CN: Yale University Press; Sherif, M., & Hovland, C. I. (1961). *Social judgment.* New Haven, CN: Yale University Press.

9. Liddy, G. G. (1980). *Will.* New York: St. Martin's.

10. See Greenwald, A. G., Brock, T. C., & Ostrom, T. M. (1968). *Psychological foundations of attitudes.* New York: Academic Press; Petty, R. E., & Cacioppo, J. T. (1981). *Attitudes and persuasion: Classic and contemporary approaches.* Dubuque, IA: Brown; Petty, R. E., Ostrom, T. M., & Brock, T. C. (1981). *Cognitive responses in persuasion.* Hillsdale, NJ: Erlbaum; Pratkanis, A. R., Breckler, S. J., & Greenwald, A. G. (1989). *Attitude structure and function.* Hillsdale, NJ: Erlbaum.

11. For more details on these principles, see (especially chapters 4 and 5) Aronson, E. (1991). *Social animal* (6th ed.). New York: W. H. Freeman.

3 MINDLESS PROPAGANDA, THOUGHTFUL PERSUASION

1. Burton, P. W. (1981). *Which ad pulled best?* Chicago: Crain; Caples, J. (1974). *Tested advertising methods.* Englewood Cliffs, NJ: Prentice-Hall;

Loudon, D. L., & Della Bitta, A. J. (1984). *Consumer behavior*. New York: McGraw-Hill; Ogilvy, D. (1983). *Ogilvy on advertising*. New York: Crown.

2. Ibid.

3. Langer, E., Blank, A., & Chanowitz, B. (1978). The mindlessness of ostensibly thoughtful action: The role of "placebic" information in interpersonal interaction. *Journal of Personality and Social Psychology, 36*, 635–642.

4. Santos, M., Leve, C., & Pratkanis, A. R. (August 1991). *Hey buddy, can you spare 17 cents? Mindfulness and persuasion*. Paper presented at the annual meeting of the American Psychological Association, San Francisco.

5. Petty, R. E., & Cacioppo, J. T. (1986). The elaboration likelihood model of persuasion. In L. Berkowitz (Ed.), *Advances in experimental social psychology* (Vol. 19; pp. 123–205). New York: Academic Press; Petty, R. E., & Cacioppo, J. T. (1986). *Communication and persuasion: Central and peripheral routes to attitude change*. New York: Springer-Verlag. See also Chaiken, S. (1980). Heuristic versus systematic information processing and the use of source versus message cues in persuasion. *Journal of Personality and Social Psychology, 39*, 752–766; Chaiken, S., Liberman, A., & Eagly, A. (1989). Heuristic versus systematic information processing within and beyond the persuasion context. In J. S. Uleman & J. A. Bargh (Eds.), *Unintended thought* (pp. 212–252). New York: Guilford.

6. Petty, R. E., Cacioppo, J. T., & Goldman, R. (1981). Personal involvement as a determinant of argument-based persuasion. *Journal of Personality and Social Psychology, 41*, 847–855.

7. Fiske, S. T., & Taylor, S. E. (1991). *Social cognition*. New York: McGraw-Hill.

4 THE RATIONALIZING ANIMAL

1. Festinger, L., Riecken, H. W., & Schachter, S. (1956). *When prophecy fails*. New York: Harper & Row.

2. Festinger, L. (1957). *A theory of cognitive dissonance*. Stanford, CA: Stanford University Press.

3. Aronson, E. (1969). The theory of cognitive dissonance: A current perspective. In L. Berkowitz (Ed.), *Advances in Experimental Social Psychology* (Vol. 4; pp. 1–34). New York: Academic Press.

4. We thank Julie Rogers for assistance in preparing this case study. For details see, Santa Cruz mourns, copes. (1989, October 21) *San Jose Mercury News*; Minutes from Santa Cruz City Council meetings of February 24, 1987, April 7, 1987, and May 12, 1987; Turner, M. E., & Pratkanis, A. R. (1991). *Groupthink as collecitive dissonance reduction: Evidence from the field and the laboratory.* Unpublished paper; San Jose State University.

5. Cialdini, R. B., & Schroeder, D. (1976). Increasing compliance by legitimizing paltry contributions: When even a penny helps. *Journal of Personality and Social Psychology*, *34*, 599–604.

6. Harris, J. (1970). *Hiroshima: A study of science, politics, and the ethics of war*. Menlo Park, CA: Addison-Wesley.

5 WORDS OF INFLUENCE

1. Bem, D. (1970). *Beliefs, attitudes, and human affairs*. Belmont, CA: Brooks/Cole.

2. Levin, I. P., & Gaeth, G. J. (1988). How consumers are affected by the frame of attribute information before and after consuming the product. *Journal of Consumer Research*, *15*, 374–378.

3. Werkmeister, W. H. (1948). *An introduction to critical thinking*. Lincoln, NB: Johnsen.

4. Fox, S. (1984). *The mirror makers*. New York: William Morrow.

5. Lutz, W. (1989). *Doublespeak*. New York: Harper & Row.

6. Orwell, G. (1949). *1984*. New York: New American Library; p. 246.

7. Allport, G. W. (1954). *The nature of prejudice*. Reading, MA: Addison-Wesley.

8. Bem, S. L., & Bem, D. J. (1973). Does sex-biased job advertising "aid and abet" sex discrimination? *Journal of Applied Social Psychology*, *3*, 6–18. For more examples of the effects of sex bias in language, see Henley, N. (1989). Molehill or mountain? What we know and don't know about sex bias in language. In M. Crawford & M. Gentry (Eds.), *Gender and thought* (pp. 59–78). New York: Springer-Verlag.

9. Ries, A., & Trout, J. (1981). *Positioning: The battle for your mind*. New York: Warner Books.

10. Miller, R. L., Brickman, P., & Bolin, D. (1975). Attribution versus persuasion as a means for modifying behavior. *Journal of Personality and Social Psychology*, *31*, 430–441.

11. Ibid.

12. Snyder, M., Tanke, E. D., & Berscheid, E. (1977). Social perceptions and interpersonal behavior: On the self-fulfilling nature of social stereotypes. *Journal of Personality and Social Psychology*, *35*, 656–666.
13. Cited in Thomson, O. (1977). *Mass persuasion in history*. Edinburgh, UK: Paul Harris, p. 111.

6 PICTURES IN OUR HEADS

1. Lippmann, W. (1922). *Public opinion*. New York: Harcourt, Brace.
2. Gerbner, G., Gross. L., Morgan, M., & Signorielli, N. (1986). Living with television: The dynamics of the cultivation process. In J. Bryant & D. Zillman (Eds.), *Perspectives on media effects* (pp. 17–40). Hillsdale, NJ: Erlbaum.
3. Quoted in *Newsweek*, December 6, 1982, p. 40.
4. Haney, C., & Manzolati, J. (1981). Television criminology: Network illusions on criminal justice realities. In E. Aronson (Ed.), *Readings about the social animal* (3rd ed.; pp. 125–136). New York: W. H. Freeman.
5. See Heath, L. (1984). Impact of newspaper crime reports on fear of crime: Multimethodological investigation. *Journal of Personality and Social Psychology*, *47*, 263–276; Linz, D. G., Donnerstein, E., & Penrod, S. (1988). Effects of long-term exposure to violent and sexually degrading depictions of women. *Journal of Personality and Social Psychology*, *55*, 758–768; Hennigan, K., Heath, L., Wharton, J. D., Del Rosario, M., Cook, T. D., & Calder, B. (1982). Impact of the introduction of television on crime in the United States: Empirical findings and theoretical implications. *Journal of Personality and Social Psychology*, *42*, 461–477.
6. Iyengar, S., & Kinder, D. R. (1987). *News that matters*. Chicago: University of Chicago Press.
7. Rogers, E. M., & Dearing, J. W. (1988). Agenda-setting research: Where has it been, Where is it going? In. J. A. Anderson (Ed.), *Communication Yearbook 11* (pp. 555–594). Beverly Hills, CA: Sage.
8. McCombs, M. E., & Shaw, D. L. (1972). The agenda setting function of mass media. *Public Opinion Quarterly*, *36*, 176–187.
9. Dilenschneider, R. L. (1990). *Power and influence*. New York: Prentice-Hall.
10. Hart, R. P. (1987). *The sound of leadership*. Chicago: University of Chicago Press.
11. Pfeffer, J. (1981). *Power in organizations*. Cambridge, MA: Ballinger.
12. Cited in Rogers and Dearing (1988). See note 7.

7 SADDAM HUSSEIN: THE HITLER WE "KNOW"

1. Gilovich, T. (1981). Seeing the past in the present: The effects of associations to familiar events on judgments and decisions. *Journal of Personality and Social Psychology, 40,* 797–808.
2. Kennedy, P. (1991, January 24). A declining empire goes to war. *Wall Street Journal.*
3. Corbett, E. P. J. (1990). *Classical rhetoric for the modern student.* New York: Oxford University Press, p. 105.
4. *U.S. News & World Report,* May 6, 1991, p. 19.
5. What did Bush win? *Newsweek,* May 13, 1991, p. 27.

8 ASKING THE *RIGHT* QUESTIONS

1. Kahneman, D., & Tversky, A. (1984). Choices, values, and frames. *American Psychologist, 39,* 341–350.
2. Meyerowitz, B. E., & Chaiken, S. (1987). The effect of message framing on breast self-examination attitudes, intentions, and behavior. *Journal of Personality and Social Psychology, 52,* 500-510.
3. Lockerbie, B., & Borrelli, S. A. (1990). Question wording and public support for Contra aid, 1983–1986. *Public Opinion Quarterly, 54,* 195–208; see also Payne, S. L. (1951). *The art of asking questions.* Princeton, NJ: Princeton University Press.
4. Loftus, E. F., & Palmer, J. C. (1974). Reconstruction of automobile destruction: An example of the interaction between language and memory. *Journal of Verbal Learning and Verbal Behavior, 13,* 585–589; Loftus, E. F. (1977). Shifting human color memory. *Memory and Cognition, 5,* 696–699.

9 THE POWER OF "DECOYS"

1. Pratkanis, A. R., Farquhar, P. H., Silbert, S., & Hearst, J. (1989). *Decoys produce contrast effects and alter choice probabilities.* Unpublished paper, University of California, Santa Cruz.
2. Kenrick, D. T., & Gutierres, S. E. (1980). Contrast effects in judgments of attractiveness: When beauty becomes a social problem. *Journal of Personality and Social Psychology, 38,* 131–140.

10 THE PSYCHOLOGY OF FACTOIDS

1. Johnson, D. M. (1945). The "phantom anesthetist" of Mattoon: A field study of mass hysteria. *Journal of Abnormal and Social Psychology, 40,* 175–186.
2. Mailer, N. (1973). *Marilyn.* New York: Galahad Books, p. 18.
3. For discussions of the psychology of rumors, see Allport, G. W., & Postman, L. (1947). *The psychology of rumor.* New York: Henry Holt; Cantril, H. (1940). *The invasion from Mars.* New York: Harper & Row; Rosnow, R. L. (1980). Psychology of rumor reconsidered. *Psychological Bulletin, 87,* 578–591; Rosnow, R. L., & Fine, G. A. (1976). *Rumor and gossip.* New York: Elsevier; Shibutani, T. (1966). *Improvised news.* Indianapolis, IN: Bobbs-Merrill.
4. Wegner, D. M., Wenzalaff, R., Kerker, R. M., & Beattie, A. E. (1981). Incrimination through innuendo: Can media questions become public answers? *Journal of Personality and Social Psychology, 40,* 822–832.
5. Kassin, S. M., Williams, L. N., & Saunders, C. L. (1990). Dirty tricks of cross-examination: The influence of conjectural evidence on the jury. *Law and Human Behavior, 14,* 373–384; Sue, S., Smith, R. E., & Caldwell, C. (1973). Effects of inadmissible evidence on the decisions of simulated jurors: A moral dilemma. *Journal of Applied Social Psychology, 3,* 345–353; Carroll, J. S., Kerr, N. L., Alfini, J. J., Weaver, F. M., MacCoun, R. J., & Feldman, V. (1986). Free press and fair trial: The role of behavioral research. *Law and Human Behavior, 10,* 187–201.
6. Kapferer, J. N. (1989). A mass poisoning rumor in Europe. *Public Opinion Quarterly, 53,* 467–481.
7. Loh, W. D. (1985). The evidence and trial procedure: The law, social policy, and psychological research. In S. M. Kassin & L. S. Wrightsman (Eds.), *The psychology of evidence and trial procedure* (pp. 13–39). Beverly Hills, CA: Sage.
8. See Francois, W. E. (1978). *Mass media law and regulation.* Columbus, OH: Grid.

11 THE CREDIBLE COMMUNICATOR

1. Aristotle. (1954). Rhetoric. In W. Roberts (Trans.), *Aristotle, rhetoric and poetics* (p. 25). New York: Modern Library.
2. Hovland, C., & Weiss, W. (1951). The influence of source credibility on communication effectiveness. *Public Opinion Quarterly, 15,* 635–650.

3. Aronson, E., & Golden, B. (1962). The effect of relevant and irrelevant aspects of communicator credibility on opinion change. *Journal of Personality*, *30*, 135–146.

12 BREAKFAST OF CHAMPIONS, JUNK FOOD FOR THE SELF

1. Mills, J., & Aronson, E. (1965). Opinion change as a function of communicator's attractiveness and desire to influence. *Journal of Personality and Social Psychology*, *1*, 173–177.
2. Eagly, A., & Chaiken, S. (1975). An attribution analysis of the effect of communicator characteristics on opinion change: The case of communicator attractiveness. *Journal of Personality and Social Psychology*, *32*, 136–144.
3. Petty, R. E., Cacioppo, J. T., & Schumann, D. (1983). Central and peripheral routes to advertising effectiveness: The moderating role of involvement. *Journal of Consumer Research*, *10*, 134–148.

13 HOW DO YOU PERSUADE IF EVERYONE KNOWS YOU ARE UNTRUSTWORTHY, UNBELIEVABLE, AND DISLIKED?

1. Oliver, R. T. (1971). *Communication and culture in ancient India and China*. Syracuse, NY: Syracuse University Press.
2. Walster (Hatfield), E., Aronson, E., & Abrahams, D. (1966). On increasing the persuasiveness of a low prestige communicator. *Journal of Experimental Social Psychology*, *2*, 325–342.
3. Eagly, A., Wood, W., & Chaiken, S. (1978). Causal inferences about communicators and their effect on opinion change. *Journal of Personality and Social Psychology*, *36*, 424–435.
4. *Santa Cruz Sentinel*, January 13, 1987, p. A8.
5. Oliver, R. T. (1971). See note 1.
6. Walster (Hatfield), E., & Festinger, L. (1962). The effectiveness of "overheard" persuasive communications. *Journal of Abnormal and Social Psychology*, *65*, 395–402.

14 THE MANUFACTURE OF CREDIBILITY

1. McGinness, J. (1970). *The selling of the president: 1968*. New York: Pocket Books, p. 160.
2. Jamieson, K. H. (1984). *Packaging the presidency*. New York: Oxford University Press.
3. Bush's cautious alter ego. *U.S. News & World Report*, March 26, 1990.
4. Ailes, R. (1988). *You are the message*. New York: Doubleday, p. 81.
5. Dilenschneider, R. L. (1990). *Power and influence*. New York: Prentice-Hall.

15 PRIZEFIGHTER SLAYS 11 WITH ONE LOOK: THE INFLUENCE OF MASS MEDIA MODELS

1. See *National Examiner*, January 2, 1990, and *National Enquirer*, January 2, 1990.
2. Phillips, D. P. (1986). Natural experiments on the effects of mass media violence on fatal aggression: Strengths and weaknesses of a new approach. In L. Berkowitz (Ed.), *Advances in Experimental Social Psychology* (Vol. 19; pp. 207–250). New York: Academic Press.
3. Bandura, A. (1973). *Aggression: A social learning analysis*. Englewood Cliffs, NJ: Prentice-Hall.
4. Bryan, J. H., & Test, M. A. (1967). Models and helping: Naturalistic studies in aiding behavior. *Journal of Personality and Social Psychology*, *6*, 400–407.
5. Baron, R. A., & Kepner, C. R. (1970). Model's behavior and attraction toward the model as determinants of adult aggresssive behavior. *Journal of Personality and Social Psychology*, *14*, 335–344.
6. Bryan, J. H., Redfield, J., & Mader, S. (1971). Words and deeds about altruism and the subsequent reinforcement power of the model. *Child Development*, *42*, 1501–1508; Bryan, J. H., & Walbek, N. H. (1970). Preaching and practicing generosity: Children's actions and reactions. *Child Development*, *41*, 329–353.

16 PACKAGES

1. "Which cereal for breakfast?" *Consumer Reports*, February 1981, pp. 68–75.

2. Comparison based on "Eating to Lower Your High Blood Cholesterol," U.S. Department of Health and Human Services, NIH Publication No. 87-2920, September 1987. Saturated fats, such as animal fat, and some vegetable fats, such as coconut oil, cocoa butter, palm oil, and hydrogenated oil, have been shown to raise cholesterol levels. Cereal manufacturers sometimes use such fats, especially coconut, palm, and hydrogenated oils in their products. Many manufacturers are in the process of reformulationg their cereals to remove such oils, so check the label before making a final decision.

3. Petty, R. E., & Cacioppo, J. T. (1984). The effects of involvement on responses to argument quantity and quality: Central and peripheral routes to persuasion. *Journal of Personality and Social Psychology, 46,* 69–81.

4. Axsom, D., Yates, S., & Chaiken, S. (1987). Audience response as a heuristic cue in persuasion. *Journal of Personality and Social Psychology, 53,* 30–40.

5. Fierman, J. (1991, June 3). The big muddle in green marketing. *Fortune,* pp. 91–101; Hume, S. (1991, January 29). MacDonald's. *Advertising Age,* p. 32.

6. Pratkanis, A. R. (1989). The cognitive representation of attitudes. In A. R. Pratkanis, S. J. Breckler, & A. G. Greenwald (Eds.), *Attitude structure and function* (pp. 71–98). Hillsdale, NJ: Erlbaum.

17 SELF-SELL

1. Lewin, K. (1947). Group decision and social change. In T. M. Newcomb & E. L. Hartley (Eds.), *Readings in social psychology* (pp. 330–344). New York: Holt.

2. Boninger, D. S., Brock, T. S., Cook, T. D., Gruder, C. L., & Romer, D. (1990). Discovery of reliable attitude change persistence resulting from a transmitter tuning set. *Psychological Science, 1,* 268–271.

3. Gregory, W. L., Cialdini, R. B., & Carpenter, K. M. (1982). Self-relevant scenarios as mediators of likelihood estimates and compliance: Does imagining make it so? *Journal of Personality and Social Psychology, 43,* 89–99.

18 NAKED ATTICS AND NEIGHBORHOOD WAR HEROES: ON VIVIDNESS IN COMMUNICATION

1. Gonzales, M. H., Aronson, E., & Costanzo, M. (1988). Increasing the effectiveness of energy auditors: A field experiment. *Journal of Applied Social Psychology, 18*, 1049–1066; Aronson, E. (1990). Applying social psychology to prejudice reduction and energy conservation. *Personality and Social Psychology Bulletin, 16*, 118–132.
2. Nisbett, R., & Ross, L. (1980). *Human inference: Strategies and shortcomings of social judgment.* Englewood Cliffs, NJ: Prentice-Hall. (We also borrowed their definition of vividness used at the beginning of this chapter.)
3. Jamieson, K. H. (1988). *Eloquence in an electronic age: The transformation of political speechmaking.* Oxford, UK: Oxford University Press.
4. Cited in Nisbett, R., & Ross, L. (1980). See note 2.

19 WHY DO THEY KEEP REPEATING THE SAME ADS?

1. These examples are found in Fox, S. (1984). *The mirror makers.* New York: Morrow.
2. Zajonc, R. B. (1968). The attitudinal effects of mere exposure. *Journal of Personality and Social Psychology, Monograph Supplement 9*, 1–27.
3. Grush, J., McKeough, K., & Ahlering, R. (1978). Extrapolating laboratory exposure research to actual political elections. *Journal of Personality and Social Psychology, 36*, 257–270; Grush, J. E. (1980). Impact of candidate expenditures, regionality, and prior outcomes on the 1976 presidential primaries. *Journal of Personality and Social Psychology, 38*, 337–347.
4. Kinder, D. R., & Sears, D. O. (1985). Public opinion and political action. In G. Lindzey & E. Aronson (Eds.), *Handbook of social psychology* (3rd ed.; pp. 659–742). New York: Random House.
5. Quoted in Herzstein, R. E. (1987). *The war that Hitler won.* New York: Paragon House, p. 31.
6. Described in Harrison, A. A. (1977). Mere exposure. In L. Berkowitz (Ed.), *Advances in experimental social psychology* (Vol. 10; pp. 39–83). New York: Academic Press.
7. Described in Cacioppo, J. T., & Petty, R. E. (1985). Central and peripheral routes to persuasion: The role of message repetition. In A. Mitchell & L. Alwitt (Eds.), *Psychological processes and advertising*

effects (pp. 91–111). Hillsdale, NJ: Erlbaum. For a recent extension, see Schumann, D. W., Petty, R. E., & Clemons, D. S. (1990). Predicting the effectiveness of different strategies of advertising variation: A test of the repetition-variation hypotheses. *Journal of Consumer Research, 17*, 192–202.

20 IF YOU HAVE NOTHING TO SAY— DISTRACT THEM

1. For a discussion of affect and persuasion, see Petty, R. E., Cacioppo, J. T., Sedikidies, C., & Strathman, A. J. (1988). Affect and persuasion. *American Behavioral Scientist, 31*, 355–371.
2. Festinger, L., & Maccoby, N. (1964). On resistance to persuasive communications. *Journal of Abnormal and Social Psychology, 68*, 359–366.
3. Osterhouse, R. A. & Brock, T. C. (1970). Distraction increases yielding to propaganda by inhibiting counterarguing. *Journal of Personality and Social Psychology, 15*, 344–358.
4. Ogilvy, D. (1983). *Ogilvy on advertising*. New York: Crown.
5. Petty, R. E., Wells, G. L., & Brock, T. C. (1976). Distraction can enhance and reduce yielding to propaganda: Thought disruption versus effort justification. *Journal of Personality and Social Psychology, 34*, 874–884.
6. Moore, D. L., Hausknecht, D., & Thamodaran, K. (1986). Time compression, response opportunity, and persuasion. *Journal of Consumer Research, 13*, 85–99.

21 IF YOU WANT TO GAIN AN INCH, ASK FOR A MILE—SOMETIMES!

1. Zimbardo, P. (1960). Involvement and communication discrepancy as determinants of opinion conformity. *Journal of Abnormal and Social Psychology, 60*, 86–94.
2. Hovland, C., Harvey, O. J., & Sherif, M. (1957). Assimilation and contrast effects in reaction to communication and attitude change. *Journal of Abnormal and Social Psychology, 55*, 244–252.
3. Aronson, E., Turner, J., & Carlsmith, J. M. (1963). Communication credibility and communication discrepancy as determinants of opinion change. *Journal of Abnormal and Social Psychology, 67*, 31–36.

22 PROTAGORAS' IDEAL: ONE-SIDED PUFFERY VERSUS TWO-SIDED DEBATE

1. Herodotus. (1942). *The Persian wars.* (G. Rawlinson, Trans.). New York: Modern Library, p. 499.
2. Aristotle. (1954). Rhetoric. In W. Roberts (Trans.), *Aristotle, rhetoric and poetics* (p. 185). New York: Modern Library.
3. Lippmann, W. (August 1939). The indispensable opposition. *The Atlantic,* pp. 186–190.
4. For a discussion of comparative advertising, see Aaker, D., & Myers, J. G. (1986). *Advertising management.* Englewood Cliffs, NJ: Prentice-Hall. (pp. 305–310).
5. Fox, S. (1984). *The mirror makers.* New York: Morrow.
6. Ries, A., & Trout, J. (1981). *Positioning: The battle for your mind.* New York: Warner.
7. Hovland, C. I., Lumsdaine, A. A., & Sheffield, F. D. (1949). *Experiments on mass communications.* Princeton, NJ: Princeton University Press.
8. Pfau, M., & Kenski, H. C. (1990). *Attack politics.* New York: Praeger.

23 THE FEAR APPEAL

1. Faust, C. H., & Johnson, T. H. (1935). *Jonathan Edwards.* New York: American Book, p. 161.
2. See Baynes, N. H. (1942). *The speeches of Adolf Hilter April 22–August 1939.* New York: Oxford University Press.
3. Leventhal, H. (1970). Findings and theory in the study of fear communications. In L. Berkowitz (Ed.), *Advances in experimental social psychology* (Vol. 5; pp. 119–186). New York: Academic Press.
4. Chu, G. C. (1966). Fear arousal, efficacy and immanency. *Journal of Personality and Social Psychology, 4,* 517–524; Rogers, R. W. (1983). Cognitive and physiological processes in fear appeals and attitude change: A revised theory of protection motivation. In J. T. Cacioppo & R. E. Petty (Eds.), *Social psychophysiology: A sourcebook* (pp. 153–176). New York: Guilford.

24 THE GRANFALLOON TECHNIQUE

1. For reviews and discussion, see Tajfel, H. (1981). *Human groups and social categories.* Cambridge, UK: Cambridge University Press; Turner, J. C. (1987). *Rediscovering the social group.* New York: Blackwell.
2. Vonnegut, K. (1963). *Cat's Cradle.* New York: Dell.
3. For illustrative studies see Wetherell, M. (1983). *Social identification, social influence, and group polarization.* Unpublished doctoral thesis, University of Bristol, UK; Abrams, D., Wetherell, M., Cochrane, S., Hogg, M. A., & Turner, J. C. (1990). Knowing what to think by knowing who you are: Self-categorization and the nature of norm formation, conformity, and group polarization. *British Journal of Social Psychology, 29,* 97–119.
4. Cialdini, R. B., Borden, R. J., Thorne, A., Walker, M. R., Freeman, S., & Sloan, L. R. (1976). Basking in reflected glory: Three (football) field studies. *Journal of Personality and Social Psychology, 36,* 463–476.
5. See, for example, Weiss, M. J. (1988) *The clustering of America.* New York: Harper & Row; Mitchell, A. (1983). *The nine American lifestyles.* New York: Warner; Riche, M. F. (July 1989). Psychographics for the 1990s. *American Demographics,* pp. 24–31, 53–55.
6. Jamieson, K. H. (1988). *Eloquence in an electronic age.* Oxford, UK: Oxford University Press.
7. For descriptions, see Abelman, R., & Neuendorf, K. (1985). How religious is religious television programming? *Journal of Communication, 35,* 98–110; Hoover, S. M. (1988). *Mass media religion: The social sources of the electronic church.* Beverly Hills, CA: Sage.

25 GUILT SELLS

1. Carlsmith, J. M., & Gross, A. E. (1969). Some effects of guilt on compliance. *Journal of Personality and Social Psychology, 11,* 232–239.

26 WHAT IS THE INFLUENCE OF ONE FLOWER GIVEN?

1. Cialdini, R. B. (1984). *Influence.* New York: Morrow.
2. Regan, D. T. (1971). Effects of a favor and liking on compliance. *Journal of Experimental Social Psychology, 7,* 627–639.

3. Cialdini, R. B., & Ascani, K. (1976). Test of a concession procedure for inducing verbal, behavioral, and further compliance with a request to give blood. *Journal of Applied Psychology*, *61*, 295–300.

27 THE COMMITTED HEART

1. Freedman, J., & Fraser, S. (1966). Compliance without pressure: The foot-in-the-door technique. *Journal of Personality and Social Psychology*, *4*, 195–202.
2. Pliner, P., Hart, H., Kohl, J., & Saari, D. (1974). Compliance without pressure: Some further data on the foot-in-the-door technique. *Journal of Experimental Social Psychology*, *10*, 17–22.
3. Greenwald, A. G., Carnot, C. G., Beach, R., & Young, B. (1987). Increasing voting behavior by asking people if they expect to vote. *Journal of Applied Psychology*, *72*, 315–318.
4. Cialdini, R. B., Cacioppo, J. T., Bassett, R., & Miller, J. (1978). Low-ball procedure for compliance: Commitment then cost. *Journal of Personality and Social Psychology*, *36*, 463–476.
5. Pentagon papers: The secret war. (1971, June 28). *Time*, p. 12.
6. White, R. (November 1971). Selective inattention. *Psychology Today*, pp. 47–50, 78–84.

28 THE PSYCHOLOGY OF SCARCITY AND THE MYSTIQUE OF PHANTOMS

1. Volokh, A. (1983). *The art of Russian cuisine*. New York: Collier.
2. See Fromkin, H. L., Olson, J. C., Dipboye, R. L., & Barnaby, D. A. (1971). *A commodity theory analysis of consumer preferences for scarce products*. Paper presented at the annual meeting of the American Psychological Association, Washington, DC; Worchel, S., Lee, J., & Adewole, A. (1975). Effects of supply and demand on ratings of object value. *Journal of Personality and Social Psychology*, *32*, 906–914; Knishinsky, A. (1982). *The effects of scarcity of material and exclusivity of information on industrial buyer perceived risk in provoking a purchase decision*. Unpublished doctoral dissertation, Arizona State University, Tempe.

3. Farquhar, P. H., & Pratkanis, A. R. (1987). *Phantom choices: The effects of unavailable alternatives on decision making.* Unpublished manuscript, Carnegie-Mellon University, Pittsburgh.

4. Pratkanis, A. R., & Farquhar, P. H. (in press). A brief history of research on phantom alternatives: Evidence for seven empirical generalizations about phantoms. *Basic and Applied Social Psychology.*

5. Mischel, W. (1974). Processes in delay of gratification. In L. Berkowitz (Ed.), *Advances in experimental social psychology,* (Vol. 7; pp. 249–92). New York: Academic Press.

6. Freeman, K., Pratkanis, A. R., & Farquhar, P. H. (1990). *Phantoms as psychological motivation: Evidence for compliance and reactance processes.* Unpublished manuscript, University of California, Santa Cruz.

7. Snyder, C. R. (August 1990). *Scarce experiences and possessions: A source of uniqueness.* Paper presented at the annual meeting of the American Psychological Association, Boston; Snyder, C. R., & Fromkin, H. L., (1980). *Uniqueness: The human pursuit of difference.* New York: Plenum.

8. Fromm, E. (1976). *To have or to be?* New York: Harper & Row.

9. Zellinger, D. A., Fromkin, H. L., Speller, D. E., & Kohn, C. A. (1975). A commodity theory analysis of the effects of age restrictions upon pornographic materials. *Journal of Applied Psychology, 60,* 94–99.

10. Farquhar, P. H., & Pratkanis, A. R. (1989). *Decision structuring with phantom alternatives.* Unpublished manuscript, Carnegie-Mellon University, Pittsburgh.

29 SUBLIMINAL SORCERY: WHO IS SEDUCING WHOM?

1. Cousins, N. (1957, October 5). Smudging the subconscious. *Saturday Review,* p. 20.

2. Key, W. B. (1973). *Subliminal seduction.* Englewood Cliffs, NJ: Signet; Key, W. B. (1976). *Media sexploitation.* Englewood Cliffs, NJ: Signet; Key, W. B. (1980). *The clam-plate orgy.* Englewood Cliffs, NJ: Signet; Key, W. B. (1989). *The age of manipulation.* New York: Holt.

3. Ibid (1973), p.1.

4. Natale, J. A. (September 1988). Are you open to suggestion? *Psychology Today,* pp. 28–30.

5. Pratkanis, A. R., & Greenwald, A. G. (1988). Recent perspectives on unconscious processing: Still no marketing applications. *Psychology & Marketing, 5,* 339–355.

6. Moore, T. E. (1982). Subliminal advertising: What you see is what you get. *Journal of Marketing*, *46*, 38–47.
7. "Phone now," said CBC subliminally—but nobody did. (1958, February 10). *Advertising Age*, p. 8.
8. Weir, W. (1984, October 15). Another look at subliminal "facts." *Advertising Age*, p. 46.
9. Pratkanis, A. R., Eskenazi, J., & Greenwald, A. G. (1989). *What you expect is what you believe (but not necessarily what you get): On the effectiveness of subliminal audiotapes.* Unpublished manuscript, University of California, Santa Cruz.
10. Greenwald, A. G., Spangenberg, E. R., Pratkanis, A. R., & Eskenazi, J. (1991). Double-blind tests of subliminal self-help audiotapes. *Psychological Science*, *2*, 119–122. Pratkanis, A. R. (May 1991). *The cargo cult science of subliminal influence.* Paper presented at the annual conference of the Committee for the Scientific Investigation of Claims about the Paranormal, Berkeley, CA.
11. Zanot, E. J., Pincus, J. D., & Lamp, E. J. (1983). Public perceptions of subliminal advertising. *Journal of Advertising*, *12*, 37–45.
12. In Re *Vance and Belknap v. Judas Priest and CBS Records*. 86-5844/86-3939. Second District Court of Nevada. August 24, 1990, p.31.

30 IS FOREWARNED FOREARMED? OR HOW TO REALLY RESIST PROPAGANDA

1. Liebert, R. M., & Sprafkin, J. (1988). *The early window*. New York: Pergamon.
2. For a review, see Cialdini, R. B., & Petty, R. E. (1981). Anticipatory opinion effects. In R. E. Petty, T. M. Ostrom, & T. C. Brock (Eds.), *Cognitive responses in persuasion* (pp. 217–235). Hillsdale, NJ: Erlbaum.
3. Freedman, J. L., & Sears, D. O. (1965). Warning, distraction, and resistance to influence. *Journal of Personality and Social Psychology*, *1*, 262–266.
4. Cialdini, R. B., Levy, A., Herman, C. P., & Evenbeck, S. (1973). Attitudinal politics: The strategy of moderation. *Journal of Personality and Social Psychology*, *25*, 100–108; Cialdini, R. B., Levy, A., Herman, C. P., Kozlowski, L. T., & Petty, R. E. (1976). Elastic shifts of opinion: Determinants of direction and durability. *Journal of Personality and Social Psychology*, *34*, 663–672.

5. Watts, W. A., & Holt, L. E. (1979). Persistence of opinion change induced under conditions of forewarning and distraction. *Journal of Personality and Social Psychology*, *37*, 778–789.

6. Petty, R. E., & Cacioppo, J. T. (1979). Effect of forewarning of persuasive intent and involvement on cognitive responses and persuasion. *Personality and Social Psychology Bulletin*, *5*, 173–176.

7. McGuire, W., & Papageorgis, D. (1961). The relative efficacy of various types of prior belief-defense in producing immunity against persuasion. *Journal of Abnormal and Social Psychology*, *62*, 327–337.

8. McAlister, A., Perry, C., Killen, J., Slinkard, L. A., & Maccoby, N. (1980). Pilot study of smoking, alcohol and drug abuse prevention. *American Journal of Public Health*, *70*, 719–721.

9. Pryor, B., & Steinfatt, T. (1978). The effects of initial belief level on inoculation theory and its proposed mechanisms. *Human Communications Research*, *4*, 217–230.

31 EDUCATION OR PROPAGANDA?

1. Zimbardo, P. G., Ebbesen, E., & Maslach, C. (1977). *Influencing attitudes and changing behavior*. Reading, MA: Addison-Wesley.

2. Vallone, R. P., Ross, L., & Lepper, M. R. (1985). The hostile media phenomenon: Biased perception and perceptions of media bias in coverage of the Beirut massacre. *Journal of Personality and Social Psychology*, *49*, 577–585.

3. Comstock, G. (1980) *Television in America*. Beverly Hills, CA: Sage.

32 ON THE INEFFECTIVENESS OF INFORMATION CAMPAIGNS

1. Canon, L. (1964). Self-confidence and selective exposure to information. In L. Festinger (Ed.), *Conflict, decision, and dissonance* (pp. 83–96). Stanford, CA: Stanford University Press.

2. Hyman, H., & Sheatsley, P. B. (1947). Some reasons why information campaigns fail. *Public Opinion Quarterly*, *11*, 412–423.

3. Entman, R. M. (1989). *Democracy without citizens*. New York: Oxford University Press.

33 WHAT IS NEWS?

1. Lippmann, W. (1922). *Public opinion*. New York: Harcourt, Brace.
2. Hale, O. J. (1964). *The captive press in the Third Reich*. Princeton, NJ: Princeton University Press.
3. Roxburgh, A. (1987). *Pravda: Inside the Soviet news machine*. New York: Braziller.
4. Steele, R. W. (1985). *Propaganda in an open society: The Roosevelt Administration and the media, 1933-1941*. Westport, CT: Greenwood Press.
5. DeParle, J. (1991, May 6). Keeping the news in step. Are the Pentagon's Gulf War rules here to stay? *New York Times*, p. A9.
6. Gans, H. J. (1979). *Deciding what's news*. New York: Vintage; Nelkin, D. (1987). *Selling science*. New York: W. H. Freeman.
7. Mark Levy, quoted in *Time*, October 1, 1979, p. 83.
8. Mann, P., & Iscoe, I. (1971). Mass behavior and community organization: Reflections on a peaceful demonstration. *American Psychologist*, *26*, 108-113.
9. Rubin, J. (1970). *Do it*. New York: Ballantine Books, p. 106.
10. Ibid, p. 37.

34 PERSUASION DIRECT

1. See Baier, M. (1983). *Elements of direct marketing*. New York: McGraw-Hill; Caples, J. (1974). *Tested advertising methods*. Englewood Cliffs, NJ: Prentice-Hall; Harper, R. (1986). *Mailing list strategies*. New York: McGraw-Hill; Stone, B. (1986). *Successful direct marketing methods*. Lincolnwood, IL: Crain.

35 HOW TO BECOME A CULT LEADER

1. Examples and details are from Galanter, M. (1989). *Cults: Faith, healing, and coercion*. New York: Oxford University Press; Kanter, R. M. (1972). *Commitment and community: Communes and utopias in sociological perspective*. Cambridge, MA: Harvard University Press; Lifton, R. J. (1963). *Thought reform and the psychology of totalism: A study of "brainwashing" in China*. New York: Norton; Osherow, N. (1988). Making sense of the nonsensical: An analysis of Jonestown.

In E. Aronson (Ed.), *Readings about the social animal* (pp. 68–86). New York: W. H. Freeman; Patrick, T., & Dulack, T. (1976). *Let our children go!* New York: Ballantine; Schein, E. H. (1961). *Coercive persuasion.* New York: Norton; Stoner, C., & Parke, J. A. (1977). *All God's children.* Radnor, PA: Chilton Book Co.; Weightman, J. M. (1983). *Making sense of the Jonestown suicides.* New York: Edwin Mellen.
2. Ibid (1976), p. 45.

36 PROPAGANDA IN THE THIRD REICH: A CASE FOR UNCERTAINTY

1. Hitler, A. (1925). *Mein kampf.* Boston: Houghton Mifflin, p. 176.
2. Jowett, G. S., & O'Donnell, V. (1986). *Persuasion and propaganda.* Beverly Hills, CA: Sage; Peterson, H. C. (1939). *Propaganda for war: The campaign against American neutrality, 1914–1917.* Norman, OK: University of Oklahoma Press.
3. For excellent discussions of Nazi and World War II propaganda, see Childers, T. (1983). *The Nazi voter.* Chapel Hill, NC: University of North Carolina Press; Doob, L. W. (1950). Goebbel's principles of propaganda. *Public Opinion Quarterly, 14,* 419–422; Hale, O. J. (1964). *The captive press in the Third Reich.* Princeton, NJ: Princeton University Press; Herzstein, R. E. (1978). *The war that Hitler won.* New York: Paragon House; Rhodes, A. (1987). *Propaganda: The art of persuasion: World War II.* Secaucus, NJ: Wellfleet Press; Rutherford, W. (1978). *Hitler's propaganda machine.* London: Bison Books; Welch, D. (1983). *Nazi propaganda.* Beckenham, Kent, UK: Croom Helm; Zeman, Z. A. B. (1964). *Nazi propaganda.* London: Oxford University Press.
4. Hitler. See note 1, p. 178.
5. Ibid, pp. 180–181.
6. Quoted in Rhodes, A. (1987). See note 3, p. 13.
7. Bronowski, J. (1973). *The ascent of man.* Boston: Little, Brown.
8. Hitler. See note 1, pp. 182–183.
9. Quoted in Rhodes, A. (1987). See note 3, p. 90.

37 PEITHO'S CHILDREN

1. For excellent discussions of the ethics and role of persuasion in society, see Alinsky, S. D. (1971). *Rules for radicals.* New York: Vintage; Entman,

R. M. (1989). *Democracy without citizens*. New York: Oxford University Press; Freire, P. (1968). *Pedagogy of the oppressed*. New York: Seabury; Qualter, T. H. (1962). *Propaganda and psychological warfare*. New York: Random House; Stone, I. F. (1988). *The trial of Socrates*. Boston, MA: Little, Brown.

2. Quoted in Alinsky, S. Ibid, p. 25.

INDEX

ANTHONY PRATKANIS is an expert on consumer behavior and persuasive tactics. An engaging classroom teacher, he began his career in the business school at Carnegie-Mellon University where he taught popular courses in advertising and consumer behavior. Dr. Pratkanis's expertise is sought by both public and private enterprises. His testimony on subliminal persuasion at the trial of CBS Records/Judas Priest was instrumental in winning that case for the defense. A frequent contributor to scientific journals and the popular press on the topics of persuasion and influence, he is an editor of *Attitude Structure and Function*. Anthony Pratkanis is currently Associate Professor of Psychology at the University of California, Santa Cruz.

ELLIOT ARONSON is Professor of Psychology at the University of California, Santa Cruz. He is generally considered to be one of the world's most versatile and distinguished psychologists; his research on reducing prejudice in public schools earned him the Gordon Allport prize for outstanding contributions to intergroup relations; he is a recipient of the American Psychological Association's Distinguished Teaching Award and the American Association for the Advancement of Science's Award for Distinguished Research in Socio-Psychology. Dr. Aronson is the author of many books including *The Jigsaw Classroom, Methods of Research in Social Psychology,* and *The Social Animal*, and he is coeditor (with Gardner Lindzey) of *The Handbook of Social Psychology*.